AF556502

VARIETY MEAT TERMINOLOGY

By

Dr. M. Prakash

Deptt. of Zoology
M.M.H. Post Graduate College
Ghaziabad (U.P.)
(India)

DISCOVERY PUBLISHING HOUSE PVT. LTD.
NEW DELHI-110 002

Published by:
Tilak Wasan

DISCOVERY PUBLISHING HOUSE PVT. LTD.
4383/4B, Ansari Road, Darya Ganj
New Delhi-110 002 (India)
Phone : +91-11-23279245, 43596064-65
Fax : +91-11-23253475
E-mail : parul.wasan@gmail.com
discoverypublishinghouse@gmail.com
web : www.discoverypublishinggroup.com

***First Edition:* 2013**

ISBN: 978-93-5056-309-0

Variety Meat Terminology

Printed at:
Dynamic Printers
Delhi

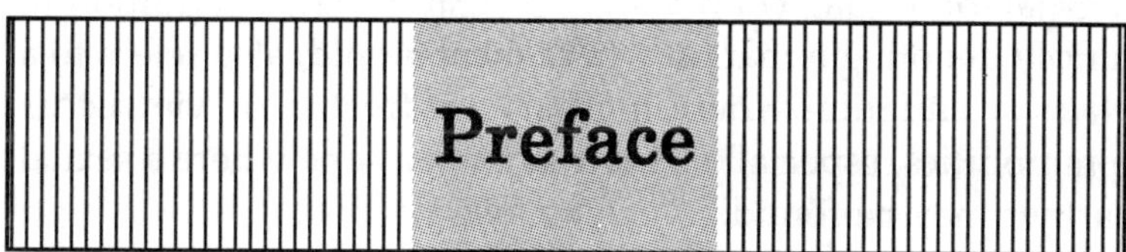

Preface

Meat is animal flesh that is used as food. Most often, this means the skeletal muscle and associated fat, but it may also describe other edible tissues such as organs, livers, skin, brains, bone marrow, kidneys, or lungs. The word *meat* is also used by the meat packing industry in a more restrictive sense—the flesh of mammalian species (pigs, cattle, lambs, etc.) raised and prepared for human consumption, to the exclusion of fish, poultry, and game.

The word *meat* comes from the Old English word *mete,* which referred to food in general. The term is related to *mad* in Danish, *mat* in Swedish and Norwegian, and *matur* in Icelandic, which also mean 'food'. The word 'mete' also exists in Old Frisian (and to a lesser extent, modern West Frisian) to denote important food, differentiating it from "swiets" (sweets) and 'dierfied' (animal feed).

One definition that refers to meat as not including fish developed over the past few hundred years and has religious influences. The distinction between fish and 'meat' is codified by the Jewish dietary law of *kashrut,* regarding the mixing of milk and meat, which does not forbid the mixing of milk and fish. Modern Jewish legal practice (*halakha*) on *kashrut* classifies the flesh of both mammals and birds as 'meat'; fish are considered to be *parve,* neither meat nor a dairy food. The Catholic dietary restriction on 'meat' on Fridays also does not apply to the cooking and eating of fish.

The Latin word *caro* 'meat' (also the root of 'carnal', referring to the 'pleasures of the flesh') is often a euphemism for sexual pleasure, effected from the function performed by fleshy organs. Thus 'meat' may refer to the human body in a sensual, or sexual, connotation. A *meat market,* in addition to simply denoting a market where meat is sold, also refers to a place or situation where humans are treated or viewed as commodities, especially a place known as one where a sexual partner may be found.

'Meat' may also be used to refer to humans humorously or indifferently. In military slang, 'meat shield' refers to soldiers sent towards an enemy to draw fire away from another unit.

Meat constituted a substantial proportion of even the earliest humans' diet, paleontological evidence suggests. Early hunter-gatherers depended on the organized hunting of large animals such as bison and deer.

The domestication of animals, of which we have evidence dating back to the end of the last glacial period (c. 10,000 years BP), allowed the systematic production of meat and the breeding of animals with a view to improving meat production. The animals which are now the principal sources of meat were domesticated in conjunction with the development of early civilizations.

—Author

Contents

CHAPTER

1

INTRODUCTION

Meat is animal flesh that is used as food. Most often, this means the skeletal muscle and associated fat, but it may also describe other edible tissues such as organs, livers, skin, brains, bone marrow, kidneys, or lungs. The word *meat* is also used by the meat packing industry in a more restrictive sense—the flesh of mammalian species (pigs, cattle, lambs, etc.) raised and prepared for human consumption, to the exclusion of fish, poultry, and game.

The word *meat* comes from the Old English word *mete,* which referred to food in general. The term is related to *mad* in Danish, *mat* in Swedish and Norwegian, and *matur* in Icelandic, which also mean 'food'. The word 'mete' also exists in Old Frisian (and to a lesser extent, modern West Frisian) to denote important food, differentiating it from "swiets" (sweets) and 'dierfied' (animal feed).

One definition that refers to meat as not including fish developed over the past few hundred years and has religious influences. The distinction between fish and 'meat' is codified by the Jewish dietary law of *kashrut,* regarding the mixing of milk and meat, which does not forbid the mixing of milk and fish. Modern Jewish legal practice (*halakha*) on *kashrut* classifies the flesh of both mammals and birds as 'meat'; fish are considered to be *parve,* neither meat nor a dairy food. The Catholic dietary restriction on 'meat' on Fridays also does not apply to the cooking and eating of fish.

The Latin word *caro* 'meat' (also the root of 'carnal', referring to the 'pleasures of the flesh') is often a euphemism for sexual pleasure, effected from the function performed by fleshy organs. Thus 'meat' may refer to the human body in a sensual, or sexual, connotation. A *meat market,* in addition to simply denoting a market where meat is sold, also refers to a place or situation where humans are treated or viewed as commodities, especially a place known as one where a sexual partner may be found.

'Meat' may also be used to refer to humans humorously or indifferently. In military slang, 'meat shield' refers to soldiers sent towards an enemy to draw fire away from another unit.

Meat constituted a substantial proportion of even the earliest humans' diet, paleontological evidence suggests. Early hunter-gatherers depended on the organized hunting of large animals such as bison and deer.

The domestication of animals, of which we have evidence dating back to the end of the last glacial period (c. 10,000 years BP), allowed the systematic production of meat and the breeding of animals with a view to improving meat production. The animals which are now the principal sources of meat were domesticated in conjunction with the development of early civilizations:

- Sheep, originating from western Asia, were domesticated with the help of dogs prior to the establishment of settled agriculture, likely as early as the eighth millennium BC. Several breeds of sheep were established in ancient Mesopotamia and Egypt by 3500-3000 BC. Presently, more than 200 sheep breeds exist.

- Cattle were domesticated in Mesopotamia after settled agriculture was established about 5000 BC, and several breeds were established by 2500 BC. Modern domesticated cattle fall into the groups *Bos taurus* (European cattle) and *Bos indicus* (zebu), both descended from the now-extinct aurochs. The breeding of beef cattle, cattle optimized for meat production as opposed to animals best suited for draught or dairy purposes, began in the middle of the 18th century.
- Domestic pigs, which are descended from wild boars, are known to have existed about 2500 BC in modern-day Hungary and in Troy; earlier pottery from Jericho and Egypt depicts wild pigs. Pork sausages and hams were of great commercial importance in Greco-Roman times. Pigs continue to be bred intensively as they are being optimized to produce meat best suited for specific meat products.

Other animals are, or have been raised or hunted for their flesh. The type of meat consumed varies much in different cultures, changes over time, and depends on different factors such as the availability of the animals and traditions.

Horses are still commonly eaten in countries such as France or Japan. Horses (and other large mammals as reindeers) were hunted during the Late Paleolithic in western Europe.

Dogs are widely consumed in China, Vietnam, the Philippines and South Korea. Dogs are also occasionally eaten in the Arctic regions. Historically, dog meat has been consumed in various part of the world, such as Hawaii, Japan, Switzerland and Mexico.

Cats are consumed in Southern China, Peru and certain rural parts of Switzerland.

Guinea pigs are raised for their flesh in the Andes.

Whales and dolphins are still being hunted, partly for their flesh, by aboriginal communities in Alaska, Siberia, Canada, by the Faroe Islands, Greenland, Iceland, Saint Vincent and the Grenadines and by two small communities in Indonesia. Modern agriculture employs a number of techniques, such as progeny testing, to make animals evolve rapidly towards having the qualities desired by meat producers. For instance, in the wake of well-publicised health concerns associated with saturated fats in the 1980s, the fat content of UK beef, pork and lamb fell from 20-26 per cent to 4-8 per cent within a few decades, both due to selective breeding for leanness and changed methods of butchery. Methods of genetic engineering aimed at improving the meat production qualities of animals are now also becoming available.

Even though it is a very old industry, meat production continues to be shaped strongly by the rapidly evolving demands of customers. The trend towards selling meat in pre-packaged cuts has increased the demand for larger breeds of cattle, which are better suited to producing such cuts. Even more animals not previously exploited for their meat are now being farmed, especially the more agile and mobile species, whose muscles tend to be developed better than those of cattle, sheep or pigs. Examples include the various antelope species, the zebra, water buffalo and camel, as well as non-mammals, such as the crocodile, emu and ostrich. Another important trend in contemporary meat production is organic farming which, while providing no organoleptic benefit to meat so produced, meets an increasing demand for numerous reasons.

Several economically important traits in meat animals are heritable to some degree and can thus be selected for by breeding. In cattle, certain growth features are controlled by recessive genes which have not so far been controlled, complicating breeding. One such trait is dwarfism; another is the doppelender or 'double muscling' condition, which causes muscle hypertrophy and thereby increases the animal's commercial value. Genetic analysis continues to reveal the genetic mechanisms that control numerous aspects of the endocrine system and, through it, meat growth and quality.

Genetic engineering techniques can shorten breeding programmes significantly because they allow for the identification and isolation of genes coding for desired traits, and for the reincorporation of these genes into the animal genome. To enable such manipulation, research is ongoing to map the entire genome of sheep, cattle and pigs. Some research has already seen commercial application. For instance, a recombinant bacterium has been developed which improves the digestion of grass in the rumen of cattle, and some specific features of muscle fibres have been genetically altered.

Experimental reproductive cloning of commercially important meat animals such as sheep, pig or cattle has been successful. The multiple asexual reproduction of animals bearing desirable traits can thus be anticipated, although this is not yet practical on a commercial scale.

Environment

Heat regulation in livestock is of great economic significance, because mammals attempt to maintain a constant optimal body temperature. Low temperatures tend to prolong animal development and high temperatures tend to retard it. Depending on their size, body shape and insulation through tissue and fur, some animals have a relatively narrow zone of temperature tolerance and others (*e.g.* cattle) a broad one. Static magnetic fields, for reasons still unknown, also retard animal development.

Nutrition

The quality and quantity of usable meat depends on the animal's *plane of nutrition, i.e.,* whether it is over- or under-fed. Scientists disagree, however, about how exactly the plane of nutrition influences carcase composition.

The composition of the diet, especially the amount of protein provided, is also an important factor regulating animal growth. Ruminants, which may digest cellulose, are better adapted to poor-quality diets, but their ruminal microorganisms degrade high-quality protein if supplied in excess. Because producing high-quality protein animal feed is expensive, several techniques are employed or experimented with to ensure maximum utilization of protein. These include the treatment of feed with formalin to protect amino acids during their passage through the rumen, the recycling of manure by feeding it back to cattle mixed with feed concentrates, or the partial conversion of petroleum hydrocarbons to protein through microbial action.

In plant feed, environmental factors influence the availability of crucial nutrients or micronutrients, a lack or excess of which can cause a great many ailments. In Australia, for instance, where the soil contains limited phosphate, cattle are being fed additional phosphate to increase the efficiency of beef production. Also in Australia, cattle and sheep in certain areas were often found losing their appetite and dying in the midst of rich pasture; this was at length found to be a result of cobalt deficiency in the soil. Plant toxins are also a risk to grazing animals; for instance, fluoracetate, found in some African and Australian plants, kills by disrupting the cellular metabolism. Certain man-made pollutants such as methylmercury and some pesticide residues present a particular hazard due to their tendency to bioaccumulate in meat, potentially poisoning consumers.

Human Intervention

Meat producers may seek to improve the fertility of female animals through the administration of gonadotrophic or ovulation-inducing hormones. In pig production, sow infertility is a common problem, possibly due to excessive fatness. No methods currently exist to augment the fertility of male animals. Artificial insemination is now routinely used to produce animals of the best possible genetic quality, and the efficiency of this method is improved through the administration of hormones that synchronize the ovulation cycles within groups of females.

Growth hormones, particularly anabolic agents such as steroids, are used in some countries to accelerate muscle growth in animals. This practice has given rise to the beef hormone controversy, an international trade dispute. It may also decrease the tenderness of meat, although research on this is inconclusive, and have other effects on the composition

of the muscle flesh. Where castration is used to improve control over male animals, its side effects are also counteracted by the administration of hormones.

Sedatives may be administered to animals to counteract stress factors and increase weight gain. The feeding of antibiotics to certain animals has been shown to improve growth rates also. This practice is particularly prevalent in the USA, but has been banned in the EU, partly because it causes antibiotic resistance in pathogenic microorganisms. Biochemical composition.

Numerous aspects of the biochemical composition of meat vary in complex ways depending on the species, breed, sex, age, plane of nutrition, training and exercise of the animal, as well as on the anatomical location of the musculature involved. Even between animals of the same litter and sex there are considerable differences in such parameters as the percentage of intramuscular fat.

Main Constituents

Adult mammalian muscle flesh consists of roughly 75 per cent water, 19 per cent protein, 2.5 per cent intramuscular fat, 1.2 per cent carbohydrates and 2.3 per cent other soluble non-protein substances. These include nitrogenous compounds, such as amino acids, and inorganic substances such as minerals.

Muscle proteins are either soluble in water (sarcoplasmic proteins, about 11.5 per cent of total muscle mass) or in concentrated salt solutions (myofibrillar proteins, about 5.5 per cent of mass). There are several hundred sarcoplasmic proteins. Most of them — the glycolytic enzymes — are involved in the glycolytic pathway, *i.e.,* the conversion of stored energy into muscle power. The two most abundant myofibrillar proteins, myosin and actin, are responsible for the muscle's overall structure. The remaining protein mass consists of connective tissue (collagen and elastin) as well as organelle tissue.

Fat in meat can be either adipose tissue, used by the animal to store energy and consisting of 'true fats' (esters of glycerol with fatty acids), or intramuscular fat, which contains considerable quantities of phospholipids and of unsaponifiable constituents such as cholesterol.

Red and White Meat

Meat can be broadly classified as 'red' or 'white' depending on the concentration of myoglobin in muscle fibre. When myoglobin is exposed to oxygen, reddish oxymyoglobin develops, making myoglobin-rich meat appear red. The redness of meat depends on species, animal age, and fibre type: Red meat contains more narrow muscle fibres that tend to operate over long periods without rest, while white meat contains more broad fibres that tend to work in short fast bursts.

The meat of adult mammals such as cows, sheep, goats, and horses is generally considered red, while domestic chicken and turkey breast meat is generally considered white.

All muscle tissue is very high in protein, containing all of the essential amino acids, and in most cases is a good source of zinc, vitamin B_{12}, selenium, phosphorus, niacin, vitamin B_6, choline, riboflavin and iron. Several forms of meat are high in vitamin K_2, which is only otherwise known to be found in fermented foods, with natto having the highest concentration. Muscle tissue is very low in carbohydrates and does not contain dietary fiber. The fat content of meat can vary widely depending on the species and breed of animal, the way in which the animal was raised, including what it was fed, the anatomical part of the body, and the methods of butchering and cooking. Wild animals such as deer are typically leaner than farm animals, leading those concerned about fat content to choose game such as venison. Decades of breeding meat animals for fatness is being reversed by consumer demand for meat with less fat.

Red meat, such as beef, pork, and lamb, contains many essential nutrients necessary for healthy growth and development in children. Nutrients in red meat include iron, zinc, vitamin B_{12}, and protein. Most meats contain a full complement of the amino acids required for the human diet. Fruits and vegetables, by contrast, are usually lacking several essential amino acids contained in meat. It is for this reason that people who abstain from eating all meat need to plan their diet carefully to include sources of all the necessary amino acids.

While each kind of meat has about the same content of protein and carbohydrates, there is a very wide range of fat content. It is the additional fat that contributes most to the calorie content of meat, and to concerns about dietary health.

Meat is produced by killing the animal in question and cutting the desired flesh out of it. These procedures are called slaughter and butchery, respectively.

Attesting to the long history of meat consumption in human civilizations, ritual slaughter has become part of the practice of several religions. These rituals, as well as other pre-industrial meat production methods such as these used by indigenous peoples, are not detailed here. This section will instead provide an overview of contemporary industrialized meat production in dedicated slaughterhouses from cattle, sheep and pigs.

Transport

Upon reaching a predetermined age or weight, livestock are usually transported *en masse* from the farm to the slaughterhouse, a process called 'live export'. Depending on its length and circumstances, this exerts stress and injuries on the animals, and some may die *en route*. Apart from being arguably inhumane, unnecessary stress in transport may adversely affect the quality of the meat. In particular, the muscles of stressed animals are low in water and glycogen, and their pH fails to attain acidic values, all of which results in poor meat quality. Consequently, and also due to campaigning by animal welfare groups, laws and industry practices in several countries tend to become more restrictive with respect to the duration and other circumstances of livestock transports.

Slaughter

Animals are usually slaughtered by being first stunned and then exsanguinated (bled out). Death results from the one or the other procedure, depending on the methods employed. Stunning can be effected through asphyxiating the animals with carbon dioxide, shooting them with a gun or a captive bolt pistol, or shocking them with electric current. In most forms of ritual slaughter, stunning is not allowed.

Draining as much blood as possible from the carcase is necessary because blood causes the meat to have an unappealing appearance and is a very good breeding ground for micro-organisms. The exsanguination is accomplished by severing the carotid artery and the jugular vein in cattle and sheep, and the anterior vena cava in pigs.

Dressing and Cutting

After exsanguination, the carcase is dressed; that is, the head, feet, hide (except hogs and some veal), excess fat, viscera and offal are removed, leaving only bones and edible muscle. Cattle and pig carcases, but not those of sheep, are then split in half along the mid ventral axis, and the carcase is cut into wholesale pieces. The dressing and cutting sequence, long a province of manual labour, is progressively being fully automated.

Conditioning

Under hygienic conditions and without other treatment, meat can be stored at above its freezing point (–1.5°C) for about six weeks without spoilage, during which time it undergoes an aging process that increases its tenderness and flavour.

During the first day after death, glycolysis continues until the accumulation of lactic acid causes the pH to reach about 5.5. The remaining glycogen, about 18 g per kg, is believed to increase the water-holding capacity and tenderness of the flesh when cooked. *Rigor mortis* sets in a few hours after death as ATP is used up, causing actin and myosin to combine into rigid actomyosin and lowering the meat's water-holding capacity, causing it to lose water ('weep'). In muscles that enter *rigor* in a contracted position, actin and myosin filaments overlap and cross-bond, resulting in meat that is tough on cooking — hence again the need to prevent pre-slaughter stress in the animal.

Over time, the muscle proteins denature in varying degree, with the exception of the collagen and elastin of connective tissue, and *rigor mortis* resolves. Because of these changes, the meat is tender and pliable when cooked just after death or after the resolution of *rigor,* but tough when cooked during *rigor.* As the muscle pigment myoglobin denatures, its iron oxidates, which may cause a brown discoloration near the surface of the meat. Ongoing proteolysis also contributes to conditioning. Hypoxanthine, a breakdown product of ATP, contributes to the meat's flavour and odour, as do other products of the discomposition of muscle fat and protein.

Spoilage and Preservation

The spoilage of meat occurs, if untreated, in a matter of hours or days and results in the meat becoming unappetizing, poisonous or infectious. Spoilage is caused by the practically unavoidable infection and subsequent decomposition of meat by bacteria and fungi, which are borne by the animal itself, by the people handling the meat, and by their implements. Meat can be kept edible for a much longer time — though not indefinitely — if proper hygiene is observed during production and processing, and if appropriate food safety, food preservation and food storage procedures are applied. Without the application of preservatives and stabilizers, the fats in meat may also begin to rapidly decompose after cooking or processing, leading to an objectionable taste known as warmed over flavour.

Meat is prepared in many ways, as steaks, in stews, fondue, or as dried meat like beef jerky. It may be ground then formed into patties (as hamburgers or croquettes), loaves, or sausages, or used in loose form (as in 'sloppy joe' or Bolognese sauce). Some meat is cured, by smoking, pickling, preserving in salt or brine (see salted meat and curing). Other kinds of meat are marinated and barbecued, or simply boiled, roasted, or fried. Meat is generally eaten cooked, but there are many traditional recipes that call for raw beef, veal or fish (tartare). Meat is often spiced or seasoned, as in most sausages. Meat dishes are usually described by their source (animal and part of body) and method of preparation.

Meat is a typical base for making sandwiches. Popular varieties of sandwich meat include ham, pork, salami and other sausages, and beef, such as steak, roast beef, corned beef, pepperoni, and pastrami. Meat can also be molded or pressed (common for products that include offal, such as haggis and scrapple) and canned.

Ethical issues regarding the consumption of meat can include objections to the act of killing animals or the agricultural practices surrounding the production of meat. Reasons for objecting to the practice of killing animals for consumption may include animal rights, environmental ethics, religious doctrine, or an aversion to inflicting pain or harm on other sentient creatures. The religion of Jainism has always opposed eating meat, and there are also many schools of Buddhism, Hinduism and Sikhism that condemn the eating of meat. Some people, while not vegetarians, refuse to eat the flesh of certain animals, such as cats, dogs, horses, or rabbits, due to cultural or religious taboo. In some cases, specific meats (especially from pigs and cows) are forbidden within religious traditions. Some people eat only the flesh of animals which they believe have not been mistreated, and abstain from the meat of animals reared in factory farms or from particular products such as foie gras and veal.

Health

Consumption of large quantities of meat, like overconsumption of any caloric food, has certain adverse effects which can include: obesity, heart disease, and constipation. The common misconception of *"I can't eat unless there is meat"* is largely due to cultural attitudes and how one is raised to think about food. In recent years, health concerns have been raised about the consumption of meat increasing the risk of cancer. In particular, red meat and processed meat were found to be associated with higher risk of cancers of the lung, esophagus, liver, and colon, among others, although also a reduced risk for some minor type of cancers. Another study found an increase risk of pancreatic cancer for red meat and pork. That study also suggests that fat and saturated fat are not likely contributors to pancreatic cancer. Animal fat, particularly from ruminants, tends to have a higher percentage of saturated fat *vs.* monounsaturated and polyunsaturated fat when compared to vegetable fats, with the exception of some tropical plant fats; consumption of which has been correlated with various health problems. The saturated fat found in meat has been associated with significantly raised risks of colon cancer, although evidence suggests that risks of prostate cancer are unrelated to animal fat consumption. USDA claims that consumption of meat as a source of protein in the human diet is crucial, have been resoundingly contradicted by recent studies.

The correlation of meat consumption to increased risk of heart disease is controversial. Some studies fail to find a link between red meat consumption and heart disease (although the same study found statistically significant correlation between the consumption of processed meat and cancer), while another study, a survey ,conducted in 1960, of 25,153 California Seventh-Day Adventists, found that the risk of heart disease is three times greater for 45-64 year old men who eat meat daily, versus those who did not eat meat. In another study in 2010 involving over one million people who ate meat found that only processed meat had an adverse risk in relation to coronary heart disease. The study suggests that eating 50g (less than 2oz) of processed meat per day increases risk of coronary heart disease by 42 per cent, and diabetes by 19 per cent. Equivalent levels of fat, including saturated fats, in unprocessed meat (even when eating twice as much per day) did not show any deleterious effects, leading the researchers to suggest that "differences in salt and preservatives, rather than fats, might explain the higher risk of heart disease and diabetes seen with processed meats, but not with unprocessed red meats."

A 2009 study by the National Cancer Institute revealed a correlation between the consumption of red meat and increased mortality from cancer and cardiovascular diseases. This study has been criticized for using an improperly validated food frequency questionnaire, which has been shown to have low levels of accuracy.

In response to changing prices as well as health concerns about saturated fat and cholesterol, consumers have altered their consumption of various meats. A USDA report points out that consumption of beef in the United States between 1970-1974 and 1990-1994 dropped by 21 per cent, while consumption of chicken increased by 90 per cent. During the same period of time, the price of chicken dropped by 14 per cent relative to the price of beef. In 1995 and 1996, beef consumption increased due to higher supplies and lower prices.

Cooking

Meat, like any food, can also transmit certain diseases, but complete cooking and avoiding recontamination reduces this possibility.

Several studies published since 1990 indicate that cooking muscle meat creates heterocyclic amines (HCAs), which are thought to increase cancer risk in humans. Researchers at the National Cancer Institute published results of a study which found that human subjects who ate beef rare or medium-rare had less than one third the risk of stomach cancer than those who ate beef medium-well or well-done. While eating muscle meat raw may be the only way to avoid HCAs fully, the National Cancer Institute states that cooking meat below 212°F (100°C) creates "negligible amounts" of HCAs. Also, microwaving meat before cooking may reduce HCAs by 90 per cent.

Nitrosamines, present in processed and cooked foods, have been noted as being carcinogenic, being linked to colon cancer. Also, toxic compounds called PAHs, or Polycyclic aromatic hydrocarbons, present in processed, smoked and cooked foods, are known to be carcinogenic.

In vitro and Imitation

Various forms of imitation meat have been created to satisfy people wishing to reduce or eliminate meat consumption for health, environmental, or ethical considerations, but who still wish to taste the flavour and texture of meat. They are typically some form of processed soybean, (tofu, tempeh), but they can also be based on wheat gluten or even fungus (quorn).

In vitro meat, also known as cultured meat, is animal flesh that has never been part of a complete, living animal. Several research projects are currently experimentally growing *in vitro* meat, but no meat has yet been produced for public consumption. The goal is to grow fully developed muscle organs, but the first generation will most likely be minced meat products.

The UN Food and Agriculture Organization (FAO) has estimated that direct emissions from meat production account for about 18 per cent of the world's total greenhouse gas emissions. The FAO figure accounts for the entire meat production cycle – clearing forested land, making and transporting fertiliser, burning fossil fuels in agricultural machinery, and the front and rear end emissions of cattle and sheep. In tracking food animal production from the feed through to the dinner table, the inefficiencies of grain fed meat, milk and egg production range from a 4:1 energy input to protein output ratio up to 54:1, in the opinion of Roger Segelken.

CHAPTER 2

OFFAL

Offal is a culinary term used to refer to the entrails and internal organs of a butchered animal. The word does not refer to a particular list of organs, but includes most internal organs other than muscles or bones. Note that as an English collective noun, the term *'offal'* is used in the same form for singular and plural — without a final 's'. People in some cultures shy away from offal as food, while others use it as everyday food, or even in delicacies that command a high price.

Offal not used directly for human or animal food is often processed in a rendering plant, producing material that is used for fertilizer or fuel.

The word shares its etymology with several German words: *Abfall'* (offall *in some Western German dialects),* afval *in Dutch and Afrikaans,* avfall *in Norwegian and Swedish and* affald *in Danish. These Germanic words all mean 'garbage', or—literally—'off-fall', referring to that which has fallen off during butchering.*

Europe

In some parts of Europe, scrotum, brain, chitterlings (pig's small intestine), trotters (feet), heart, head (of pigs, calves, sheep and lamb), kidney, liver, "lights" (lung), sweetbreads (thymus or pancreas), fries (testicles), tongue, snout (nose), tripe (reticulum) and maws (stomach) from various mammals are common menu items.

United Kingdom

The traditional Scottish haggis consists of sheep stomach stuffed with a boiled mix of liver, heart, lungs, rolled oats and other ingredients. In the UK Midlands, faggots are made from ground or minced pig offal (mainly liver and cheek), bread, herbs and onion wrapped in pig's caul. Steak and kidney pie (typically featuring veal or beef kidneys) is widely known and enjoyed in Britain and Ireland. Brawn is a British English term for 'head cheese', or the collection of meat and tissue found on an animal's skull (typically a pig) that is cooked, chilled and set in gelatin.

Another British and Irish food is black pudding, consisting of congealed pig's blood with oatmeal made into sausage-like links with pig intestine as a casing, then boiled and is usually fried on preparation. Melton Mowbray pork pies are made in part from pig trotters. Pressed and sliced ox tongue remains popular amongst older UK residents for use in sandwiches. *Luncheon Tongue* refers to reformed tongue pieces rather than slices of the whole tongue. Both kinds of tongue are found in tinned form and in slices. Home pressing and cooking of tongue appears to have died out over the last fifty years. Bleached *tripe* was a popular dish in Northern England with many specialist tripe shops in industrial areas: these too have almost all closed.

In Norway the smalahove is a traditional dish, usually eaten around and before Christmas time, made from a sheep's head. The skin and fleece of the head is torched, the brain removed, and the head is salted, sometimes smoked, and dried. The head is boiled for about 3 hours and served with mashed rutabaga and potatoes. The ear and eye (one half of a head is one serving) are normally eaten first, as they are the fattiest area and must be eaten warm.The head is often eaten from the front to the back, working around the bones of the skull. Smalahove is considered by some to be unappealing or even repulsive. It is mostly enjoyed by enthusiasts, and is often served to tourists and braver visitors.

Other Norwegian specialities include Smalaføtter, which is a traditional dish similar to Smalahove, but instead of a sheep's head it is made of lamb's feet. Syltelabb is boiled, salt-cured pig's trotter, and is known as a Christmas delicacy for enthusiasts. Syltelabb is usually sold cooked and salted. In 2006 the World Cup in Syltelabb eating was held in Brokelandsheia Norway where Norwegian comedian Kristopher Schau participated.

In Denmark a version of liver pâté, known as 'leverpostej' in Danish, used as a spread (often in an open sandwich on rye bread) is considered a national dish. The most common main ingredients of *leverpostej* are pork liver, lard and anchovies, but numerous alternative recipes exist. The 5.5 million Danes consume roughly 14,000 tons of *leverpostej* per year, the most popular commercial brand being Stryhn's. Versions of brawn (often served on rye bread as an open sandwich with garnish of dijon mustard and pickled beetroot) and blood sausage (served pan-fried with muscovado) are eaten mainly during wintertime, *e.g.* as part of the traditional Danish Christmas lunch or 'julefrokost'.

Iceland has its own version of both haggis and brawn. The Icelandic haggis called 'slátur' (slaughter) is made in two versions: 'Blóðmör' (bloodlard), a sheep's stomach stuffed with a mixture of sheep's blood, rolled oats and cut up bits of sheep's fat, and 'lifrarpylsa' (liver sausage), which consists of sheep stomach stuffed with a mixture of ground lamb's liver, rolled oats and cut-up bits of mutton. The Icelandic brawn 'Svið' is made from singed sheep heads, and it is eaten either hot or cold off the bone or set in gelatin.

Sweden has a version of the British black pudding called 'blodpudding' (blood pudding) and the Dutch also have their version of black pudding, called "Bloedworst" (bloodsausage).

The Scottish haggis is called 'pölsa' or 'lungmos' (mashed lung). The Swedish 'pölsa' is made of some offal like liver or heart, onions, rolled barley and spices and is served with boiled potatoes, fried eggs and sliced beetroot. 'Blodpudding' is mostly served sliced and fried with lingonberry preserve, grated carrot and fried bacon. Other popular offal dishes are 'levergryta' (liver stew) 'leverpastej' (liver pâté).

Finland also has it's own version of black pudding, mustamakkara. There is also liver sausage, usually eaten as a spread on bread, similarly to the Danish leverpostej. Liver is also eaten in various other forms including fried slices and minced liver patties. Liver casserole, traditionally made with minced liver, rice, butter, onions, egg, syrup and usually raisins, used to be mainly a Christmas dish, but is now available and eaten all year round. There are also many traditional and modern game recipes that use offal.

Especially in southern Germany, some offal varieties are served in regional cuisine. The Bavarian expression *Kronfleischküche* includes skirt steak and offal as well, *e.g.* Milzwurst, a sausage containg small pieces of spleen, and even dishes based on udder. Swabia is famous for *Saure Kutteln* — sour tripes, served steaming hot with fried potatoes. *Herzgulasch* is a (formerly cheaper) type of goulash using heart. Liver is part of various recipes, such as some sorts of Knödel and Spätzle, and in Liverwurst. As a main dish, together with cooked sliced apple and onion rings, liver (*Leber Berliner Art*, liver Berlin style) is a famous recipe from the German capital. Helmut Kohl's preference for Saumagen was a challenge to various political visitors during his terms as German Chancellor. *Markklößchen* are small dumplings made with bone marrow; they are served as part of *Hochzeitssuppe* (wedding soup), a soup served at marriages in some German regions. In Bavaria, lung stew is served with Knödel, dumplings.

In the French city of Marseille, lamb's trotters and a package of lamb tripe are a traditional food under the name '*pieds et paquets*'. In France, chitterlings sausage is regarded as a delicacy called *andouillette*.

In Poland offal and blood are used to prepare kaszanka. It's a traditional blood sausage in Polish cuisine (now only somewhat popular) made of a mixture of pig's blood, pig offal and buckwheat or barley usually served fried with onions or grilled.

Southern Europe

In Italy consumption of entrails and internal organs is quite widespread. Among the most popular preparations are fried or stewed brain; boiled stomach (trippa), often served with tomato sauce; lampredotto (the fourth stomach of the cow), boiled in broth and seasoned with parsley sauce and chili; liver (stir-fried with onions, roasted); kidneys; heart and coronaries (coratella or animelle); head, eyes, and testicles of pig; and several preparations based on chicken entrails. Pajata is a traditional dish from Rome. It refers to the intestines of an 'un-weaned' calf, *i.e.*, only fed on its mother's milk. The calf is killed soon after nursing. The intestines are cleaned, but the milk is left inside. When cooked, the combination of heat and the enzyme rennet in the intestines coagulates the milk and creates a sort of thick, creamy, cheese-like sauce. Pajata and tomatoes are often used to prepare a typical sauce for rigatoni. In Sicily, many enjoy a type of sandwich called 'pani ca meusa', or bread with spleen and caciocavallo cheese. In Brooklyn, New York, where it is also commonly eaten, it goes by the name 'vastedda'.

In Spain, the visceral organs are used in many traditional dishes, but the use of some of them is falling out of favour with the younger generations. Some traditional dishes are *callos* (cow tripe, very traditional in Madrid and Asturias), liver (often prepared with onion or with garlic and parsley, and also as breaded steaks), kidneys (often prepared with sherry wine or grilled), brains (of sheep), *criadillas* (bull testicles), braised cow's tongue, pig's head and feet (in Catalonia; pig feet are also traditionally eaten with snails), pork brains (part of the traditional 'tortilla sacromonte' in Granada) and pigs' ears (mostly in Galicia). There are also many varieties of blood sausage (morcilla), with flavours and textures ranging from very spicy to very mild. Some of the strongest are as hard in texture as chorizo or salami, while others are very soft, and some types include rice, giving the stuffing a haggis-like appearance. 'Morcillas' are added to soups, or just boiled on their own, in which case the cooking liquid is discarded. They are sometimes grilled and rarely fried. Also coagulated, boiled blood is a typical dish in Valencia (cut into cubes and often prepared with onion and/or tomato sauce).

In Portugal traditionally, the whole animal's visceral organs are used in many dishes. Trotters (also known as *chispe*), tripe and pig's ears are cooked in bean broths. The cow's brain (*Mioleira*) is also a delicacy, although consumption has decreased since Creutzfeld-Jakob outbreak. The blood of the pig is used to produce a very peculiar form of black pudding known as *farinhato* that includes flour and seasonings. Chicken feet are also used in soups.

In Greece (and similarly in Turkey, Albania and the Republic of Macedonia), *splinantero* consists of liver, spleen, and small intestine, roasted over an open fire. A festive variety is *kokoretsi* (from Turkish *kokoreç*, Macedonian *kukurek*): pieces of lamb offal (liver, heart, lungs, spleen, kidney and fat) are pierced on a spit and covered by washed small intestine wound around in a tube-like fashion. The kokoretsi is then roasted over a coal fire. It is a traditional dish for Easter. Another traditional Easter food is *magiritsa*: a soup made with lamb offal and lettuce in a white sauce, eaten at midnight on Easter Sunday to break the fast of lent. *Tzigerosarmas* (from Turkish *ciger sarmasi*, meaning 'liver wrap') and *gardoumba* are two varieties of *splinantero* and *kokoretsi* made in different sizes and with extra spices to improve the taste.

Eastern Europe

In Romania, there is a dish similar to haggis called *drob*, which is served at Easter. Romanian peasants make a kind of traditional sausage from pork offal, called *caltabos* — the main difference being that *drob* is enclosed in abdominal membranes (*prapore*) of the animal, while chitterlings is used for *caltabos*. A popular dish of tripe soup called ciorba de burta is similar to shkembe chorba (from Turkish *iskembe çorbasi*). There is also a two-fold variation on the concept of head cheese: *piftie* which does contain gelatin, is served cold and is usually only made from pork or beef (traditionally only pork), but does not contain as much head material (usually only the lower legs and ears are used since they contain large amounts of gelatin) and *pacele* which is exclusively made of meat and tissue found on the head (save for the eyes and usually only made from lamb; addition of brain and tongue varies by local habit). Pacele is made by first boiling the head whole (to soften the meat and make it easier to peel off) and then peeling/scraping off all meat and tissue from it. A generous amount of garlic or garlic juice (*mujdei*) is then added and the dish is served warm.

Finally, there are many dishes in Romania that are based on whole offal, such as: grilled pig and cow kidney (served with boiled or steam cooked vegetables—usually peas and carrot slices); butcher's brain (usually lamb's brains, rolled in batter and deep-fried); tongue and olives stew (mostly done with cow tongue) and many others.

The Armenian traditional dish known as khash is a traditional meal with inexpensive ingredients, originating in the Shirak region. The main ingredient in khash is pig's or cow's feet, although other animal parts, such as the ears and tripe, may also be used. Formerly a nutritious winter food for the poor, it is now considered a delicacy, and is enjoyed as a festive winter meal.

In Bulgaria, Republic of Macedonia and Turkey, shkembe chorba is a widespread soup variety made from tripe.

Latin America

In some Latin American countries, such as Mexico, almost all internal parts and organs are consumed regularly. Chicken hearts, gizzards and livers are usually eaten fried or boiled, either alone, or in broth. Brainstem is served as soup, *sopa de médula*. The tongue is boiled to make tacos. Eyes are eaten as *tacos de ojo*. *Tripas* (intestines) are also eaten, but normally in tacos rather than stews. A popular dish is the "*pancita*", a stew of beef stomach. Tripe is also used to make *menudo* and *mondongo*. Cow's head is usually eaten as "Tacos de Cabeza", which include every part of the head: lips, cheeks, eyes, etc. Sheep's or goat's head are also eaten in as part of the barbacoa, the "Montalayo" is dish made of chopped organs, spiced with Adobo, and cooked inside of the sheep stomach. This is known as "Menudo de Birria" in the Pacific states and is made with goat parts instead of sheep. Chopped carrots and potatoes can be added, as well as peas. Pork brains are considered a delicacy and are eaten in the deep fried Quezadillas de Sesos. Beef and pork liver are regularly eaten pan-fried with onion or breaded and deep-fried. The pork ears, feet and snout are pickled and eaten in tostadas. Elsewhere, as in Peru, beef heart is used for *anticuchos* - a sort of brochette.

In Brazil, *churrasco* (barbecue) often includes chicken hearts, roasted on a big skewer. The typical *feijoada* sometimes contains pork trimmings (ears, feet and tail). Gizzard stews, fried beef liver and beef stomach stews used to be more popular dishes in the past, but are nonetheless still consumed. *Buchada*, a popular dish from the northeast of the country, consists of the diced organs of a goat, which are seasoned and then sewn inside the goat's stomach and boiled.

In Argentina, Chile and Uruguay, the traditional *asado* is often made along with several offal types (called "Achuras"), like *chinchulines* and *tripa gorda* (chitterlings), *mollejas* (sweetbreads) and *riñón* (cow's kidney). Brains, *sesos*, are used to make ravioli stuffing. Tongue is usually boiled, sliced and marinated with a mixture of oil, vinegar, salt, chopped peppers and garlic. Testicles (*criadillas*) are eaten mostly in cattle-raising regions.

Africa

In South Africa offal is enjoyed by South Africans of diverse backgrounds. Due to the popularity of this dish, it is one of the few customs that white (especially Afrikaners) and black South Africans share.

Offal dishes in South Africa do not really consist of any organs and are mostly limited to stomach skin, sheeps head, shin and very rarely brains. With regards the sheep head, it has over the years gained many nicknames such as 'skobo' (township colloquial term meaning head) and 'smiley' (referring to the expression of the head when cooked).

There are numerous recipes to cook the above mentioned items available on many South African websites. One of the more popular way to cook offal in South Africa is to cook it with small potatoes in a curry sauce served on rice. Alternatively it can served with samp or maize rice.

Asia

In China, many organs and animal-parts are used for food or traditional Chinese medicine. Since pork is the most consumed meat in China, popular pork offal dishes include stir-fried pork kidneys with oyster sauce, ginger and scallions, "???? - Wu Geng Chang Wang" a spicy stew with preserved mustard, tofu, pork intestine slices and congealed pork blood cubes. "??? - Zha Fei Chang," deep fried pork intestine slices and dipped in a sweet bean sauce is commonly offered by street hawkers. Pork tongue slices with salt and sesame oil is also a popular dish, especially in Sichuan province. Braised pork ear strips in soy sauce, five-spice powder and sugar is a common 'cold plate' appetizer available as hawker food or in major local supermarkets. Stir-fried pork kidneys and/or liver slices with oyster sauce, ginger and scallions or in soups is a regular dish in southern provinces. Pork blood soup is at least 1,000 years old since the Northern Song Dynasty, when the quintessential Chinese restaurant and eateries became popular. Pork blood soup and dumplings, jiaozi, were recorded as food for night labourers in Kaifeng. In Shanghai cuisine, the soup has evolved into the well-known 'Suan La Tang', Hot and Sour Soup, with various additional ingredients. As well as pork, the offal of other animals is used in traditional Chinese cooking, most commonly cattle, duck, and chicken.

Perhaps the best examples of taking offal dishes to culinary heights are seen in Hong Kong, where all Chinese regional cuisines converge. For example, shops of the Cantonese '*Siu mei*", Barbecue Delicacies, have achieved its foundation of influence here. Besides the popular *cha siu* and crispy skin pork, and all the other poultry, there are also the roasted chicken liver with honey, and the very traditional, and very expensive now, 'Gum Chin Gai', another honey roasted dimsum that is a sandwich of a piece each of pork fat, pork/chicken liver, ginger and cha siu.

The use of offals in dim sum does not stop there. In dim sum restaurants, the feet of chicken, ducks and pork are offered in various cooking styles. For example, the pork feet in sweet vinegar stew is a popular bowl now besides its traditional function as supplement for postpartum mother care. Young ginger stems, boiled eggs, and blanched pork feet are stew in sweet black rice vinegar for a few hours to make this 'Jui Kerk Gieng'. 'Ap Kerk Jat' is a piece each of ham, shiitake mushroom and deep fried fish maw wrapped with dried bean curd sheet in the duck feet and steamed. The use of fish offal in Cantonese cuisine is not limited to the maw. For example, there is the folksy dish of 'Tung Gong Yu Wan Bo', a casserole with the lips of fresh water large head fish; and shark fin soup.

In the more pragmatic folksy eateries, however, maximum utilization of the food resource is the traditional wisdom. The fish is completely made use of. Deep fried fish skin is a side dish in the fish ball noodle shop. The intestine is steamed with egg and other ingredients in the Hakka cuisine. The bones are wrapped in a cotton bag to boil in the soup for noodles.

Chaozhou cuisine shows its best manifestation also in Hong Kong. The goose meat, liver (foie gras), blood, intestine, feet, neck and tongue are all major ingredients to various dishes. There is also the must-try soup, pork stomach with whole pepper corns and pickled mustard.

The use of beef organs is classically represented in noodle shops here. Each respectable operation has its own recipe for preparing the stews of brisket, intestine, lung, and varieties of tripe. The big pots are often placed facing the street and next to the entrance such that the mouth-watering aroma is the best draw for the shop's business.

Contrary to a common Westerners' disgust for these dishes due to cultural unfamiliarity and sanitary concerns, these offal items are very well cleaned. The pork intestines' tough inner skin (which is exposed to bolus and pre-fecal materials) is completely removed. Then, the intestine is exhaustively soaked, cleaned and rinsed. The nephrons (urine carrying and extracting vessels) of pork kidneys are skilfully excised, and the kidneys are soaked for several hours and cleaned.

The use of the pancreas, liver, kidney, gall bladder, lung and even bronchus of various farm animals together with herbs in Chinese medicine have strong empirical theories and studies are being conducted to try to understand their nature in modern scientific terms. However, there are other strange offal usages in folk practice. Taoist and rural folk beliefs have their influence. The idea of essences and energy, heat and cold, are key. Snake wine with a live snake heart is thought to promote stamina due to the "essences of energy and heat", which is derived from a snake's attributes, such as aggressive behaviour (fiery) and venom (energy). When bears were more common in the Chinese northeast, bears claw and dried bear offal were used as medicines, seen as a source of vitality. Dry deer antlers are still a common medicine, thought to provide 'yang energy' to complement the male sex and the tail, 'yin energy' for the female sex. Extractions of animal penises and testes are still believed to contribute to better male performance and those of the embryo and uterus to the eternal youth of the female. However, these are being marginalized as synthetic hormones get more popular and affordable.

The Cantonese and Vietnamese consumed monkey brains, but this is now rare to non-existent, and primarily offered to rich, Western tourists. Strange items are more associated in the Chinese southeast, Vietnam and Southeast Asia, where the tropical diversity and use of exotic items captured the

Westerner's imagination during the era of colonialism up to the Vietnam War and is still a target of interest for adventure-seeking Western tourists.

In Korea, offal usage is very similar to mainland China but less frequent. Grilled intestine slices and pork blood are both consumed. Headcheese prepared with pork head meat was quite popular in the past. Steamed pork intestines are easy to found in traditional markets. The popular traditional Korean sausage called soondae is steamed pork small intestines filled with pork blood, seasoned noodles, and vegetables. Pork feet steamed in a special stock are considered delicacy in Korea. Beef stomach and intestines are still quite popular for cooking. It is not difficult to find grilled chicken hearts, gizzards, and feet in traditional street bars. Medicinal usages are also similar to mainland China and less common with offal uses. Korea traditional medicine focuses more on simpler, herbaceous materials and plants, such as ginseng, jujube and ginger.

In Indonesia and Malaysia, cow and goat organs are very popular fried or in soups or satay and almost all of the parts of the animal are eaten. Cow's stomach (*babat*) and intestine (*iso*) are popular, fried or in soup, in Javanese cuisine. Cow's lung, called *paru,* coated in cooked rice and spices (turmeric and coriander) and fries is often eaten as a snack or side dish. In Malaysia, cow or goat lung, called *paru,* coated in turmeric and fried is often served as a side dish to rice, especially in the ever popular nasi lemak. Tripe is used in a few dishes either stir fried or in a gravy. Tripe is also consumed as satay. Liver is deep fried or stir fried in some vegetable dishes. Liver is also sometimes made into a spicy dish called rendang. Cow or goat tongue is sliced and fried, sometimes in a spicy sauce. Brain is sometimes consumed but is not very popular in urban areas. Giblets of chicken and duck are commonly consumed too.

In Singapore, pig's organ soup is a common feature of hawker centres. Due to Singapore's proximity and ethnic makeup, many of the items written for Indonesia and Malaysia above are also found in Singapore.

In Japan chicken offal is often skewered and grilled over charcoal as *yakitori*, to be served alongside drinks in an *izakaya* (Japanese food-pub). Offal originating from cattle is also an ingredient in certain dishes (see *yakiniku*). However, Japanese culture mostly disdains offal use from large animals due to the lack of a long tradition of meat-eating, since Buddhist Japan was a largely vegetarian nation (except for the consumption of fish and seafood) prior to the late 19th century. During the Sino-Japanese War, Japanese troops took pigs from Chinese farmers and slaughtered the animals only for the major muscles (no head, feet and fully disemboweled).

In the Philippines, people eat practically every part of the pig, including snout, intestines, ears, and innards. *Dinuguan* is a particular type of blood-stew (depending on region) made using pig intestines, pork meat and sometimes ears and cheeks usually with a vinegar base, and green chili peppers. *Bopis* (bópiz in Spanish) is a spicy Filipino dish made out of pork lungs and heart sautéed in tomatoes, chilies and onions. *Isaw* is another treat enjoyed mostly in the Philippines which is a kebab made with pig's large intestine pieces barbecued and dipped in vinegar before eating. Crispy *Pata* is popular, consisting of pig's feet that have been boiled until tender, cut into pieces, and then deep fried.

In Pakistan, the goat's brain (*maghaz*), feet (*paey*), head (*siri*), stomach (*ojhari* or *but*), tongue (*zabaan*), liver (*kalayji*), kidney (*gurda*), udder (*kheeri*) and testicles (*kapooray*) as well as chickens' heart and liver are enjoyed. One popular dish, *Kata-Kat*, is a combination of spices, brains, liver, kidneys and other organs.

In India, lamb and goat brain sauted and stir fried with spices (often called *bheja fry*) is commonly available in all non-vegetarian restaurants. In Maharashtra, a strong-smelling dish called *rakti*, made of heavily spiced porcine offal and cartilaginous tissue, is considered a homely indulgence by the local Christian community (observant Muslims avoid pork products). However, the most popular offal is that of goats, especially in South India. Goat intestines are cooked into various spicy dishes, usually a dry curry with spices. Goat blood is also reduced to a dry stir fry with spices and coconut scrapings.

In Bangladesh, a bull's or goat's brain (*magoze*), feet (*paya*), head (*matha*), stomach skin (*bhuri*), tongue (*zihba*), liver (*kalija*), kidney (*gurda*), and heart ('deel') are delicacies. Chickens' heart, gizzard and liver are also enjoyed.

In Nepal, a goat's brain (*gidi*), feet (*khutta*), head (*tauko*), stomach skin (*bhudri*), tongue (*jibro*), liver (*kalejo*), kidney, lungs(*phokso*), fried intestines (*aandra*), fried solidified blood (*ragati*) and to a lesser extent testicles are considered delicacies and are in very high demand in Dashain when families congregate and enjoy them with whiskey and beer. Chickens' heart and liver are also enjoyed but it is chicken's gizzards that are truly prized.

In Lebanon, lamb brain is used in *nikhaat* dishes and sometimes as a sandwich filling. A tradition practiced less often today would be to eat fish eyes either raw, boiled, or fried. Another popular dish in the region surrounding is *korouch* which is rice-stuffed sheep intestine.

In Iran, tongue (*zabaan*), feet (*paa*) or Kaleh Pacheh, sheep liver (*jigar*), heart (*qalb*), lungs (*shosh*), testicles (*dombalan*) and kidneys are used as certain types of *kebab* and have a high popularity among people, as well as sheep intestines and stomach, though the latter is boiled. Sheep brains and tongue, alongside knee joints, as a formal breakfast dish called *kale pache* (lit. 'head and leg'), are boiled in water with beans and eaten with traditional bread.

North America

In the United States, the giblets of chickens, turkeys and ducks are much more commonly consumed than the organs of mammals, except for the liver, which is eaten quite commonly. Ground chicken livers, mixed with chicken fat and onions, called *chopped liver,* is a meal made with offal in the United States.

In some parts of the country the euphemism 'variety meats' is used for mammal organ meat. Some ethnic groups have traditional dishes made from lungs (such as *lungen stew*). Pepper Pot soup, frequently served in Philadelphia, is made from tripe (beef stomach).

Mammal offal is somewhat more popular in the American South, where some recipes include chitterlings, livers, brain, and hog maw. Scrapple, sometimes made from pork offal, is somewhat common in the Mid-Atlantic US, particularly in areas with Amish communities. Fried-brain sandwiches are a specialty in the Ohio River Valley. Traditional recipes for turkey gravy typically include the bird's giblets. Rocky Mountain oysters or *prairie oysters* (beef testicles) are a delicacy eaten in some cattle-raising parts of the western US and Canada. Turkey Fries (testicles) are served in restaurants in Nebraska.

Australia

In Australia offal is most commonly consumed in meat pies, or in ethnic dishes.

Food standards require that products containing offal be labeled as such. The presence of brain, heart, kidney, liver, tongue or tripe must be declared either by specific type or more generally as offal. Other offal, such as blood, pancreas, spleen and thymus must be declared by name.

Health and Food Safety Issues

The offal of certain animals is unsafe to consume:

The internal organs of the fugu pufferfish are highly toxic — in Japan, fugu can only be prepared by trained master chefs, working under extremely strict regulations, sanitary conditions, and licensing. Even a residual portion of fugu toxin can be fatal.

The liver of the polar bear is unsafe to eat because it is very high in vitamin A and can cause hypervitaminosis A, a dangerous disorder. This has been recognized since at least 1597 when Gerrit de Veer wrote in his diary that, while taking refuge in the winter in Nova Zemlya, he and his men became gravely ill after eating polar-bear liver.

Some animal intestines are very high in coliform bacteria and need to be washed and cooked thoroughly to be safe for eating.

Nervous system tissue can be contaminated with TSE prions, which cause bovine spongiform encephalopathy (BSE, 'mad cow disease'); in some jurisdictions these offal are classified as specified risk materials and are subject to special regulations.

Offal very high in purines can precipitate an acute attack of gout in someone with the condition.

Offal can be very high in cholesterol and saturated fats, including kidneys, stomach, intestines, heart, tongue and liver.

The practice of feeding raw offal to dogs on farms and ranches can spread echinococcosis, a potentially fatal parasitic disease of animals and humans.

CHAPTER 3

BEEF

Beef is the culinary name for meat from bovines, especially domestic cattle. Beef can be harvested from cows, bulls, heifers or steers. It is one of the principal meats used in the cuisine of the Middle East, Pakistan, Australia, Argentina, Europe and the United States, and is also important in Africa, parts of East Asia, and Southeast Asia. Beef is considered a taboo food in some cultures, especially in Indian culture, and thence is eschewed by Hindus and Jains; it is also discouraged among some Buddhists.

Beef muscle meat can be cut into steak, roasts or short ribs. Some cuts are processed (corned beef or beef jerky), and trimmings, usually mixed with meat from older, leaner cattle, are ground, minced or used in sausages. The blood is used in some varieties of blood sausage. Other parts that are eaten include the oxtail, tongue, tripe from the reticulum or rumen, glands (particularly the pancreas and thymus, referred to as sweetbread), the heart, the brain (although forbidden where there is a danger of bovine spongiform encephalopathy, BSE), the liver, the kidneys, and the tender testicles of the bull (known in the US as *calf fries, prairie oysters,* or *Rocky Mountain oysters*). Some intestines are cooked and eaten as-is, but are more often cleaned and used as natural sausage casings. The lungs and the udder are considered unfit for human consumption in the US. The bones are used for making beef stock.

Beef from steers and heifers is equivalent, except for steers having slightly less fat and more muscle, all treatments being equal. Depending on economics, the number of heifers kept for breeding varies. Older animals are used for beef when they are past their reproductive prime. The meat from older cows and bulls is usually tougher, so it is frequently used for mince (UK)/ground beef (US). Cattle raised for beef may be allowed to roam free on grasslands, or may be confined at some stage in pens as part of a large feeding operation called a feedlot (or concentrated animal feeding operation), where they are usually fed a ration of grain, protein, roughage and a vitamin/ mineral preblend.

In absolute numbers, the United States, the European Union, Brazil, and the People's Republic of China are the world's four largest consumers of beef. On a per capita basis, Uruguayans eat the most beef at 58.2 kg annually per person; people in the US eat 40.2 kg annually, while those in the EU eat 16.9 kg.

The world's largest exporters of beef are Brazil, Australia, and the United States. Beef production is also important to the economies of Argentina, Mexico, New Zealand, Nicaragua, Russia, and Uruguay.

The flesh of bovines has been eaten by hunters from prehistoric times; some of the earliest known cave paintings, such as those of Lascaux show aurochs in hunting scenes. Domestication of cattle occurred around 8000 BC, providing ready access to beef, milk and leather. Most cattle originated in the Old World, with the exception of bison hybrids. Examples include the Wagyu from Japan, Ankole-Watusi from Egypt, and longhorn Zebu from the Indian subcontinent. It is unknown when exactly cooking beef came into being. Cattle were widely used across the Old World for draft animals (oxen), milk production, or specifically for meat production, depending on local needs and resources. With mechanization of farming, some breeds were specifically bred to increase meat yield, like Chianina and Charolais or to improve texture, such as the Murray Grey, Angus or Wagyu. Some breeds (dual-purpose) have been selected for both meat and milk production, *e.g.* Brown Swiss (Braunvieh).

The word *beef* is from Latin bovinus (cognate to beef), in contrast to *cow*, which is from Middle English 'cou' (both words have the same Indo-European root *g?ou- . After the Norman Conquest, the French-speaking nobles who ruled England naturally used French words to refer to the meats they were served. Thus the animal was called *cu* (cow) by the Anglo-Saxon peasants, but the meat was called *boef* (ox) (Modern French *boeuf*) by the French nobles —who did not often deal with the live animal — when it was served to them.

This is one example of the common English dichotomy between the words for animals (with largely Germanic origins) and their meat (with Romanic origins) that is also found in such English word-pairs as pig/pork and sheep/mutton.

Beef is first divided into primal cuts. These are basic sections from which steaks and other subdivisions are cut. Since the animal's legs and neck muscles do the most work, they are the toughest; the meat becomes more tender as distance from *hoof and horn* increases. Different countries have different cuts and names.

The American cultural anthropologist Margaret Mead wrote in the American Anthropological Journal of the American Anthropological Association, "cultures that divide and cut beef specifically to consume are the Koreans and the Bodi tribe in East Africa. The French and English make 35 differentiations to the beef cuts, 51 cuts for the Bodi tribe, while the Koreans differentiate beef cuts into a staggering 120 different parts."

The following is a list of the American primal cuts. Beef carcasses are split along the axis of symmetry into 'halves', then across into front and back 'quarters' (forequarters and hindquarters).

Forequarter Cuts

The chuck is the source of bone-in chuck steaks and roasts (arm or blade), and boneless clod steaks and roasts, most commonly. The trimmings and some whole boneless chucks are ground for hamburgers.

The rib contains part of the short ribs, rib eye steaks, prime rib, and standing rib roasts.

The *brisket* is used for barbecue, corned beef and pastrami.

The foreshank or *shank* is used primarily for stews and soups; it is not usually served any other way due to it being the toughest of the cuts.

The plate is the other source of short ribs, used for pot roasting, and the outside skirt steak, which is used for fajitas. The remainder is usually ground, as it is typically a cheap, tough, and fatty meat.

Hindquarter Cuts

The loin has two subprimals, or three if boneless:

- the short loin, from which club, T-bone, and Porterhouse steaks are cut if bone-in, or strip loin (N.Y. strip) and filet mignon if boneless;
- the sirloin, which is less tender than short loin, but more flavorful, and can be further divided into top sirloin and bottom sirloin (including tri-tip); and
- the tenderloin, which is the most tender. It can be removed as a separate subprimal, and cut into fillets, tournedos or tenderloin steaks or roasts (such as for beef Wellington), or can be left on wedge or flat-bone sirloin and T-bone and Porterhouse loin steaks.

The round contains lean, moderately tough, lower fat (less marbling) cuts, which require moist cooking or lesser degrees of doneness. Some representative cuts are round steak, eye of round, top round and bottom round steaks and roasts.

The flank is used mostly for grinding, except for the long and flat flank steak, best known for use in London broil, and the inside skirt steak, also used for fajitas. Flank steaks were once one of the most affordable steaks, because they are substantially tougher than the more desirable loin and rib steaks. Many recipes for flank steak use marinades or moist cooking methods, such as braising, to improve the tenderness and flavour. This, in turn, increased the steaks' popularity; when combined with natural leanness, increased prices have resulted.

Special Beef Designations

Certified Angus Beef (CAB) is a specification-based, branded-beef programme which was founded in 1978 by Angus cattle producers to increase demand for their breed of cattle, by promoting the impression that Angus cattle have consistent, high-quality beef with superior taste. The brand is owned by the American Angus Association and its 35,000 rancher members. The terms *Angus Beef* or *Black Angus Beef* are loosely and commonly misused and/or confused with CAB; this is especially common in the foodservice industry. The brand or name Certified Angus Beef cannot be legally used by an establishment that is not licensed to do so.

Certified Hereford Beef is beef certified to have come from Hereford cattle.

Grass-fed beef cattle have been raised exclusively on forage. Grain-fed beef cattle are raised primarily on forage, but are 'finished' in a feedlot.

Kobe beef is from cattle of the Wagyu breed, raised and fattened in the hills above Kobe, Hyogo Prefecture, Japan. During the fattening period, the cattle are hand-fed (using high-energy feed, including beer and beer mash) for tenderness and high fat content, and hand-massaged to reduce stress.

Halal beef has been certified to have been processed in a prescribed manner in accordance with Muslim dietary laws.

Kosher beef has been certified to have been processed in a prescribed manner in accordance with Jewish dietary laws.

Organic beef is produced without added hormones, pesticides, or other chemicals, though requirements for labelling it *organic* vary widely.

The European Union recognises the following Protected Designation of Origin beef brands:

Spain - Carne de Ávila, Carne de Cantabria, Carne de la Sierra de Guadarrama, Carne de Morucha de Salamanca, Carne de Vacuno del País o Euskal Okela.

France - Taureau de Camargue, Boeuf charolais du Bourbonnais, Boeuf de Chalosse, Boeuf du Maine

Portugal - Carne Alentejana, Carne Arouquesa, Carne Barrosã, Carne Cachena da Peneda, Carne da Charneca, Carne de Bovino Cruzado dos Lameiros do Barroso, Carne dos Açores, Carne Marinhoa, Carne Maronesa, Carne Mertolenga, Carne Mirandesa

United Kingdom - Orkney Beef, Scotch Beef, Welsh Beef

Belgium - Belgian Blue

USDA Beef Grades

In the United States, the USDA Agricultural Marketing Service (AMS) operates a voluntary beef grading programme. The meat processor pays for a trained AMS meat grader to grade whole carcasses at the abattoir. Users are required to comply with Food Safety and Inspection Service (FSIS) grade labelling procedures. The official USDA grade designation can appear in one or any combination of the following ways: container markings, individual bags, legible roller brand appearing on the meat itself, or by a USDA shield stamp that incorporates the quality and/or yield grade.

There are eight beef quality grades. The grades are based on two main criteria: the degree of marbling (intramuscular fat) in the beef, and the maturity (estimated age of the animal at slaughter). Some meat scientists object to the current scheme of USDA grading since it is not based on direct measurement of tenderness, although marbling and maturity are indicators of tenderness. Most other countries' beef grading systems mirror the US model. Most beef offered for sale in supermarkets is graded US Choice or Select. US Prime beef is sold to hotels and upscale restaurants. Beef that would rate as US Standard or less is almost never offered for grading.

Utility, Cutter, and Canner grade are rarely used in foodservice operations and primarily used by processors and canners.

There are five beef yield grades — 1 to 5, which estimate the yield of saleable product, with YG 1 having the highest and YG 5 the lowest. Although consumers rarely see or are aware of it, yield grade was an important marketing tool for packers and retailers. The conversion from carcass and bone-in primals to boneless, trimmed cuts has reduced the importance.

Traditionally, beef sold in steakhouses and supermarkets has been advertised by its USDA grade; however, many restaurants and retailers have recently begun advertising beef on the strength of brand names and the reputation of a specific breed of cattle, such as black Angus.

To improve tenderness of beef, it often is aged (i.e., stored refrigerated) to allow endogenous proteolytic enzymes to weaken structural and myofibrillar proteins. Wet aging is accomplished using vacuum packaging to reduce spoilage and yield loss. Dry aging involves hanging primals (usually ribs or loins) in humidity-controlled coolers. Outer surfaces dry out and can support growth of molds (and spoilage bacteria, if too humid), resulting in trim and evaporative losses. Evaporation concentrates the remaining proteins and increases flavour intensity; the molds can contribute a nut-like flavour. The majority of the tenderizing effect occurs in the first 10 days, although two to three days allow significant effects. Boxed beef, stored and distributed in vacuum packaging, is, in effect, wet aged during distribution. Premium steakhouses dry age for 21 to 28 days or wet age up to 45 days for maximum effect on flavour and tenderness. Meat from less tender cuts or older cattle can be mechanically tenderized by forcing small, sharp blades through the cuts to disrupt the proteins. Also, solutions of exogenous proteolytic enzymes (papain, bromelin or ficin) can be injected to augment the endogenous enzymes. Similarly, solutions of salt and sodium phosphates can be injected to soften and swell the myofibrillar proteins. This improves juiciness and tenderness. Salt can improve the flavour, but phosphate can contribute a soapy flavour.

Moist Heat

Moist heat cooking methods include braising, pot roasting, and stewing.

Stewing

Simmering meat, whole or cut into bite-size pieces, in a water-based liquid with flavourings.

Braising

Cooking meats, in a covered container, with small amounts of liquids (usually seasoned or flavoured). Unlike stewing, braised meat is not fully immersed in liquid, and usually is browned before the oven step.

Meat has usually been cooked in water which is just simmering; higher temperatures make meat tougher. Since thermostatic temperature control became available, cooking at temperatures well below boiling, 65°C (149°F) to 90°C (194°F), for prolonged periods has become possible; this is just hot enough to dissolve connective tissue and kill bacteria, with minimal toughening.

Raw Beef

Steak tartare is a French dish made from finely chopped or ground (minced) raw meat (often beef). More accurately, it is scraped so as not to let even the slightest of the sinew fat get into the scraped meat. It is often served with onions, capers, seasonings such as fresh ground pepper and Worcestershire sauce, and sometimes raw egg. The Belgian dish *filet américain* is also made of finely chopped ground beef, though it is seasoned differently, and either eaten as a main dish or can be used as a dressing for a sandwich. *Kibbeh nayyeh* is a similar Lebanese dish. And in Ethiopia, a ground raw meat dish called *tire siga* or *kitfo* is eaten.

Carpaccio of beef is a thin slice of raw beef dressed with olive oil, lemon juice and seasoning. Often, the beef is partially frozen before slicing to allow very thin slices to be cut.

Yukhoe is a variety of *hoe,* raw dishes in Korean cuisine which is usually made from raw ground beef seasoned with various spices or sauces. The beef part used for *yukhoe* is tender rump steak. For the seasoning, soy sauce, sugar, salt, sesame oil, green onion, and ground garlic, sesame seed, black pepper and juice of *bae* (Korean pear) are used. The beef is mostly topped with the yolk of a raw egg.

Cured or Smoked Beef

Bresaola is an air-dried, salted beef that has been aged about two to three months until it becomes hard and a dark red, almost purple, colour. It is lean, has a sweet, musty smell and is tender. It originated in Valtellina, a valley in the Alps of northern Italy's Lombardy region. Bündnerfleisch is a similar product from neighbouring Switzerland.

Pastrami is often made from beef; raw beef is salted, then partly dried and seasoned with various herbs and spices, and smoked.

Corned beef is a cut of beef cured or pickled in a seasoned brine. The corn in *corned beef* refers to the grains of coarse salts (known as corns) used to cure it. The term *corned beef* can denote different styles of brine-cured beef, depending on the region. Some, like American-style corned beef, are highly seasoned and often considered delicatessen fare.

Beef jerky is dried, salted, smoked beef popular in the United States.

Biltong is a cured, salted, air dried beef popular in South Africa.

Spiced beef is a cured and salted joint of round, topside, or silverside, traditionally served at Christmas in Ireland. It is a form of salt beef, cured with spices and saltpetre, intended to be boiled or broiled in Guinness or a similar stout, and then optionally roasted for a period after.

Religious Prohibitions

Hindus and Indian Buddhists generally consider killing cattle and eating beef a taboo, and Jains are forbidden to eat any kind of meat. Though the Indo-Aryans ate beef and served it to guests, bovines have been highly revered as sacred to mankind in Indian culture since the Indus Valley Civilization. The role of cattle, especially cows, as a source of milk, meat, dairy products, and their relative importance to the pastoral Aryans allowed this special status; and this rose to prominence with the advent of the Jain tradition and Hindu revivalism during the Gupta period.

During the season of Lent, Catholics traditionally give up all meat and poultry products as a religious act of fasting. Prior to Pope Paul VI's *Paenitemini*, canonical law strictly stated meat was forbidden on all Fridays, a violation of which could be a mortal sin. Pope Paul VI's revisions relaxed the policy; now, the common interpretation is that meat is only forbidden on Ash Wednesday and Fridays in the season of Lent, although the fact that some form of penance is still asked of Catholics on Fridays leads many to continue the traditional abstention from beef and poultry.

Jews refrain from eating meat and poultry (and drinking wine, among other restrictions) during The Nine Days of mourning leading up to the fast of Tisha B'Av.

Beef is a good source of minerals, such as zinc, selenium, phosphorus and iron, and B vitamins. Red meat is the most significant dietary source of carnitine and, like any other meat (pork, fish, veal, lamb etc.), is a source of creatine.

Health Concerns

A study released in 2007 by the World Cancer Research Fund reported "strong evidence that red meat and processed meats are causes of bowel cancer" and recommends people eat less than 500 grams (18 oz) of cooked red meat weekly, and as little processed meat as possible. The report also recommends that average consumption in populations should not exceed 300 grams (11 oz) per week, stating this goal "corresponds to the level of consumption of red meat at which the risk of colorectal cancer can clearly be seen to rise." Lean beef, with its high selenium and vitamin B_{12} content, may actually lower the risk of colon cancer.

The Harvard School of Public Health recommends consumers eat red meat sparingly as it has high levels of undesirable saturated fat. Nevertheless, a meta-analysis of the most current epidemiological studies that appeared in the *American Journal of Clinical Nutrition* indicated "[T]here is no significant evidence for concluding that dietary saturated fat is associated with an increased risk" of coronary heart disease or cardiovascular disease. Like some other animal products (such as whole milk), red meat provides a rich source of conjugated linoleic acid, which may protect against several diseases, along with the saturated fat. Beef's high content of vitamins B_6 and B_{12} may help lower homocysteine.

Mad Cow Disease

In 1984, the use of meat and bone meal in cattle feed resulted in the world's first outbreak of bovine spongiform encephalopathy (BSE or, colloquially, mad cow disease) in the United Kingdom.

Since then, other countries have had outbreaks of BSE:

In May 2003, after a cow with BSE was discovered in Alberta, Canada, the American border was closed to live Canadian cattle, but was reopened in early 2005.

Argentine Beef

Beef is a key component of traditional Argentine cuisine.

Argentina has the world's highest consumption rate of beef, at 65 kg a year per capita. In 2006, livestock farmers kept between 50 and 55 million head of cattle, mostly in the fertile pastures of the Pampas. The country is currently the third largest beef exporter in the world after Brazil and Australia. The national government applies a 15 per cent tax on beef exports and has applied further restrictions since March 2006 to keep domestic prices low.

Current Export Restrictions

On 8 March 2006, after unsuccessfully trying to control the rising prices of beef in the internal market (26% since the beginning of that year), the Argentine government banned beef exports for 180 days (with the exception of pre-arranged shipments and the Hilton Quota). On 26 May, the ban was replaced by a quota, to be in force between June and November, equivalent to 40 per cent of the amount of beef exported in the same period of 2005.

These measures met harsh criticism from livestock farmers, the meat processing industry, and the export sector; some analysts have said that it will be useless in the long term and harm Argentina's international image, besides causing large monetary losses. Other analysts have said it is the only adequate measure that deals with inflation and that the industry is the only one in Argentina profitable enough to sustain such a policy.

Cattle were first introduced into Argentina in 1536 by Spanish Conquistadors. Due to the geographic conditions on the Pampas and an insufficiently large internal market, the cattle multiplied rapidly. Railway construction within Argentina and the invention of refrigerated trains and ships in the late 19th century created an external export market and Argentina's beef export industry started to thrive. The reversed seasons between the Northern and Southern Hemispheres meant that Argentine beef came onto the market at a time of year when beef was less readily available in the Northern Hemisphere, which further increased the potential export market in the United States and European markets.

Following the increasing demand for high quality beef, new breeds and selective crossbreeding have been developed.

Argentine beef and its production have played a major part in the Culture of Argentina, from the *asado* to the history of the *gauchos* of the Pampas. Landowners became wealthy from beef production and export, and *estancia* owners built large houses, important buildings in Buenos Aires and elsewhere, and contributed to politics, philanthropy and society. The agricultural show *La Rural* each winter in Buenos Aires became a major part of the social season since it started in 1886.

In Chile heightened taxes for the import of Argentine cattle in 1905 led to the Meat riots, one of the first massive protests in Santiago. The price of meat was kept artificially high by the government, by means of the combination of a special tariff applied to cattle imports from Argentina, in order to protect the domestic producers, and a runaway inflation. The riots lasted from October 22 until October 27, and between 200 and 250 people were killed over this period, while more than 500 were injured. The financial losses were staggering. This revolt emphasized that the social problems were far more serious than what the authorities believed.

Foot-and-mouth Disease Crisis

Argentina's cattle industry had become one of the most important economic factors of the country, as worldwide, Argentina had become the fourth largest beef exporter. As such, it was devastating news when, in 2001, for the first time after 60 years, new cases of foot-and-mouth diseases (FMD) were announced. Although FMD is in most cases harmless to people, it is a highly contagious (between animals) viral disease which requires the slaughter of infected animals. Argentine beef was banned by more than 60 countries, including the United States and Canada, as they were afraid of allowing the disease to spread among their own cattle.

After an aggressive vaccination programme, the OIE (Office International des Epizooties) declared in 2003 that Argentina had regained "foot-and-mouth free with vaccination" status. A few years later, new cases of FMD were discovered in a herd of cattle in a northern province of Argentina. As a result, Chile banned the import of Argentine meat.

Food Safety or Quality labels are rarely used in Argentina and a major initiative has been called for on this issue. There is no label certified by the government. The unsatisfactory situation concerning Food Safety becomes immediately clear by looking at the fact that the Argentine National Inspection Services audited and approved only 35 slaughterhouses in 2003 on Good Manufacturing Practices and Hazard Analysis and Critical Control Point (HACCP).

However, farmers as well as the export industry started to realize that there is a steadily increasing demand for safer and more reliable brands. To meet customer expectations, several initiatives have been taken. There are certificates handed out by private organizations, such as breed associations. For instance, the Argentine Angus Association established a *Carne Angus Certificada* to ensure that only meat coming from an Angus is described as Angus. Furthermore, the association supports other certificates like the *Ternero Angus Certificado.*

Besides the breed associations, different pilot projects have been initiated. The *Pampas Del Salado* project is an example of these; its approach has been to ear-tag calves in order to assure their origin and quality. However, most of those projects have only scant participation; certificates and labels will only gain reputation and acceptance among consumers only if there is a sufficiently large percentage of producers participating.

Promotion of Argentine Beef

In order to increase sales in foreign countries and to improve the production and reliability of beef produced in Argentina, a public non-governmental organization, the IPCVA (*Instituto de Promoción de la Carne Vacuna Argentina*— The Argentine Beef Promotion Institute) was founded in December 2001. Furthermore, the IPCVA is also concerned with promotional work in Argentina itself.

The IPCVA is made up of a range of partners involved in Argentine Beef production and export, from experienced cattle farmers to managers. This broad expertise in various fields aims to allow the IPCVA to organize beef production and beef sales professionally. As a fairly young institution, the IPCVA has had to define an image which allows the identification of the main product, beef. Three key factors influence this image: history, tradition, and prestige. All of them are considered to be USP's (Unique selling própositions).

International and National Promotion

Several activities have been undertaken to make Argentine beef better known in the world:

- The IPCVA participated in the International Food and Drink Exhibition (IFE) held in London, United Kingdom in March.
- An Argentine Beef Festival was arranged last February in Helsinki, Finland. In order to promote the product, a big Banquet was held at the Helsinki Oasis Hotel with the Argentine Ambassador.
- Representatives of the IPCVA traveled to Washington DC, USA to negotiate a special contract to ease export of Argentine Beef to the North American market.
- Qualitative soundings are being developed in the main cities of the European Union to better know consumers' preferences in order to design specific promotion campaigns.

However, with the export restrictions for beef set by the Argentine government, these measures may be of little use. Therefore, the IPCVA also focuses on promotion work in Argentina.

The IPCVA is developing the first beef consumption map in Argentina. Through complete research of the domestic market, an 'X-Ray' of the beef consumption in the whole country will be set up and used for marketing and promotion purposes.

'Las Leonas' Secret' Las Leonas, the Argentine women's field hockey team, has a contract with the IPCVA to eat Argentine beef. This prestigious sport is seen as key to promoting the meat, especially because prestige is one of the key factors of the Argentine beef image.

Funding of the IPCVA

These huge promotions are expensive. Therefore the IPCVA arranged to get the following contributions for its budget:

- 1.25 Argentine pesos from producers per killed animal
- 0.55 Argentine pesos from packers per packed animal

This adds up to 1.80 Argentine pesos per slaughtered animal. At a killing rate of 13 million animals per year, it totals 23,400,000 Argentine pesos. This is a budget of around •6,325,000 per year (March 28, 2006).

Goals of the IPCVA

The long term goals of the IPCVA are described as follows on their website:

- Identify and create demand for Argentine beef products in domestic and foreign markets.
- Design and develop marketing strategies to improve Argentine beef products' competitiveness overseas.
- Plan and develop promotion strategies to contribute to the improvement of domestic consumption levels.
- Work to consolidate Argentine beef quality and security, contributing to the efficiency of productive and industrial processes.

The IPCVA has become a major instrument to improve the international competitiveness of Argentine beef.

Quality of Argentine Beef

Beef quality is dependent on the diet provided to cattle and their living conditions. The two different farming regimes used for beef production in Argentina are grass pasture and feedlot-based farming.

Argentina's rainfall and largely temperate climate result in high quality pastures, which may, however, not be suitable for more intensive agriculture. The Humid Pampa (*Pampa Húmeda*) is the most important and best-known cattle-producing region, as it has vast and open pastures. Grass-fed beef is believed to be healthier than beef from feedlots, as it contains less saturated fat and more omega 3 fatty acids than grain-fed beef, and so does not contribute so much to raising cholesterol in humans. Although the latter diet is increasing, grass-fed beef is still the most popular in Argentina.

Grass-fed cattle are living under more natural conditions, and are less likely to have hormone implants. On the other hand, the technique requires large amounts of expensive land and a larger number of trained staff. Additionally, it takes longer to raise the animal.

As beef is increasingly mass-produced, farming techniques with the ultimate goal of fattening the animals are evolving; the most common of these is grain-fed beef cattle held in feedlots. But as the animals, denied physical effort and stocked together, get fatter; beer is often used to calm them. In order to prevent disease on farms and feedlots, the animals are fed antibiotics. The feedlot diet guarantees constant and controlled results, year-round productivity as it is not as dependent on climate and does not require so much land. Taking into consideration all these factors, it is thus the cheaper diet, but there are suggestions it is less beneficial for the welfare of the animals and for the health-giving qualities and flavour of the meat.

The high consumption per capita shows that beef is profoundly integrated into traditional Argentine cuisine. In fact, only Uruguay eats more beef per capita than Argentina. However, as can be seen, beef exports are not an essential part of the Argentine economy. This is in large part because Argentina consumes most of its beef and the industry has been prevented from orienting itself to an export industry. Secondary reasons include the restrictive rules and regulations on beef of importing countries. For instance, Argentina agreed with the United States on an annual restriction of 20,000 tons. While these rules were not always in place in previous years/ decades, Argentina still has not become a massive exporter of beef, but an exporter nonetheless.

Even while beef exports are not fully developed for a larger contribution to the Argentine economy, Argentina has been a major player in the world beef market for many years, due in large part to the reputation of Argentine beef.

CATTLE BREEDS

Shorthorn

Originally from northeast England, the shorthorn was introduced to Argentina in 1826 and was the first foreign breed to enter the country. As in many other countries, Argentina's selection was designated to produce not only meat but milk as well.

Nowadays, Argentina's Shorthorn breed has been bred to greatly improve its meat quality thanks to hybridisation (crossbreeding) as has been demonstrated at the National Agropecuarian Technology Centre.

Characteristics: considerable size; wide back and forequarters. A couple of centuries ago, they used to lack symmetry and uniformity.

Hereford

Produced with the objective of responding to England's food market expansion during Britain's industrial revolution the Hereford is known for its high yield of beef. It was first introduced to Argentina in 1858, and is characterized by its juice and flavour consistency. Just as the Argentina's Shorthorn has evolved, so did the Argentine Hereford through crossbreeding with local breeds.

Characteristics: high yield of beef; wide back; early maturity; rustling ability and hardiness.

Aberdeen Angus

Originally from Scotland, the Aberdeen Angus were first introduced to Argentina by Don Carlos Guerrero in 1879.

They are generally found in temperate climates. Instead of focussing on crossbreeding in order to strength their qualities, Argentine farmers decided to focus on a purebred evolution based on natural and high-quality nutrition.

Characteristics: maternal skills; highly fertile; growth capacity; climate adaptation; thin skin; short and smooth hair.

Holando-Argentina

Derived from the Holstein, it was first introduced from The Netherlands in 1880, to the fertile regions the Pampas, and devoted to the production of both beef and milk.

Zebu

Originally from India, the Zebu is an animal used for pulling loads. Many different breeds can be found spread over the world since they were crossbred in order to pass on their tolerance to hot weather and strength.

Characteristics: light coloured; clear hump between the shoulders; large horns; hot climate and insect tolerance.

Charolais

Brought to Argentina around 1910, the Charolais breed is originally from France. Focusing on size and strength, farmers paid little attention to their quality of meat and therefore to refinement. Characteristics: wide opened and round horns; long and tall; projecting shoulders and deep hips.

Recipes with Argentine Beef

Beef is traditionally cooked over charcoal flame (as an *asado*) and served often as part of a wider selection of grilled meat, with chimichurri as a relish.

General Treatment and Cooking of Beef Meat

The following points are a summary how to treat and cook beef meat correctly. These guidelines were set up by the IPCVA (Instituto de Promoción de la Carne Vacuna Argentina).

To ease cooking and to make the meat lighter, fat should be removed except for pieces that are to be grilled.

For the eye round, totally separate the outside fat, and remove the film that covers it with a sharp knife. Then season the beef before cooking it.

To cook beef brown the meat on all sides. Then take it out of the pan, and add it again once the liquid of the recipe is being added.

In order not to lose the beef's natural juices once arranged in the platter, paint the meat with its own juice, or use the juice as ingredient for the sauce.

When doing the beef in the oven always seal the meat first. This stops the loss of juices. (Seal in a Frying pan, or in the oven at high heat).

To freeze beef, freeze quantities that you will be able to use for future meals. Preferably cut the beef in small pieces to freeze it. This way it will be easier to defrost it, and the fibres will not break.

Cooked meat should be frozen with its sauce.

Jerky (Food)

Jerky is meat that has been cut into strips, trimmed of fat, marinated in a seasoned sweet rub or liquid, and dried or smoked with low heat (usually under 70°C/160°F) or is occasionally just salted and sun-dried. The result is a sweet (occasionally semisweet or savory) snack which can be eaten immediately, or which can be stored for months without refrigeration.

The word 'jerky' comes from the Quechua term *charqui,* which means *to burn (meat).*

Jerked meat was one of the first human-made products and was a crucially important food preservation technique for survival.

Any particular preparation or recipe for jerky typically uses only one type of meat. Around the world, meat from domestic and wild animals is used to make jerky. Meats from domestic animals include beef, pork, goat and mutton or lamb. Wild animals including deer, elk, caribou, kudu, springbok, kangaroo, bison and moose are also used. Recently, other animals such as turkey, ostrich, salmon, alligator, tuna, emu and horse are also used.

The meat must be dried quickly, to limit bacterial growth during the critical period where the meat is not yet dry. To do this, the meat is thinly sliced, or pressed thinly, in the case of ground meat. The strips of meat are dried at low temperatures, to avoid cooking it, or overdrying it to the point where it is brittle.

In present-day factories, large jerky ovens are made of insulated panels. Inside these low-temperature drying ovens are many heater elements and fans. The ovens have exhaust ports to remove the moisture-laden air. The combination of fast-moving air and low heat dries the meat to the desired moisture content within a few hours. The raw, marinated jerky strips are placed on racks of nylon-coated metal screens which have been sprayed with a light vegetable oil to allow the meat to be removed easily. The screen trays are placed closely in layers on rolling carts which are then put in the drying oven.

Some additional form of chemical preservative, such as sodium nitrite, is often used in conjunction with the historical salted drying procedure to prepare jerky. Smoking is the most traditional method, as it preserves, flavors, and dries the meat simultaneously. Salting is the most common method used today, as it both provides seasoning to improve the flavor as well as preserve the meat. While some methods involve applying the seasonings with a marinade, this can increase the drying time by adding moisture to the meat.

Much like numerous types of foods produced, there are some jerky products that are made naturally and organically. Natural and organic jerky makers use meat from animals which are raised on organic feed and are minimally processed. These animals are not treated with hormone enhancement and are not fed animal byproducts. Additionally, these jerky products may be gluten free.

Packaging

After the jerky is dried to the proper moisture content to prevent spoilage, it is cooled, then packaged in resealable plastic bags, either nitrogen gas flushed or vacuumed packed. To prevent the oxidation of the fat, the sealed packages often contain small pouches of oxygen absorber. These small packets are filled with iron particles which react with oxygen, removing the O_2 from the sealed jerky package, and from the air that is introduced after the seal is broken (due to partial consumption).

Most of the fat must be trimmed off prior to drying the meat, as fat does not dry, thus creating the potential for spoilage as the fat becomes rancid (modern vacuum packing and chemical preservatives have served to help prevent these risks).

Because of the necessary low fat and moisture content, jerky is high in protein. A 30 g (about 1 oz) portion of lean meat, for example, contains about 7 g of protein. By removing 15 g of water from the meat, the protein ratio is doubled to nearly 15 g of protein per 30 g portion. In some low moisture varieties, a 30 g serving will contain 21 grams of protein, and only one gram of fat. This leads to the high price of such brands of jerky, as it takes 90 g of 99 per cent lean meat to generate that 30 gram serving.

Unpackaged fresh jerky made from sliced, whole muscle meat has been available in specialty stores in Hong Kong at least since the 1970s. The products are purchased by kilograms, and customers choose from 10 to 20 types of meat used to make the product. Some are sold in strands instead of slices. Macau has opened numerous specialty shops also, many of which are franchise extensions of stores from Hong Kong. Compared to the sealed packaged versions, unpackaged jerky has a relatively short shelf life.

This type of jerky has also become very popular in convenience stores in the USA. This product is called 'slab' jerky and is usually marketed in plexiglass containers.

Regulation

Most nations have regulations pertaining to the production of dried meat products. There are strict requirements to ensure safe and wholesome production of jerky products. Factories are required to have inspectors and sanitation plans. In the United States, the U.S. Department of Agriculture (USDA) is responsible for that oversight. Many European Union countries presently prohibit the importation of meat products, including jerky, without additional and extensive customs documentation, and further inspections.

Availability

Traditional jerky, made from sliced, whole muscle meat, is readily available in the United States and Canada in varying meats, brands and qualities, both as packaged and unpackaged. These products are available in nearly every convenience store, gas station, supermarket, and variety shop in those countries.

A similar, less expensive product is made with finely ground meat, mixed with flavors, then the mush is processed into thin dried strips. The finished item labeled as jerky, but with the qualifier 'ground and formed'. This product is widely available in general interest stores, such as supermarkets and convenience stores.

Also popular is shredded dry jerky sold in containers resembling snuff or dip. Jerky made in the traditional style is also a ubiquitous staple of farmers' markets in rural areas all over North America.

In addition to being quite common in the United States and Canada, jerky is also gaining popularity in supermarkets, convenience stores and online retailers. In Australia, New Zealand and the United Kingdom, jerky products are available and becoming more common. They are carried by some major supermarkets, and now also smaller stores. In China, in addition to the more traditional forms of jerky, there is also a similar product which is usually made from pork called pork chip.

A similar product is quite popular in Rome, Italy, and its hinterland: it is called *coppiette* and was originally made with horse or donkey meat, but it is now generally made with pork. Coppiette are seasoned with red pepper and fennel seeds. Coppiette were usually eaten while drinking wine (mostly white) in Roman osterie.

In Ethiopia jerky is called *qwant'a*. In addition to salt, it is seasoned with black pepper and either berbere or awaze. however, it differs very much in production process and taste.

Since 1996, jerky has been selected by astronauts as space food several times for space flight due to its light weight and high level of nutrition.

Veal

Veal is the meat of young cattle (calves), as opposed to beef from older cattle. Though veal can be produced from a calf of either sex and any breed, most veal comes from male calves of dairy cattle breeds. Veal has a tender texture.

There are five types of veal:

- **Bob veal**, from calves that are slaughtered when only a few days old (70-150 lb.) up to 150 lb.
- **Formula-fed (or 'milk-fed') veal**, from calves that are raised on a milk formula supplement. The meat colour is ivory or creamy pink, with a firm, fine, and velvety appearance. They are usually slaughtered when they reach 18-20 weeks of age (450-500 lb).
- **Non-formula-fed ('red' or 'grain-fed') veal**, from calves that are raised on grain, hay, or other solid food, in addition to milk. The meat is darker in colour, and some additional marbling and fat may be apparent. Usually marketed as calf, rather than veal, at 22-26 weeks of age (650-700 lb).
- **Rose veal** UK is from calves reared on farms in association with the UK RSPCA's Freedom Food programme. Its name comes from its pink colour, which is a result of the calves being slaughtered at around 35 weeks.

- **Free-raised veal**, The veal calves are raised in the pasture, have unlimited access to mother's milk and pasture grasses. They are not administered hormones or antibiotics. These conditions replicate those used to raise authentic pasture-raised veal. The meat is a rich pink color. Free-raised veal are typically lower in fat than other veal. Calves are slaughtered at about 24 weeks of age.

The veal industry's support for the dairy industry goes beyond the purchase of surplus calves. It also buys large amounts of milk by-products. Almost 70 per cent of veal feeds (by weight) are milk products. Most popular are whey and whey protein concentrate (WPC), by-products of the manufacture of cheese. Milk by-products are sources of protein and lactose. Skimmed milk powder, casein, buttermilk powder and other forms of milk by-products are used from time to time.

Veal has been an important ingredient in Italian and French cuisine since ancient times. The veal is often in the form of cutlets, such as the Italian cotoletta or the famous Austrian dish Wiener Schnitzel. Some classic French veal dishes include: fried escalopes, fried veal grenadines (small thick fillet steaks), stuffed paupiettes, roast joints and blanquettes. As veal is lower in fat than many meats, care must be taken in preparation to ensure that it does not become tough. Veal is often coated in preparation for frying or eaten with a sauce. Veal Parmigiana is a common Italian-American dish consisting of breaded veal cutlets.

In addition to providing meat, the bones of calves are used to make a stock that forms the base for sauces and soups such as demi-glace. The stomachs are also used to produce rennet, used in the production of cheese. Calf offal is also widely regarded as the most prized of animal offal. Most valued are the liver, sweetbreads, kidney, and bone marrow. The head, brains, tongue, feet, and mesentery are also valued.

Veal is a byproduct of the dairy industry and comes from male dairy calves. Veal in the United States contributes $250 million to the American dairy industry. To produce milk, cows must be lactating, and to be lactating, they must get pregnant and give birth. Approximately 50 per cent of all calves born in dairy farming are male. Since female calves are used to produce milk and beef, use of male calves is limited, outside of breeding.

Newborn calves are given a varied amount of time with their mothers, which can be anything from a few hours to a few days. Free raised calves are raised alongside their mothers, and always have access to their mother's milk.

Housing

There are primarily three different types of housing used for veal calves: hutches, stalls, or various types of group housing.

While calves are young and most vulnerable to disease, they are kept in hutches, which keep them isolated and restricts movement so as to prevent muscle from developing, as the taste of veal raised in this manner is considered desirable.

Free-raised or pasture-raised veal calves require no housing, barns, or facilities. Calves freely roam open pastures with their mothers and herd.

Feeding

Milk-fed veal calves consume a diet consisting of milk replacer, formulated with mostly milk-based proteins with added vitamins and minerals to provide a balanced nutritional solution. This type of diet relates to infant formula and is also one of the most common diets used for calves in the veal industry.

Grain-fed calves normally consume a diet of milk replacer for the first 6-8 weeks. The calves then move onto a grain-based diet (mostly corn-based), that contains many vitamins and minerals.

Free raised calves are raised on an open pasture and receive of diet of milk, grass, and fresh water. Furthermore, free raised calves do not receive drugs such as hormones or antibiotics, which is often a focus of criticism amongst animal welfare organizations.

Animal Welfare

Multiple animal welfare organizations, who strongly focus on factory farming, attempt to educate consumers about several veal production procedures that they consider to be inhumane. This education has proven successful in creating pressure on the industry, resulting in recently announced changes in the methods used by the veal industry.

A strong animal welfare movement concerning veal started in the 1980s with the release of photographs of veal calves tethered in crates where they could barely move. After the release of these photographs, veal sales have plummeted, and have never recovered.

Many veal farmers listened to the concern of their customers and have started improving conditions in their veal farms.

The American Veal Association has announced they plan to phase out the use of crates by 2017, which is often the main focus of controversy in veal farming. Strauss Brands is the first veal packer in the US to raise veal calves in a completely tether free and group raised since December 31, 2008.

Criticism with veal crates revolve around the facts that the veal calves are highly restricted in movement; have unsuitable flooring; spend their entire lives indoors; experience prolonged sensory, social, and exploratory deprivation; and are more susceptible to high amounts of stress and disease. However, according to the Veal Quality Assurance Programme and Veal Issues Management Programme industry fact sheet, and the Ontario Veal Association, individual housing systems are important for disease control, and in reducing the possibility of physical injury. Furthermore, they state that it also allows for veal farmers to provide more personal attention to veal calves, being in individual crates.

Alternative agricultural practices for using male dairy calves include raising bob veal (slaughter at 2 or 3 days old), raising calves as 'red veal' without the severity of dietary restrictions needed to create pale meat (resulting in fewer antibiotic treatments and fewer slaughtered calves), and as dairy beef.

When it comes to the centuries-old method of free raised veal, calves never experience the stress of confinement, separation from their mothers and herd-mates, or an unnatural diet. Many veal producers are realizing this, and the demand for free raised veal is rapidly increasing.

In 2007, less than 5 per cent of veal calves were raised in a group environment. In 2009, this had increased to 35 per cent.

Vermont Bob Veal Slaughterhouse Closure

In November 2009, a slaughterhouse certified as an organic processor in Vermont specializing in bob veal was closed after a series of cases of inhumane treatment towards veal calves. Inhumane treatment, in this situation, involved calves that appeared to have been skinned alive, kicked, dragged, and repeatedly shocked with electric prods.

In a hidden-camera investigation by the HSUS, a USDA Food Safety and Inspection Service inspector was shown coaching a slaughterhouse worker on ways to avoid having the facility being shut down. The facility, Bushway Packing, was shut down by the USDA with the Vermont Agriculture Agency.

Drug Usage in Veal

The USDA does not approve the use of hormones on veal calves for any reason, with the exclusion for use in ruminating cattle, which is not related to veal. They do, however, approve the use of antibiotics in veal raising to treat or prevent disease. There is no check in order to see that farmers and veal producers do not use antibiotics for reasons other than preventing or treat diseases.

In 2004, an official of the USDA found a lump on a veal calf in a Wisconsin veal farm. This lump turned out to be an illegal hormone implant (such implants are only allowed legally for beef cattle). PETA claims that the American Veal Association has confessed that this practice has been going for 30 years.

The USDA has expressed concern that the use of illegal drugs might be widespread in the veal industry.

The USDA claims, in relation to penicillin, the following:

- "Penicillin is not used in calf raising: tetracycline has been approved but is not widely used."

Veal Crate Bans

The following shows where veal crates have been banned, or are currently in the process of being banned:

Europe

Veal crates became illegal in the UK in 1990, and a full ban has been placed for the entire European Union, as of 2007. Switzerland, with its substantial dairy industry, continues to use crates.

Veal calf production as such is not allowed in many Northern European countries, such as in Finland. As in Finland giving feed, drink or other nutrition which is known to be dangerous to the health of the animal to an animal which is being cared for is prohibited, as well as failing to give nutrients the lack of which is known to cause the animal to fall ill. Finnish animal welfare decree and Finnish Animal Welfare Act.

CHAPTER

4

MEAT OF DOMESTIC SHEEP

Lamb, mutton, and hogget (New Zealand and Australia) are the meat of domestic sheep. The meat of a sheep in its first year is *lamb*; that of a juvenile sheep older than 1 year is *hogget*; and the meat of an adult sheep is *mutton*.

The strict definitions for lamb, hogget and mutton vary considerably between countries. In New Zealand for example, they are defined as follows:

- ***Lamb*** — a young sheep under 12 months of age which does not have any permanent incisor teeth in wear.
- ***Hogget*** — a young male sheep or maiden ewe having no more than two permanent incisors in wear.
- ***Mutton*** — a female (ewe) or castrated male (wether) sheep having more than two permanent incisors in wear.

In Australia the definitions are extended to include ewes and rams, as well as being stricter on the definition for lamb which is:

- ***Lamb*** — 0 permanent incisors; female or castrate entire male ovine 0–12 months (note that the Australian definition requires 0 permanent incisors, whereas the New Zealand definition allows 0 incisors 'in wear'.)

Under current United States federal regulations, only the term 'lamb' is used:

- ***Lamb*** – ovine animals of any age, including ewes and rams.

The terms 'mutton' and 'hogget' are essentially unknown in the United States.

The younger the lamb is, the smaller the lamb will be; however, the meat will be more tender. Sheep mutton is meat from a sheep over two years old, and has a less tender flesh. In general, the darker the colour, the older the animal. Baby lamb meat will be pale pink, while regular lamb is pinkish-red.

Other definitions include:

- ***Lamb*** – a young sheep that is less than one year old.
- ***Baby lamb*** – a milk-fed lamb between six and eight weeks old.
- ***Spring lamb*** – a milk-fed lamb, usually three to five months old, born in late winter or early spring and sold usually before July 1.
- ***Yearling lamb*** – a young sheep between 12 and 24 months old.
- ***Milk-fed lamb*** – meat from an unweaned lamb, typically 4 to 6 weeks old and weighing 5.5 to 8 kg; this is almost unavailable in countries such as the USA and the UK, where it is considered uneconomic. The flavour and texture of milk-fed lamb when grilled (such as the tiny lamb chops known as *chuletillas* in Spain) or roasted (*lechazo asado* or *cordero lechal asado*) is generally thought to be finer than that of older lamb. The areas in northern Spain where this can be found include Asturias, Cantabria, Castile and León, and La Rioja. Milk-fed lambs (and kids) are especially prized for Easter in Greece, when they are roasted on a spit.

- ***Sucker lambs*** — a term used in Australia includes young milk-fed lambs as well as slightly older lambs up to about 7 months of age which are also still dependent on their mothers for milk. Carcases from these lambs usually weigh between 14 and 30 kg. Older weaned lambs which have not yet matured to become mutton are known as old-season lambs.
- ***Saltbush mutton*** — a term used in Australia for the meat of mature Merinos which have been allowed to graze on atriplex plants.
- ***Salt marsh lamb*** (also known as 'saltmarsh lamb' or by its French name, *agneau de pré-salé*) — the meat of sheep which graze on salt marsh in coastal estuaries that are washed by the tides and support a range of salt-tolerant grasses and herbs such as samphire, sparta grass, sorrel and sea lavender. Depending on where in the world the salt marsh is located, the nature of the plants may be subtly different. Salt marsh lamb has long been appreciated in France and is growing in popularity in the United Kingdom. Places where salt marsh lamb are reared in the UK include Harlech and the Gower Peninsula in Wales, the Somerset Levels and Morecambe Bay.

In many Eastern countries including the Indian sub-continent, Malaysia and Singapore, the term *mutton* refers to goats' meat (which is properly called *chevon*) and usually not to sheep's meat. Often, the mutton curries of the Indian cuisine use goat meat when cooked at home.

The meat of a lamb is taken from the animal between one month and one year old, with a carcase (*carcass* in American English) weight of between 5.5 and 30 kilograms (12 and 65 lbs). This meat generally is more tender than that from older sheep and appears more often on tables in some Western countries. Hogget and mutton have a stronger flavour than lamb because they contain a higher concentration of species-characteristic fatty acids and are preferred by some. Mutton and hogget also tend to be tougher than lamb (because of connective tissue maturation) and are therefore better suited to casserole-style cooking, as in Lancashire hotpot, for example.

Lamb is often sorted into three kinds of meat: forequarter, loin, and hindquarter. The forequarter includes the neck, shoulder, front legs, and the ribs up to the shoulder blade. The hindquarter includes the rear legs and hip. The loin includes the ribs between the two.

Lamb chops are cut from the rib, loin, and shoulder areas. The rib chops include a rib bone; the loin chops include only a chine bone. Shoulder chops are usually considered inferior to loin chops; both kinds of chop are usually grilled. Breast of lamb (baby chops) can be cooked in an oven.

Leg of lamb is a whole leg; saddle of lamb is the two loins with the hip. Leg and saddle are usually roasted, though the leg is sometimes boiled. Roasted leg and saddle may be served anywhere from rare to well-done.

Forequarter meat of sheep, as of other mammals, includes more connective tissue than some other cuts, and, if not from a young lamb, is best cooked slowly using either a moist method, such as braising or stewing, or by slow roasting or American barbecuing. It is, in some countries, sold pre-chopped or diced.

Lamb shank definitions vary, but generally include:

- Lamb shank is cut from the arm of shoulder, contains leg bone and part of round shoulder bone, and is covered by a thin layer of fat and fell (a thin, paperlike covering).
- Lamb shank is a cut of meat from the upper part of the leg.

According to Jewish Kosher law, sheep may be eaten but as with cows, they must be killed while conscious and the sciatic nerve, as well as certain types of fat on the back half of the animal, may not be eaten. This makes certain cuts, such as leg or steaks, very difficult to produce in some countries. Thin strips of fatty mutton can be cut into a substitute for bacon called macon. Similar rules apply for the Islamic dietary code, known as *Halal*.

Meat from sheep features prominently in several cuisines of the Mediterranean, for example in Greece; in North Africa and the Middle East; in the Basque culture, both in the Basque country of Europe and in the shepherding areas of the Western United States. In Northern Europe, mutton and lamb feaure in many traditional dishes, including those of the North Atlantic islands and of the United Kingdom, particularly in the western and northern uplands, Scotland and Wales. It is also very popular in Australia. Lamb and mutton are very popular in Central Asia and South Asia, and in certain parts of China – where other red meats may be eschewed for religious or economic reasons – and in India, Iran and Pakistan. Barbecued mutton is also a specialty in some areas of the United States and Canada. However, meat from sheep is generally consumed far less in North America than in many European and Asian cuisines.

Lamb's liver, known as *lamb's fry* in Australia, is eaten in many countries and, along with the lungs and heart, is a major ingredient in the traditional Scottish dish of haggis. Lamb testicles, also known as *lamb's fries* (a term also used for other lamb offal), is another delicacy. Lamb's liver is the most common form of offal eaten in the UK, traditionally used in the family favourite (and pub grub staple) of liver with onions and/or bacon and mashed potatoes. Split grilled lamb kidneys are a popular breakfast item in Ireland, often eaten on 16 June especially, in the mistaken belief that Leopold Bloom ate one in *Ulysses*, whereas he actually ate a pork kidney.

Sheep

Sheep (*Ovis aries*) are quadrupedal, ruminant mammals typically kept as livestock. Like all ruminants, sheep are members of the order Artiodactyla, the even-toed ungulates. Although the name 'sheep' applies to many species in the genus *Ovis*, in everyday usage it almost always refers to *Ovis aries*. Numbering a little over one billion, domestic sheep are also the most numerous species of sheep.

Sheep are most likely descended from the wild mouflon of Europe and Asia. One of the earliest animals to be domesticated for agricultural purposes, sheep are raised for fleece, meat (lamb, hogget or mutton) and milk. A sheep's wool is the most widely used animal fibre, and is usually harvested by shearing. Ovine meat is called lamb when from younger animals and mutton when from older ones. Sheep continue to be important for wool and meat today, and are also occasionally raised for pelts, as dairy animals, or as model organisms for science.

Sheep husbandry is practised throughout the majority of the inhabited world, and has been fundamental to many civilizations. In the modern era, Australia, New Zealand, the southern and central South American nations, and the British Isles are most closely associated with sheep production.

Sheep-raising has a large lexicon of unique terms which vary considerably by region and dialect. Use of the word *sheep* began in Middle English as a derivation of the Old English word *sceap*; it is both the singular and plural name for the animal. A group of sheep is called a flock, herd or mob. Adult female sheep are referred to as ewes, intact males as rams or occasionally tups, castrated males as wethers, and younger sheep as lambs. Many other specific terms for the various life stages of sheep exist, generally related to lambing, shearing, and age.

Being a key animal in the history of farming, sheep have a deeply entrenched place in human culture, and find representation in much modern language and symbology. As livestock, sheep are most-often associated with pastoral, Arcadian imagery. Sheep figure in many mythologies—such as the Golden Fleece—and major religions, especially the Abrahamic traditions. In both ancient and modern religious ritual, sheep are used as sacrificial animals.

Domestic sheep are relatively small ruminants, usually with a crimped hair called wool and often with horns forming a lateral spiral. Domestic sheep differ from their wild relatives and ancestors in several respects, having become uniquely neotenic as a result of selective breeding by humans. A few primitive breeds of sheep retain some of the characteristics of their wild cousins, such as short tails. Depending on breed, domestic sheep may have no horns at all (polled), or horns in both sexes (as in wild sheep), or in males only. Most horned breeds have a single pair, but a few breeds may have several.

Another trait unique to domestic sheep (as compared to wild ovines, not other livestock) is their wide variation in colour. Wild sheep are largely variations of brown hues, and variation with species is extremely limited. Colours of domestic sheep range from pure white to dark chocolate brown and even spotted or piebald. Selection for easily dyeable white fleeces began early in sheep domestication, and as white wool is a dominant trait it spread quickly. However, coloured sheep do appear in many modern breeds, and may even appear as a recessive trait in white flocks. While white wool is desirable for large commercial markets, there is a niche market for coloured fleeces, mostly for handspinning. The nature of the fleece varies widely among the breeds, from dense and highly crimped, to long and hair-like. There is variation of wool type and quality even among members of the same flock, so wool classing is a step in the commercial processing of the fibre.

Depending on breed, sheep show a range of heights and weights. Their rate of growth and mature weight is a heritable trait that is often selected for in breeding. Ewes typically weigh between 45 and 100 kilograms (99 and 220 lb), and rams between 45 and 160 kilograms (99 and 350 lb). Mature sheep have 32 teeth. As with other ruminants, the front teeth in the lower jaw bite against a hard, toothless pad in the upper jaw. These are used to pick off vegetation, then the rear teeth grind it before it is swallowed. There are eight lower front teeth in ruminants, but there is some disagreement as to whether these are eight incisors, or six incisors and two incisor-shaped canines. This means that the dental formula for sheep is either I:0/4 C:0/0 P:3/3 M:3/3, or I:0/3 C:0/1 P:3/3 M:3/3. There is a large toothless gap between the front 'biting' teeth and the rear 'grinding' teeth.

For the first few years of life it is possible to calculate the age of sheep from their front teeth, as a pair of milk teeth is replaced by larger adult teeth each year, the full set of eight adult front teeth being complete at about four years of age. The front teeth are then gradually lost as sheep age, making it harder for them to feed and hindering the health and productivity of the animal. For this reason, domestic sheep on normal pasture begin to slowly decline from four years on, and the average life expectancy of a sheep is 10 to 12 years, though some sheep may live as long as 20 years.

Sheep have good hearing, and are sensitive to noise when being handled. Sheep have horizontal slit-shaped pupils, possessing excellent peripheral vision; with visual fields of approximately 270° to 320°, sheep can see behind themselves without turning their heads. However, sheep have poor depth perception; shadows and dips in the ground may cause sheep to baulk. In general, sheep have a tendency to move out of the dark and into well-lit areas, and prefer to move uphill when disturbed. Sheep also have an excellent sense of smell, and, like all species of their genus, have scent glands just in front of the eyes, and interdigitally on the feet. The purpose of these glands is uncertain, but those on the face may be used in breeding behaviours. The foot glands might also be related to reproduction, but alternative reasons, such as secretion of a waste product or a scent marker to help lost sheep find their flock, have also been proposed.

Sheep and goats are closely related as both are in the subfamily Caprinae. However, they are separate species, so hybrids rarely occur, and are always infertile. A hybrid of a ewe and a buck (a male goat) is called a sheep-goat hybrid (only a single such animal has been confirmed), and is not to be confused with the genetic chimera called a geep. Visual differences between sheep and goats include the beard and divided upper lip unique to goats. Sheep tails also hang down, even when short or docked, while the short tails of goats are held upwards. Sheep breeds are also often naturally polled (either in both sexes or just in the female), while naturally polled goats are rare (though many are polled artificially).

Males of the two species differ in that buck goats acquire a unique and strong odor during the rut, whereas rams do not.

The domestic sheep is a multi-purpose animal, and the more than 200 breeds now in existence were created to serve these diverse purposes. Some sources give a count of a thousand or more breeds, but these numbers cannot be verified. Almost all sheep are classified as being best suited to furnishing a certain product: wool, meat, milk, hides, or a combination in a dual-purpose breed. Other features used when classifying sheep include face colour (generally white or black), tail length, presence or lack of horns, and the topography for which the breed has been developed. This last point is especially stressed in the UK, where breeds are described as either upland (hill or mountain) or lowland breeds. A sheep may also be of a fat-tailed type, which is a dual-purpose sheep common in Africa and Asia with larger deposits of fat within and around its tail.

Breeds are also grouped based on how well they are suited to producing a certain type of breeding stock. Generally, sheep are thought to be either 'ewe breeds' or 'ram breeds'. Ewe breeds are those that are hardy, and have good reproductive and mothering capabilities — they are for replacing breeding ewes in standing flocks. Ram breeds are selected for rapid growth and carcase quality, and are mated with ewe breeds to produce meat lambs. Lowland and upland breeds are also crossed in this fashion, with the hardy hill ewes crossed with larger, fast-growing lowland rams to produce ewes called mules, which can then be crossed with meat-type rams to produce prime market lambs. Many breeds, especially rare or primitive ones, fall into no clear category.

Breeds are categorized by the type of their wool. Fine wool breeds are those that have wool of great crimp and density, which are preferred for textiles. Most of these were derived from Merino sheep, and the breed continues to dominate the world sheep industry. Downs breeds have wool between the extremes, and are typically fast-growing meat and ram breeds with dark faces. Some major medium wool breeds, such as the Corriedale, are dual-purpose crosses of long and fine-wooled breeds and were created for high-production commercial flocks. Long wool breeds are the largest of sheep, with long wool and a slow rate of growth. Long wool sheep are most valued for crossbreeding to improve the attributes of other sheep types. For example: the American Columbia breed was developed by crossing Lincoln rams (a long wool breed) with fine-wooled Rambouillet ewes.

Coarse or carpet wool sheep are those with a medium to long length wool of characteristic coarseness. Breeds traditionally used for carpet wool show great variability, but the chief requirement is a wool that will not break down under heavy use (as would that of the finer breeds). As the demand for carpet-quality wool declines, some breeders of this type of sheep are attempting to use a few of these traditional breeds for alternative purposes. Others have always been primarily meat-class sheep.

A minor class of sheep are the dairy breeds. Dual-purpose breeds that may primarily be meat or wool sheep are often used secondarily as milking animals, but there are a few breeds that are predominantly used for milking. These sheep do produce a higher quantity of milk and have slightly longer lactation curves. In the quality of their milk, fat and protein content percentages of dairy sheep vary from non-dairy breeds but lactose content does not.

A last group of sheep breeds is that of fur or hair sheep, which do not grow wool at all. Hair sheep are similar to the early domesticated sheep kept before woolly breeds were developed, and are raised for meat and pelts. Some modern breeds of hair sheep, such as the Dorper, result from crosses between wool and hair breeds. For meat and hide producers, hair sheep are cheaper to keep, as they do not need shearing. Hair sheep are also more resistant to parasites and hot weather.

With the modern rise of corporate agribusiness and the decline of localized family farms, many breeds of sheep are in danger of extinction. The Rare Breeds Survival Trust of the UK lists 22 native breeds as having only 3,000 registered animals (each), and the American Livestock Breeds Conservancy lists 14 as having fewer than 10,000. Preferences for breeds with uniform characteristics and fast growth have pushed heritage (or heirloom) breeds to the margins of the sheep industry. Those that remain are maintained through the efforts of conservation organizations, breed registries, and individual farmers dedicated to their preservation.

Sheep are exclusively herbivorous mammals. Most breeds prefer to graze on grass and other short roughage, avoiding the taller woody parts of plants that goats readily consume. Both sheep and goats use their lips and tongues to select parts of the plant that are easier to digest or higher in nutrition. Sheep, however, graze well in monoculture pastures where most goats fare poorly. Like all ruminants, sheep have a complex digestive system composed of four chambers, allowing them to break down cellulose from stems, leaves, and seed hulls into simpler carbohydrates. When sheep graze, vegetation is chewed into a mass called a bolus, which is then passed into the first chamber: the rumen. The rumen is a 19 to 38-litre (5 to 10 gal) organ in which feed is fermented via a symbiotic relationship with the bacteria, protozoa, and yeasts of the gut flora. The bolus is periodically regurgitated back to the mouth as cud for additional chewing and salivation. Cud chewing is an adaptation allowing ruminants to graze more quickly in the morning, and then fully chew and digest feed later in the day. This is beneficial as grazing, which requires lowering the head, leaves sheep vulnerable to predators, while cud chewing does not.

During fermentation, the rumen produces gas that must be expelled; disturbances of the organ, such as sudden changes in a sheep's diet, can cause the potentially fatal condition of bloat, when gas becomes trapped in the rumen. After fermentation in the rumen, feed passes in to the reticulum and the omasum; special feeds such as grains may bypass the rumen altogether. After the first three chambers, food moves in to the abomasum for final digestion before processing by the intestines. The abomasum is the only one of the four chambers analogous to the human stomach (being the only one that absorbs nutrients for use as energy), and is sometimes called the 'true stomach'.

Sheep follow a diurnal pattern of activity, feeding from dawn to dusk, stopping sporadically to rest and chew their cud. Ideal pasture for sheep is not lawn-like grass, but an array of grasses, legumes and forbs. Types of land where sheep are raised vary widely, from pastures that are seeded and improved intentionally to rough, native lands. Common plants toxic to sheep are present in most of the world, and include (but are not limited to) oak and acorns, tomato, yew, rhubarb, potato, and rhododendron.

Sheep are largely grazing herbivores, unlike browsing animals such as goats and deer that prefer taller foliage. With a much narrower face, sheep crop plants very close to the ground and can overgraze a pasture much faster than cattle. For this reason, many shepherds use managed intensive rotational grazing, where a flock is rotated through multiple pastures, giving plants time to recover. Paradoxically, sheep can both cause and solve the spread of invasive plant species. By disturbing the natural state of pasture, sheep and other livestock can pave the way for invasive plants. However, sheep also prefer to eat invasives such as cheatgrass, leafy spurge, kudzu and spotted knapweed over native species such as sagebrush, making grazing sheep effective for conservation grazing. Research conducted in Imperial County, California compared lamb grazing with herbicides for weed control in seedling alfalfa fields. Three trials demonstrated that grazing lambs were just as effective as herbicides in controlling winter weeds. Entomologists also compared grazing lambs to insecticides for insect control in winter alfalfa. In this trial, lambs provided insect control as effectively as insecticides. Other than forage, the other staple feed for sheep is hay, often during the winter months. The ability to thrive solely on pasture (even without hay) varies with breed, but all sheep can survive on this diet. Also included in some sheep's diets are minerals, either in a trace mix or in licks.

Naturally, a constant source of potable water is also a fundamental requirement for sheep. The amount of water needed by sheep fluctuates with the season and the type and quality of the food they consume. When sheep feed on large amounts of new growth and there is precipitation (including dew, as sheep are dawn feeders), sheep need less water. When sheep are confined or are eating large amounts of cured hay, more water is typically needed. Sheep also require clean water, and may refuse to drink water that is covered in scum or algae.

Sheep are one of the few livestock animals raised for meat today that have never been widely raised in an intensive, confined animal feeding operation (CAFO). Although there is a growing movement advocating alternative farming styles, a large percentage of beef cattle, pigs, and poultry are still produced under such conditions. In contrast, only some sheep are regularly given high-concentration grain feed, much less kept in confinement. Especially in industrialized countries, sheep producers may fatten market lambs before slaughter (called 'finishing') in feedlots. Many sheep breeders flush ewes and rams with a daily ration of grain during breeding to increase fertility. Ewes are also flushed during pregnancy to increase birth weights, as 70 per cent of a lamb's growth occurs in the last five to six weeks of gestation. Otherwise, only lactating ewes and especially old or infirm sheep are commonly provided with grain. Feed provided to sheep must be specially formulated, as most cattle, poultry, pig, and even some goat feeds contain levels of copper that are lethal to sheep. The same danger applies to mineral supplements such as salt licks.

Sheep are an important part of the global agricultural economy. However, their once-vital status has been largely replaced by other livestock species, especially the pig, chicken, and cow. China, Australia, India, and Iran have the largest modern flocks, and serve both local and exportation needs for wool and mutton. Other countries such as New Zealand have smaller flocks but retain a large international economic impact due to their export of sheep products. Sheep also play a major role in many local economies, which may be niche markets focused on organic or sustainable agriculture and local food customers. Especially in developing countries, such flocks may be a part of subsistence agriculture rather than a system of trade. Sheep themselves may be a medium of trade in barter economies.

Domestic sheep provide a wide array of raw materials. Wool was one of the first textiles, although in the late 20th century wool prices began to fall dramatically as the result of the popularity and cheap prices for synthetic fabrics. For many sheep owners, the cost of shearing is greater than the possible profit from the fleece, making subsisting on wool production alone practically impossible without farm subsidies. Fleeces are used as material in making alternative products such as wool insulation. In the 21st century, the sale of meat is the most profitable enterprise in the sheep industry, even though far less sheep meat is consumed than chicken, pork or beef.

Sheepskin is likewise used for making clothes, footwear, rugs, and other products. Byproducts from the slaughter of sheep are also of value: sheep tallow can be used in candle and soap making, sheep bone and cartilage has been used to furnish carved items such as dice and buttons as well as rendered glue and gelatin. Sheep intestine can be formed into sausage casings, and lamb intestine has been formed into surgical sutures, as well as strings for musical instruments and tennis rackets. Sheep droppings, which are high in cellulose, have even been sterilized and mixed with traditional pulp materials to make paper. Of all sheep byproducts, perhaps the most valuable is lanolin: the water-proof, fatty substance found naturally in sheep's wool and used as a base for innumerable cosmetics and other products.

Some farmers who keep sheep also make a profit from live sheep. Providing lambs for youth programmes such as 4-H and competition at agricultural shows is often a dependable avenue for the sale of sheep. Farmers may also choose to focus on a particular breed of sheep in order to sell registered purebred animals, as well as provide a ram rental service for breeding. The most valuable sheep ever sold to date was a purebred Texel ram that fetched £231,000 at auction. The previous record holder was a Merino ram sold for £205,000 in 1989. A new option for deriving profit from live sheep is the rental of flocks for grazing; these 'mowing services' are hired in order to keep unwanted vegetation down in public spaces and to lessen fire hazard.

Despite the falling demand and price for sheep products in many markets, sheep have distinct economic advantages when compared with other livestock. They do not require the expensive housing, such as that used in the intensive farming of chickens or pigs. They are an efficient use of land; roughly six sheep can be kept on the amount that would suffice for a single cow or horse. Sheep can also consume plants, such as noxious weeds, that most other animals will not touch, and produce more young at a faster rate. Also, in contrast to most livestock species, the cost of raising sheep is not necessarily tied to the price of feed crops such as grain, soybeans and corn. Combined with the lower cost of quality sheep, all these factors combine to equal a lower overhead for sheep producers, thus entailing a higher profitability potential for the small farmer. Sheep are especially beneficial for independent producers, including family farms with limited resources, as the sheep industry is one of the few types of animal agriculture that has not been vertically integrated by agribusiness.

Sheep meat and milk were one of the earliest staple proteins consumed by human civilization after the transition from hunting and gathering to agriculture. Sheep meat prepared for food is known as either mutton or lamb. 'Mutton' is derived from the Old French *moton,* which was the word for sheep used by the Anglo-Norman rulers of much of the British Isles in the Middle Ages. This became the name for sheep meat in English, while the Old English word *sceap* was kept for the live animal. Throughout modern history, 'mutton' has been limited to the meat of mature sheep usually at least two years of age; 'lamb' is used for that of immature sheep less than a year.

In the 21st century, the nations with the highest consumption of sheep meat are the Persian Gulf states, New Zealand, Australia, Greece, Uruguay, the United Kingdom and Ireland. These countries eat 14-40 lbs (3-18 kg) of sheep meat per capita, per annum. Sheep meat is also popular in France, Africa (especially the Maghreb), the Caribbean, the rest of the Middle East, India, and parts of China. This often reflects a past history of sheep production. In these countries in particular, dishes comprising alternative cuts and offal may be popular or traditional. Sheep testicles-called animelles or lamb fries—are considered a delicacy in many parts of the world. Perhaps the most unusual dish of sheep meat is the Scottish haggis, composed of various sheep innards cooked along with oatmeal and chopped onions inside its stomach. In comparison, countries such as the U.S. consume only a pound or less (under 0.5 kg), with Americans eating 50 pounds (22 kg) of pork and 65 pounds (29 kg) of beef. In addition, such countries rarely eat mutton, and may favour the more expensive cuts of lamb: mostly lamb chops and leg of lamb.

Though sheep's milk may be drunk rarely in fresh form, today it is used predominantly in cheese and yogurt making. Sheep have only two teats, and produce a far smaller volume of milk than cows. However, as sheep's milk contains far more fat, solids, and minerals than cow's milk, it is ideal for the cheese-making process. It also resists contamination during cooling better because of its much higher calcium content. Well-known cheeses made from sheep milk include the Feta of Bulgaria and Greece, Roquefort of France, Manchego from Spain, the Pecorino Romano (the Italian word for sheep is *pecore*) and Ricotta of Italy. Yogurts, especially some forms of strained yogurt, may also be made from sheep milk. Many of these products are now often made with cow's milk, especially when produced outside their country of origin. Sheep milk contains 4.8 per cent lactose, which may affect those who are intolerant.

CHAPTER 5

RED MEAT

Red meat in traditional culinary terminology is meat which is red when raw and not white when cooked. Red meat includes the meat of most adult mammals and some fowl (*e.g.* ducks). In the nutritional sciences, red meat includes *all* mammal meat.

Gastronomic

In gastronomy, red meat is darker-coloured meat, as contrasted with white meat. The exact definition varies by time, place, and culture, but the meat of adult mammals such as cows, sheep, and horses is invariably considered red, while chicken and rabbit are invariably considered white. The meat of young mammals such as milk-fed veal calves and sheep, and pigs is traditionally considered white; while the meat of duck and goose is considered red. Game is sometimes put in a separate category altogether (French *viandes noires* 'black meats').

Red meat does not refer to how well a piece of meat is cooked. Nor does it refer to its colouration after cooking.

Nutritional

The main determinant of the nutritional definition of the colour of meat is the concentration of myoglobin. The white meat of chicken has under 0.05 per cent; chicken thigh has 0.18-0.20 per cent; pork and veal have 0.1-0.3 per cent; young beef has 0.4-1.0 per cent; and old beef has 1.5-2.0 per cent.

According to the USDA all meats obtained from livestock are red meats because they contain more myoglobin than chicken or fish.

Red meat is a source of iron. Red meat also contains protein, levels of creatine, minerals such as zinc and phosphorus, and vitamins such as niacin, vitamin B_{12}, thiamin and riboflavin. Red meat is the richest source of Alpha Lipoic Acid, a powerful antioxidant.

Food Pyramid

The 1992 edition of the USDA food guide pyramid has been criticized for not distinguishing between red meat and other types of meat. The 2005 edition, MyPyramid, recommends lean forms of red meat.

HEALTH RISKS

Cancer

The American Institute for Cancer Research and World Cancer Research Fund stated in their report "Food, Nutrition, Physical Activity, and the Prevention of Cancer: a Global Perspective" that there is 'convincing' evidence that red meat intake increases the risk for colorectal cancer, and that there is 'suggestive' evidence that it increases the risk of oesophageal, lung, pancreatic and endometrial cancer. As a result, they recommend limiting intake of red meat to less than 300g (11 oz, or about three burgers) per week.

Some studies have linked consumption of large amounts of red meat with breast cancer, stomach cancer, lymphoma, bladder cancer, lung cancer and prostate cancer (although other studies have found no relationship between red meat and prostate cancer.

A 2009 study by the National Cancer Institute revealed a correlation between the consumption of red meat and increased mortality from cancer and cardiovascular diseases, as well as increased mortality from all causes. This study has been criticized for using an improperly validated food frequency questionnaire, which has been shown to have low levels of accuracy.

Colorectal Cancer

Many studies have found a link between red meat intake and colorectal cancer. Professor Sheila Bingham of the Dunn Human Nutrition Unit attributes this to the haemoglobin and myoglobin molecules which are found in red meat. She suggests these molecules, when ingested trigger a process called nitrosation in the gut which leads to the formation of carcinogens. Others have suggested that it is due to the presence of carcinogenic compounds called heterocyclic amines, which are created in the cooking process. However, this may not be limited to red meat, since a study from the Harvard School of Public Health found that people who ate skinless chicken five times or more per week increased their risk of developing bladder cancer by 52 per cent.

The AICR and WCRF consider the evidence that red meat causes colorectal cancer 'convincing'.

Cardiovascular Diseases

Red meat consumption is associated with cardiovascular diseases, possibly because of its high content of saturated fat. Specifically, increased beef intake is associated with fatal ischemic heart disease.

A 1999 study funded by the National Cattlemen's Beef Association, an advocacy group for beef producers, involved 191 persons with high cholesterol on diets where at least 80 per cent of the meat intake came from either lean red meat in one group, or lean white meat in another. The results of this study showed nearly identical cholesterol, and triglyceride levels in both groups. This study suggests that lean red meat may play a role in a low-fat diet for persons with high cholesterol.

Red meat consumption is also associated with acute coronary syndrome, as well as stroke. It has also been associated with greater intima-media thickness, an indicator of artherosclerosis.

Diabetes

Red meat intake has been associated with an increased risk of type II diabetes. Interventions in which red meat is removed from the diet can lower albuminuria levels. Replacing red meat with a low protein or chicken diet can improve glomerular filtration rate.

Other findings have suggested that the association may be to saturated fat, trans fat and dietary cholesterol, rather than red meat per se. An additional confound is that processed meat intake is associated with diabetes.

Goat Meat

Goat meat is the meat of the domestic goat *(Capra aegagrus hircus)*. It is often called chevon or mutton when the meat comes from adults, and is called cabrito or just kid when from young animals. While 'goat' is usually the name for the meat found in common parlance, producers and marketers may prefer to use the French-derived word chevon (from *chèvre*), since market research in the United States suggests that 'chevon eater' is more palatable to consumers than 'goat eater'. Cabrito is a word of Spanish origin, and refers specifically to young, milk-fed goat. In the English-speaking islands of the Caribbean, and in some parts of Asia, particularly Bangladesh, Nepal, Pakistan and India, the word 'mutton' is often used colloquially to describe both goat and lamb meat, despite technically only referring to sheep meat.

Although cited in a New York Times article as "the most widely-consumed meat in the world," , in total consumption goat is a distant fourth globally behind pork, beef, and chicken. Goat is a staple of Africa, Asia and South/Central America, and a delicacy in a few European cuisines. The cuisines most well-known for their use of goat include Middle Eastern, North African, Indian, Pakistani, Mexican, and Caribbean cuisine.

Goat has historically been less commonplace in American, Canadian and Northern European cuisines, but is finding a hold in some niche markets. While in the past goat meat in the West was confined to ethnic markets, it can now be found in a few upscale restaurants and purveyors, especially in cities such as New York and San Francisco. Bill Niman of Niman Ranch has recently turned to raising goats and he, along with other North American producers, tends to focus on pasture-based methods of farming.

Goat can be prepared in a variety of ways including stewed, curried, baked, grilled, barbecued, minced, canned, fried, or made into sausage. Goat jerky is also another popular variety. Furthermore, in Okinawa (Japan) goat meat is served raw in thin slices as 'yagisashi'. In India, the rice-preparation of mutton biryani uses goat meat as its primary ingredients to produce a rich taste. 'Curry goat' is a common traditional Indo-Caribbean dish.

Cabrito is specifically goat kid, a regional specialty especially common in Latin cuisines such as Mexican, Peruvian,Brazilian, and Argentine, and is usually slow roasted. Southern Italian and Greek cuisines are also both known for serving roast goat in celebration of Easter. In the alpine regions of central Europe, goat dishes also are an Easter staple, often braised (Bavaria) or breaded and fried (Tyrol).

Goat has a reputation for strong, gamey flavour, but can be mild depending on how it is raised and prepared. Despite being classified as red meat, goat is leaner and contains less cholesterol and fat than both lamb and beef. This makes it healthier to eat, but can require low-heat, slow cooking to preserve tenderness and moisture.

CHAPTER

6

SLAUGHTERHOUSE

A slaughterhouse or abattoir is a facility where animals are killed for consumption as food products.

Approximately 45-50 per cent of the animal can be turned into edible products (meat). About 15 per cent are waste, and the remaining 40-45 per cent of the animal are turned into byproducts such as leather, soaps, candles (tallow), and adhesives. In the United States, around nine billion animals are slaughtered every year (this includes about 150.4 million cattle, bison, sheep, hogs, and goats and 8.9 billion chickens, turkeys, and ducks) in 5,700 slaughterhouses and processing plants employing 527,000 workers; in 2007, 28.1 billion pounds of beef were consumed in the U.S. alone. In Canada, 650 million animals are killed annually. In the European Union, the annual figure is 300 million cattle, sheep, and pigs, and four billion chickens.

Slaughterhouses which process meat unfit for human consumption are sometimes referred to as Knacker's yards or Knackeries.

Slaughtering animals on a large scale poses significant logistical problems and public health concerns, with public aversion to meat packing in many cultures influencing the location of slaughterhouses. In addition, some religions stipulate certain conditions for the slaughter of animals so that practices within slaughterhouses vary.

There has been criticism of the methods of preparation, herding, and killing within some slaughterhouses, and in particular of the speed with which the slaughter is sometimes conducted. Investigations by animal welfare and animal rights groups have indicated that a proportion of these animals are being skinned or gutted while apparently still alive and conscious. There has also been criticism of the methods of transport of the animals, who are driven for hundreds of miles to slaughterhouses in conditions that often result in crush injuries and death en route. Slaughtering animals is opposed by most vegetarians and animal rights groups on ethical grounds.

Slaughterhouses act as the starting point of the meat industry, where stock come from farms/market to enter the food chain. They have existed as long as there have been settlements too large for individuals to rear their own stock for personal consumption.

Early maps of London show numerous stockyards in the periphery of the city, where slaughter occurred in the open air. A term for such open-air slaughterhouse is a shambles. There are streets named 'The Shambles' in some English towns (*e.g.* Worcester, York) which got their name from having been the site on which butchers killed and prepared animals for consumption.

In the latter part of the 20th century, the layout and design of most US slaughterhouses has been significantly influenced by the work of Dr. Temple Grandin. It was her fascination with patterns and flow that first led her to redesign the layout of cattle holding pens.

While Grandin's primary objective is to help slaughterhouse operators improve efficiency and profit, she suggested that reducing the stress and suffering of animals being led to slaughter may help achieve this aim. In particular she applied an intuitive understanding of animal psychology to design pens and corrals which funnel a herd of animals arriving at a slaughterhouse into a single file ready for slaughter. Her corrals employ long sweeping curves so that each animal is prevented from seeing what lies ahead and just concentrates on the hind quarters of the animal in front of it. This design also attempts to override the animals' survival instincts and prevent them from reversing direction.

Grandin now claims to have designed over 54 per cent of the slaughterhouses in the United States as well as many other slaughterhouses around the world.

The slaughterhouse process differs by species and region and may be controlled by civil law as well as religious laws such as Kosher and Halal laws. A typical procedure follows:

- Cattle (mostly steers and heifers, some cows, and even fewer bulls) are received by truck or rail from a ranch, farm, or feedlot.
- Cattle are herded into holding pens.

Cattle are rendered unconscious by applying an electric shock of 300 volts and 2 amps to the back of the head, effectively stunning the animal, or by use of a captive bolt pistol to the front of the cow's head (a pneumatic or cartridge-fired captive bolt). Swine can be rendered unconscious by CO_2/inert gas stunning. (This step is prohibited under strict application of Halal and Kashrut codes.)

Animals are hung upside down by both of their hind legs on the processing line.

The carotid artery and jugular vein are severed with a knife, blood drains, causing death through exsanguination.

The head is removed, as well as front and rear feet. Prior to hide removal, care is taken to cut around the digestive tract to prevent fecal contamination later in the process.

The hide/skin is removed by down pullers, side pullers and fisting off the pelt (sheep and goats). Hides can also be removed by laying the carcase on a cradle and skinning with a knife.

The internal organs are removed and inspected for internal parasites and signs of disease. The viscera are separated for inspection from the heart and lungs, referred to as the 'pluck'. Livers are separated for inspection, tongues are dropped or removed from the head, and the head is sent down the line on the head hooks or head racks for inspection of the lymph nodes for signs of systemic disease.

The carcase is inspected by a government inspector for safety. (This inspection is performed by the Food Safety Inspection Service in the U.S., and Canadian Food Inspection Agency in Canada.)

Carcases are subjected to intervention to reduce levels of bacteria. Common interventions are steam, hot water, and organic acids.

Carcases (typically cattle and sheep only) can be electrically stimulated to improve meat tenderness.

Carcases are chilled to prevent the growth of microorganisms and to reduce meat deterioration while the meat awaits distribution.

The chilled carcase is broken down into primal cuts and subprimals for boxed meat unless customer specifies for intact sides of meat. Beef and horse carcases are always split in half and then quartered, pork is split into sides only and goat/veal/mutton and lamb is left whole.

The remaining carcase may be further processed to extract any residual traces of meat, usually termed advanced meat recovery or mechanically separated meat, which may be used for human or animal consumption.

Waste materials such as bone, lard or tallow, are sent to a rendering plant. Also, lard and tallow can be used for the production of biodiesel or heating oil.

The wastewater, consisting of blood and fecal matter, generated by the slaughtering process is sent to a waste water treatment plant.

The meat is transported to distribution centres that then distribute to retail markets.

International Variations

The standards and regulations governing slaughter-houses vary considerably around the world. In many countries the slaughter of animals is regulated by custom and tradition rather than by law. In the non-Western world, including the Arab world, the Indian sub-continent, etc., both forms of meat are available: one which is produced in modern mechanized slaughterhouses, and the other from local butcher shops.

In some communities animal slaughter may be controlled by religious laws, most notably halal for Muslims and kashrut for Jewish communities. These both require that the animals being slaughtered should be conscious at the point of death, and as such animals cannot be stunned prior to killing. This can cause conflicts with national regulations when a slaughterhouse adhering to the rules of kosher preparation is located in some Western countries. In Islamic and Jewish law, captive bolts and other methods of pre-slaughter paralysis are generally not permissible, due to it being forbidden for an animal to be killed prior to slaughter. Various halal food authorities have more recently permitted the use of a recently developed fail-safe system of head-only stunning where the shock is less painful and non-fatal, and where it is possible to reverse the procedure and revive the animal after the shock.

In many societies, traditional cultural and religious aversion to slaughter led to prejudice against the people involved. In Japan, where the ban on slaughter of livestock for food was lifted only in the late 19th century, the newly found slaughter industry drew workers primarily from villages of *burakumin*, who traditionally worked in occupations relating to death (such as executioners and undertakers). In some parts of western Japan, prejudice faced by current and former residents of such areas (*burakumin* 'hamlet people') is still a sensitive issue. Because of this, even the Japanese word for 'slaughter' (?? *tosatsu*) is deemed politically incorrect by some pressure groups as its inclusion of the kanji for 'kill' supposedly portrays those who practice it in a negative manner.

Some countries have laws that exclude specific animal species or grades of animal from being slaughtered for human consumption, especially those that are taboo food. The former Indian Prime Minister Atal Behari Vajpayee suggested in 2004 introducing legislation banning the slaughter of cows throughout India, as Hinduism holds cows as sacred and considers their slaughter unthinkable and offensive. This was often opposed on grounds of religious freedom. The slaughter of cows and the importation of beef into the nation of Nepal are strictly forbidden. Several U.S. states have banned the slaughter and consumption of dogs. The sale and consumption of horse meat is illegal in The United States, although horses are slaughtered for meat export to Europe and Japan for human consumption and for the U.S. pet food market.

Most countries have laws in regard to the treatment of animals at slaughterhouses. In the United States, there is the Humane Slaughter Act of 1958, a law requiring that all swine, sheep, cattle, and horses be stunned unconscious with just one application of a stunning device by a trained person before being shackled and hoisted up on the line (chickens are exempt from this Act). The United States Department of Agriculture (USDA) is opposed to the Humane Slaughter Act, and violations of the Act carry no penalties. Since stopping the line to re-knock conscious animals causes 'down time' and results in lower profits, the Humane Slaughter Act is usually bypassed and ignored by USDA supervisors (Eiznitz 1997). There is some debate over the enforcement of this act. This act, like those in many countries, exempts slaughter in accordance to religious law, such as kosher shechita and dhabiha halal. Most strict interpretations of kashrut require that the animal be fully sensible when its carotid artery is cut.

The novel *The Jungle* detailed unsanitary conditions in slaughterhouses and the meatpacking industry during the 1800s. This led directly to an investigation commissioned directly by the President, and to the passage of the Meat Inspection Act and the Pure Food and Drug Act of 1906, which established the Food and Drug Administration. A much larger body of regulation deals with the public health and worker safety regulation and inspection.

For her book *Slaughterhouse,* Gail Eisnitz, chief investigator for the Humane Farming Association (HFA), interviewed slaughterhouse workers in the U.S. who say that, because of the speed with which they are required to work, animals are routinely skinned while apparently alive, and still blinking, kicking, and shrieking. Eisnitz argues that this is not only cruel to the animals, but also dangerous for the human workers, as cows weighing several thousands of pounds thrashing around in pain are likely to kick out and debilitate anyone working near them.

According to the HFA, Eiznitz interviewed slaughterhouse workers representing over two million hours of experience, who, without exception, told her that they have beaten, strangled, boiled, and dismembered animals alive, or have failed to report those who do. The workers described the effects the violence has had on their personal lives, with several admitting to being physically abusive or taking to alcohol and other drugs.

The HFA alleges that workers are required to kill up to 1,100 hogs an hour, and end up taking their frustration out on the animals. Eisnitz interviewed one worker, who had worked in ten slaughterhouses, about pig production. He told her:

> "Hogs get stressed out pretty easy. If you prod them too much, they have heart attacks. If you get a hog in the chute that's had the shit prodded out of him and has a heart attack or refuses to move, you take a meat hook and hook it into his bunghole. You try to do this by clipping the hipbone. Then you drag him backwards. You're dragging these hogs alive, and a lot of times the meat hook rips out of the bunghole. I've seen hams — thighs — completely ripped open. I've also seen intestines come out. If the hog collapses near the front of the chute, you shove the meat hook into his cheek and drag him forward".

It is observed that animals lose weight when stressed and meat loses taste quality. This does motivate companies to try to control the stress levels of animals as much as possible.

Over the last few decades, some research has been done toward making slaughterhouses more humane; one well-known scientist in this field is Temple Grandin.

Historically, some doubted that fish could experience pain. However, laboratory experiments have shown that fish do react to painful stimuli (*e.g.* injections of bee venom) in a similar way to mammals. The expansion of fish farming as well as animal welfare concerns in society has led to research into more humane and faster ways of killing fish. In large-scale operations like fish farms, stunning fish with electricity or putting them into water saturated with nitrogen so that they cannot breathe, results in death more rapidly than just taking them out of the water. For sport fishing, it is recommended that fish be killed soon after catching them by hitting them on the head followed by bleeding out, or by stabbing the brain with a sharp object (called pithing or ike jime in Japanese).

Major Slaughterhouses

The largest slaughterhouse in the world is operated by the Smithfield Packing Company in Tar Heel, North Carolina. It is capable of butchering over 32,000 pigs a day. In the US, the majority of major meat packing plants are located in the Midwestern and High Plains regions.

In vitro Meat

A 2009 article in h+ magazine (published by Humanity+) predicts that as a result of the introduction of *in vitro* meat, the slaughterhouse will eventually become an unneeded institution when animal meat is created from the DNA of the animal instead of its dead carcase. Only sentimental values will keep the butcher stores and slaughter houses open as people switch to *in vitro* meat.

CHAPTER

7

CHICKEN (FOOD)

Chicken is the fowl derived from chickens. It is the most common type of poultry in the world, and is prepared as food in a wide variety of ways, varying by region and culture.

The modern chicken is a descendant of Red Junglefowl hybrids along with the Grey Junglefowl first raised thousands of years ago in the northern parts of the Indian subcontinent.

Chicken as a meat has been depicted in Babylonian carvings from around 600 BC. Chicken was one of the most common meats available in the Middle Ages. It was widely believed to be easily digested and considered to be one of the most neutral foodstuff. It was eaten over most of the Eastern hemisphere and a number of different kinds of chicken such as capons, pullets and hens were eaten. It was one of the basic ingredients in the so-called white dish, a stew usually consisting of chicken and fried onions cooked in milk and seasoned with spices and sugar.

Chicken consumption in the US increased during World War II due to a shortage of beef and pork. In Europe, consumption of chicken overtook that of beef and veal in 1996, linked to consumer awareness of Bovine spongiform encephalopathy or B.S.E.

Modern varieties of chicken such as the Cornish Cross, are bred specifically for meat production, with an emphasis placed on the ratio of feed to meat produced by the animal. The most common breeds of chicken consumed in the US are Cornish and White Rock.

Chickens raised specifically for food are called broilers. In the United States, broilers are typically butchered at a young age. Modern Cornish Cross hybrids, for example, are butchered as early as 8 weeks for fryers and 12 weeks for roasting birds.

Capons (castrated cocks) produce more and fattier meat. For this reason, they are considered a delicacy and were particularly popular in the [Middle Ages].

Typically, the muscle tissue (breast, legs, thigh, etc.), liver, heart, and gizzard are processed for food. Chicken feet are commonly eaten, especially in Caribbean and Chinese cuisine. Chicken wings refers to a serving of the wing sections of a chicken.

Exotic parts like pygostyle (chicken's buttocks) and testicles are commonly eaten in East Asia and some parts of South East Asia.

Chicken eggs are commonly eaten. Chicken is considered poultry rather than meat.

Health Issues

Chicken meat is generally considered healthy (in contrast to red meat), however, due to a significant inclusion of cholesterol (as in most meats) it should be avoided in excess , especially for conditions in sensitivity of it (the exact conditions around cholesterol intake from animal products (limit, effects, etc.) is debated). The cholesterol issue is also apparent on the animal's eggs (particularly the yolk), and is more pronounced in certain parts of the body.

Chicken generally includes low fat in the meat itself (castrated roosters excluded), however it is highly concentrated on its skin, which should be avoided when low intake of fat is necessary.

Cooking method is highly related to health issues related to chicken, with steam cooking with skin removed being considered one of the healthiest, and fried with trans fats one of the worst.

However according to a 2006 Harvard School of Public Health study of 135,000 people, people who ate grilled skinless chicken 5 or more times a week had a 52 per cent higher chance of developing bladder cancer compared to people who didn't. However, such strong associations were not found in individuals regularly consuming chicken with skin intact.

Juvenile chickens, of less than 28 days of age at slaughter in the United Kingdom are marketed as poussin. Mature chicken is sold as small, medium or large.

Whole mature chickens are marketed in the United States as fryers, broilers, and roasters. Fryers are the smallest size, and the most common, as chicken reach this size quickly. Most dismembered packaged chicken would be sold whole as fryers. Broilers are larger than fryers. They are typically sold whole. Roasters, or roasting hens, are the largest chickens sold and are typically more expensive. These names reflect the most appropriate cooking method for the surface area to volume ratio. As the size increases, the volume (which determines how much heat must enter the bird for it to be cooked) increases faster than the surface area (which determines how fast heat can enter the bird). For a fast method of cooking, such as frying, a small bird is appropriate: frying a large piece of chicken results in the inside being undercooked when the outside is ready.

Chicken is also sold in dismembered pieces. Pieces may include quarters, or fourths of the chicken. A chicken is typically cut into two leg quarters and two breast quarters. Each quarter contains two of the commonly available pieces of chicken. A leg quarter contains the thigh, drumstick and a portion of the back; a leg has the back portion removed. A breast quarter contains the breast, wing and portion of the back; a breast has the back portion and wing removed. Pieces may be sold in packages of all of the same pieces, or in combination packages. Whole chicken cut up refers to either the entire bird cut into 8 individual pieces. (8-piece cut); or sometimes without the back. A 9-piece cut (usually for fast food restaurants) has the tip of the breast cut off before splitting. Pick of the Chicken, or similar titles, refers to a package with only some of the chicken pieces. Typically the breasts, thighs, and legs without wings or back. Thighs and breasts are sold boneless and/or skinless. Dark meat (legs, drumsticks and thighs) pieces are typically cheaper than white meat pieces (breast, wings). Chicken livers and/or gizzards are commonly available packaged separately. Other parts of the chicken, such as the neck, feet, combs, etc. are not widely available except in countries where they are in demand, or in cities that cater to ethnic groups who favour these parts.

There are many fast food restaurant chains on both a national and global scale that sell exclusively or primarily in poultry products including KFC (global), Red Rooster (Australia), Hector Chicken (Belgium) and CFC (Indonesia). Most of the products on the menu in such eateries are fried or breaded and are served with french fries.

Raw chicken can be frozen for up to two years without significant changes in flavour or texture. Chicken is typically eaten cooked as when raw it often contains salmonella. Raw or rare chicken dishes appear in Ethiopian cuisine and Japanese cuisine.

Chicken can be cooked in many ways. It can be made into sausages, skewered, put in salads, grilled, breaded and deep-fried, or used in various curries. There is significant variation in cooking methods amongst cultures. Historically common methods include roasting, baking, broasting, and frying. Today, chickens are frequently cooked by deep frying and prepared as fast foods such as fried chicken, chicken nuggets, chicken lollipops or buffalo wings. They are also often grilled for salads or tacos.

Chickens often come with labels such as 'roaster', which suggest a method of cooking based on the type of chicken. While these labels are only suggestions, ones labeled for stew often do not do well when cooked with other methods.

Some chicken breast cuts and processed chicken breast products include the moniker 'with Rib Meat'. This is a misnomer, as it is the small piece of white meat that overlays the scapula, and is removed with the breast meat. The breast is cut from the chicken and sold as a solid cut, while the leftover breast and true rib meat is stripped from the bone through mechanical separation for use in chicken franks, for example. Breast meat is often sliced thinly and marketed as chicken slices, an easy filling for sandwiches. Often, the tenderloin (pectoralis minor) is marketed separately from the breast (pectoralis major). In the US, 'tenders' can be either tenderloins or strips cut from the breast.

Chicken bones are hazardous to health as they tend to break into sharp splinters when eaten, but they can be simmered with vegetables and herbs for hours or even days to make chicken stock.

In Asian countries it is possible to buy bones alone as they are very popular for making chicken soups, which are said to be healthy. In Australia the rib cages and backs of chickens after the other cuts have been removed are frequently sold cheaply in supermarket delicatessen sections as either 'chicken frames' or 'chicken carcasses' and are purchased for soup or stock purposes.

In many factory farms, chickens are routinely administered with the feed additive Roxarsone, a relatively benign organoarsenic compound which partially decomposes into inorganic arsenic compounds in the flesh of chickens, and in their feces, which are often used as a fertilizer. The compound is used to control stomach pathogens and promote growth. A *Consumer Reports* study in 2004 reported finding "no detectable arsenic in our samples of muscle" but found "A few of our chicken-liver samples has an amount that according to EPA standards could cause neurological problems in a child who ate 2 ounces of cooked liver per week or in an adult who ate 5.5 ounces per week." However, the amounts found in these livers averaged to 460 part per billion; an amount still less than the 2,000 parts per billion limit set by the FDA. The FDA has found there to be no significant impact for the use of Roxarsone in the production of chicken, turkey or swine.

Poultry Farming

Poultry farming is the practice of raising poultry,(also known as such as raggle fraggle)chickens, turkeys, ducks, and geese, as a subcategory of animal husbandry, for the purpose of farming meat or eggs for food.

More than 50 billion chickens are reared annually as a source of food, for both their meat and their eggs. Chickens farmed for meat are called broilers, whilst those farmed for eggs are called egg-laying hens. In total, the UK alone consumes over 29 million eggs per day. Some hens can produce over 300 eggs a year. Chickens will naturally live for 6 or more years. After 12 months, the hen's productivity will start to decline. This is when most commercial laying hens are slaughtered.

The majority of poultry are raised using intensive farming techniques. According to the Worldwatch Institute, 74 per cent of the world's poultry meat, and 68 per cent of eggs are produced this way. One alternative to intensive poultry farming is free range farming.

Friction between these two main methods has led to long term issues of ethical consumerism. Opponents of intensive farming argue that it harms the environment and creates health risks, as well as abusing the animals themselves. Advocates of intensive farming say that their highly efficient systems save land and food resources due to increased productivity, stating that the animals are looked after in state-of-the-art environmentally controlled facilities. A few countries have banned cage system housing, including Sweden and Switzerland. Consumers can still purchase lower cost eggs from other countries' intensive poultry farms.

Free range poultry farming consists of poultry permitted to roam freely instead of being contained in any manner. In the UK, the Department for Environment, Food and Rural Affairs says that a free range chicken must have daytime access to open-air runs during at least half of their life. Unlike in the United States, this definition also applies to eggs. The European Union regulates marketing standards for egg farming which specifies a minimum condition for Free Range Eggs states that "hens have continuous daytime access to open-air runs, except in the case of temporary restrictions imposed by veterinary authorities". In free-range broiler systems, the chickens are given continuous access to an outdoor range during the daytime and sheds where they are housed at night. Free-range chickens grow more slowly than intensive chickens. They live at least 56 days. In the EU each chicken must have one square metre of outdoor space.

Free range poultry production requires that the poultry have access to the outside. In some cases this means the poultry are raised on pasture, enabling the poultry to move around, forage for their natural diet and live in cleaner conditions than those in batteries. In some farms, the manure from free range poultry can be used to benefit crops.

The benefits are also a reduced growth rate and opportunities for natural behaviour such as pecking, scratching, foraging and exercise outdoors, as well as fresh air and daylight. Because they grow slower and have opportunities for exercise free-range chickens have better leg and heart health and a much higher quality of life.

Finding suitable land with adequate drainage to minimise worms and coccidial oocysts, suitable protection from prevailing winds, good ventilation, access and protection from predators can be difficult. Excess heat, cold or damp can have a harmful effect on the animals and their productivity. Unlike battery farms, free range farmers have little control over the food their animals come across which can lead to unreliable productivity.

Some free range farming in the UK, which accounts for 26 per cent of production, has also come under criticism concerning animal welfare. This is due to some large scale free range farms where social abnormalities arise due to having large numbers of birds in an outdoor space. Beak trimming due to cannibalism and infighting is common in this form of poultry farming as well as in batteries. Diseases are common and the animals are vulnerable to predators. In South-East Asia, a lack of disease control in free range farming has been associated with outbreaks of Avian influenza.

In organic systems, chickens are also free-range. Organic chickens are slower growing, more traditional breeds and live typically for around 81 days. They grow at half the rate of intensive chickens. They have a larger space allowance outside (at least 2 square metres and sometimes up to 10 square metres per bird).

While often confused with free-range farming, yarding is actually a separate method of poultry culture by which chickens and cows are raised together. The distinction is that free-range poultry are either totally unfenced, or the fence is so distant that it has little influence on their freedom of movement. Yarding is common technique used by small farms in the Northeastern US.

Daily releases out of hutches or coops allows for instinctual nature for the chickens with protections from predators. The hens usually lay eggs either on the ground of the coop or in baskets if provided by the farmer. This technique can be complicated if used with roosters though, mostly because of difficulty getting them into the coop and to clean the coop while it is inside. This territorial nature is apparent while outside in which they have a brood of hens and sometimes even informal land claims. This can endanger people unaware of the existence of the territories who are attacked by the larger birds.

In egg-producing farms, birds are typically housed in rows of battery cages. Environmental conditions are automatically controlled, including light duration, which mimics summer daylength. This stimulates the birds to continue to lay eggs all year round. Normally, significant egg production only occurs in the warmer months. Critics argue that year-round egg production stresses the birds more than normal seasonal production.

Meat chickens, commonly called broilers, are floor-raised on litter such as wood shavings or rice hulls, indoors in climate-controlled housing. Poultry producers routinely use nationally approved medications, such as antibiotics, in feed or drinking water, to treat disease or to prevent disease outbreaks arising from overcrowded or unsanitary conditions. In the U.S., the national organization overseeing chicken production is the Food and Drug Administration (F.D.A.). Some F.D.A. approved medications are also approved for improved feed utilization.

In egg-producing farms, cages allow for more birds per unit area, and this allows for greater productivity and lower space and food costs, with more efforts put into egg-laying. In the U.S., for example, the current recommendation by the United Egg Producers is 67 to 86 in^2 (430 to 560 cm^2) per bird, which is about 9 inches by 9 inches. Modern poultry farming is very efficient and allows meat and eggs to be available to the consumer in all seasons at a lower cost than free range production, and the poultry have no exposure to predators.

The cage environment of egg producing does not permit birds to roam. The closeness of chickens to one another frequently causes cannibalism. Cannibalism is controlled by de-beaking (removing a portion of the bird's beak with a hot blade so the bird cannot effectively peck). Another condition that can occur in prolific egg laying breeds is osteoporosis. This is caused from year-round rather than seasonal egg production, and results in chickens whose legs cannot support them and so can no longer walk. During egg production, large amounts of calcium are transferred from bones to create eggshell. Although dietary calcium levels are adequate, absorption of dietary calcium is not always sufficient, given the intensity of production, to fully replenish bone calcium.

Under intensive farming methods, a meat chicken will live less than six weeks before slaughter. This is half the time it would take traditionally. This compares with free-range chickens which will usually be slaughtered at 8 weeks, and organic ones at around 12 weeks.

In intensive broiler sheds, the air can become highly polluted with ammonia from the droppings. This can damage the chickens' eyes and respiratory systems and can cause painful burns on their legs (called hock burns) and feet. Chickens bred for fast growth have a high rate of leg deformities because they cannot support their increased body weight. Because they cannot move easily, the chickens are not able to adjust their environment to avoid heat, cold or dirt as they would in natural conditions. The added weight and overcrowding also puts a strain on their hearts and lungs. In the U.K., up to 19 million chickens die in their sheds from heart failure each year.

Indoor with Higher Welfare

Chickens are kept indoors but with more space (around 12 to 14 birds per square metre). They have a richer environment for example with natural light or straw bales that encourage foraging and perching. The chickens grow more slowly and live for up to two weeks longer than intensively farmed birds. The benefits of higher welfare indoor systems are the reduced growth rate, less crowding and more opportunities for natural behaviour.

Humane Treatment

Animal welfare groups have frequently criticized the poultry industry for engaging in practices which they believe to be inhumane. Many animal rights advocates object to killing chickens for food, the "factory farm conditions" under which they are raised, methods of transport, and slaughter. Compassion Over Killing and other groups have repeatedly conducted undercover investigations at chicken farms and slaughterhouses which they allege confirm their claims of cruelty.

Conditions in intensive chicken farms may be unsanitary, allowing the proliferation of diseases such as salmonella and E. coli. Chickens may be raised in total darkness; hens are most often kept in crowded wire battery cages with space less than that of a sheet of paper per hen, as opposed to cage-free or free range. Rough handling and crowded transport during various weather conditions and the failure of existing stunning systems to render the birds unconscious before slaughter have also been cited as welfare concerns.

Another animal welfare concern is the use of selective breeding to create heavy, large-breasted birds, which can lead to crippling leg disorders and heart failure for some of the birds. Concerns have been raised that companies growing single varieties of birds for eggs or meat are increasing their susceptibility to disease.

A common practice among hatcheries is the culling of newly born male chicks of egg laying breeds, since they don't lay eggs, and do not grow fast enough to be profitable for meat.

Debeaking

Laying hens are routinely de-beaked when young to prevent fighting. This is bad because beaks are sensitive, the usual practice of trimming them without anaesthesia is considered inhumane by some. De-beaked chickens will peck much less than chickens with beaks, which animal behaviourist Temple Grandin attributes to guarding against pain. The United Egg Producers says that de-beaking is not painful. It is also argued that the procedure causes life-long chronic pain and discomfort and decreased ability to eat or drink.

Intelligence

Some groups which advocate for more humane treatment of chickens claim that chickens are intelligent. Dr. Chris Evans of Macquarie University claims that their range of 20 calls, problem solving skills, use of representational signaling, and the ability to recognize each other by facial features demonstrate the intelligence of chickens.

DESTRUCTIVE PRACTICES THAT POSE SERIOUS RISK TO HUMANS

Antibiotics

Antibiotics have been used on poultry in large quantities since the 1940s, when it was found that the byproducts of antibiotic production, fed because the antibiotic-producing mold had a high level of vitamin B_{12} after the antibiotics were removed, produced higher growth than could be accounted for by the vitamin B_{12} alone. Eventually it was discovered that the trace amounts of antibiotics remaining in the byproducts accounted for this growth.

The mechanism is apparently the adjustment of intestinal flora, favouring "good" bacteria while suppressing 'bad' bacteria, and thus the goal of antibiotics as a growth promoter is the same as for probiotics. Because the antibiotics used are not absorbed by the gut, they do not put antibiotics into the meat or eggs.

Antibiotics are used routinely in poultry for this reason, and also to prevent and treat disease. Many contend that this puts humans at risk as bacterial strains develop stronger and stronger resistances. Critics point out that, after six decades of heavy agricultural use of antibiotics, opponents of antibiotics must still make arguments about theoretical risks, since actual examples are hard to come by. Those antibiotic-resistant strains of human diseases whose origin is known originated in hospitals rather than farms.

A proposed bill in the United States Congress would make the use of antibiotics in animal feed legal only for therapeutic (rather than preventative) use, but it has not been passed. However, this may present the risk of slaughtered chickens harbouring pathogenic bacteria and passing them on to humans that consume them.

In October 2000, the U.S. Food and Drug Administration (FDA) discovered that two antibiotics were no longer effective in treating diseases found in factory-farmed chickens; one antibiotic was swiftly pulled from the market, but the other, Baytril, was not. Bayer, the company which produced it, contested the claim and as a result, Baytril remained in use until July 2005.

Arsenic

Chicken feed can also include Roxarsone, an antimicrobial drug that also promotes growth. Roxarsone was used as a broiler starter by about 70 per cent of the broiler growers between 1995 to 2000. The drug has generated controversy because it contains arsenic, which is highly toxic to humans. This arsenic could be transmitted through run-off from the poultry yards. A 2004 study by the U.S. magazine Consumer Reports reported "no detectable arsenic in our samples of muscle" but found "A few of our chicken-liver samples has an amount that according to EPA standards could cause neurological problems in a child who ate 2 ounces of cooked liver per week or in an adult who ate 5.5 ounces per week." The U.S. Food and Drug Administration (FDA), however, is the organization responsible for the regulation of foods in America, and all samples tested were "far less than the... amount allowed in a food product."

Growth Hormones

Chickens grow much more rapidly than they once did and some consumers have concluded that this rapid growth is due to the use of hormones in these animals. Some consumers believe that the increasingly earlier onset of puberty in humans is the result of the liberal use of such hormones. However, hormone use in poultry production is illegal in the United States. Similarly, no chicken meat for sale in Australia is fed hormones. Furthermore, several scientific studies have documented the fact that chickens grow rapidly because they are bred to do so. A small producer of natural and organic chickens confirmed this assumption.

"If this were 1948, you might have something to worry about. Using hormones to boost egg production was a brief fad in the Forties, but was abandoned because it didn't work. Using hormones to produce soft-meated roasters was used to some extent in the Forties and Fifties, but the increased growth rates of broilers made the practice irrelevant—the broilers got as big as anyone wanted them to get when they were still young enough to be soft-meated without chemicals".

The only hormone that was ever used in any quantity on poultry (DES) was banned in 1959, after everyone but a few die-hard farmers had given them up as a silly idea. Hormones are now illegal in poultry and eggs. The people who advertise 'No hormones' are either woefully ignorant or are indulging in cynical fear-mongering, maybe both.

E. coli

According to Consumer Reports, "1.1 million or more Americans [are] sickened each year by undercooked, tainted chicken." A USDA study discovered *E. coli* in 99 per cent of supermarket chicken, the result of chicken butchering not being a sterile process. However, the same study also cautions that the type of *E. coli* turned up was in every case a non-lethal form distinct from the more dangerous 'O157:H7' strain. Many of these chickens, furthermore, had relatively low levels of contamination. Feces tend to leak from the carcass until the evisceration stage, and the evisceration stage itself gives an opportunity for the interior of the carcass to receive intestinal bacteria. (So does the skin of the carcass, but the skin presents a better barrier to bacteria and reaches higher temperatures during cooking). Before 1950, this was contained largely by not eviscerating the carcass at the time of butchering, deferring this until the time of retail sale or in the home. This gave the intestinal bacteria less opportunity to colonize the edible meat. The development of the 'ready-to-cook broiler' in the 1950s added convenience while introducing risk, under the assumption that end-to-end refrigeration and thorough cooking would provide adequate protection. *E. coli* can be killed by proper cooking times, but there is still some risk associated with it, and its near-ubiquity in commercially farmed chicken is troubling to some. Irradiation has been proposed as a means of sterilizing chicken meat after butchering.

Avian Influenza

There is also a risk that crowded conditions in chicken farms will allow avian influenza (bird flu) to spread quickly. A United Nations press release states: "Governments, local authorities and international agencies need to take a greatly increased role in combating the role of factory-farming, commerce in live poultry, and wildlife markets which provide ideal conditions for the virus to spread and mutate into a more dangerous form..."

Efficiency

Farming of chickens on an industrial scale relies largely on high protein feeds derived from soybeans; in the European Union the soybean dominates the protein supply for animal feed, and the poultry industry is the largest consumer of such feed. Two kilograms of grain must be fed to poultry to produce 1 kg of weight gain. However, for every gram of protein consumed, chickens yield only 0.33 g of edible protein.

Chickens are omnivores. In the wild, they often scratch at the soil to search for seeds, insects and even larger animals such as lizards or young mice.

Chickens may live for five to ten years, depending on the breed. In commercial intensive farming, a meat chicken generally lives six weeks before slaughter. A free range or organic meat chicken will usually be slaughtered at about 14 weeks. Hens of special laying breeds may produce as many as 300 eggs a year. After 12 months, the hen's egg-laying ability starts to decline, and commercial laying hens are then slaughtered and used in processed foods, or sold as 'soup hens'. The world's oldest chicken, a hen, died of heart failure at the age of 16 according to the Guinness Book of World Records.

Roosters can usually be differentiated from hens by their striking plumage of long flowing tails and shiny, pointed feathers on their necks (*hackles*) and backs (*saddle*) which are typically of brighter, bolder colors than those of females of the same species. However, in some breeds, such as the Sebright, the rooster has only slightly pointed neck feathers, the same color as the hen's. The identification must be made by looking at the comb, or eventually from the development of spurs on the male's legs (in a few breeds and in certain hybrids the male and female chicks may be differentiated by color). Adult chickens have a fleshy crest on their heads called a *comb or cockscomb*, and hanging flaps of skin either side under their beaks called *wattles*. Both the adult male and female have wattles and combs, but in most breeds these are more prominent in males. A *muff* or *beard* is a mutation found in several chicken breeds which causes extra feathering under the chicken's face, giving the appearance of a beard.

Domestic chickens are not capable of long distance flight, although lighter birds are generally capable of flying for short distances, such as over fences or into trees (where they would naturally roost). Chickens may occasionally fly briefly to explore their surroundings, but generally do so only to flee perceived danger.

Chickens are gregarious birds and live together in flocks. They have a communal approach to the incubation of eggs and raising of young. Individual chickens in a flock will dominate others, establishing a 'pecking order', with dominant individuals having priority for food access and nesting locations. Removing hens or roosters from a flock causes a temporary disruption to this social order until a new pecking order is established. Adding hens—especially younger birds—to an existing flock can lead to violence and injury.

Hens will try to lay in nests that already contain eggs, and have been known to move eggs from neighbouring nests into their own. Some farmers use fake eggs made from plastic or stone (or golf balls) to encourage hens to lay in a particular location. The result of this behavior is that a flock will use only a few preferred locations, rather than having a different nest for every bird.

Hens can also be extremely stubborn about always laying in the same location. It is not unknown for two (or more) hens to try to share the same nest at the same time. If the nest is small, or one of the hens is particularly determined, this may result in chickens trying to lay on top of each other.

Roosters crowing (a loud and sometimes shrill call) is a territorial signal to other roosters. However, crowing may also result from sudden disturbances within their surroundings. Hens cluck loudly after laying an egg, and also to call their chicks. Chickens also give a low 'warning call' when they think they see a predator approaching.

In 2006, scientists researching the ancestry of birds 'turned on' a chicken recessive gene, *talpid2*, and found that the embryo jaws initiated formation of teeth, like those found in ancient bird fossils. John Fallon, the overseer of the project, stated that chickens have "...retained the ability to make teeth, under certain conditions... ."

When a rooster finds food, he may call other chickens to eat first. He does this by clucking in a high pitch as well as picking up and dropping the food. This behaviour may also be observed in mother hens to call their chicks and encourage them to eat.

To initiate courting, some roosters may dance in a circle around or near a hen ('a circle dance'), often lowering his wing which is closest to the hen. The dance triggers a response in the hen's brain, and when the hen responds to his 'call', the rooster may mount the hen and proceed with the fertilization.

The domestic chicken is descended primarily from the Red Junglefowl (*Gallus gallus*) and is scientifically classified as the same species. As such it can and does freely interbreed with populations of red jungle fowl. Recent genetic analysis has revealed that at least the gene for yellow skin was incorporated into domestic birds through hybridization with the Grey Junglefowl (*G. sonneratii*). It is believed by some that a single domestication event occurring in the region of modern Thailand created the modern chicken with minor transitions separating the modern breeds. Others believe that the intensive interbreeding which occurred in the past gave the modern chicken multiple origins in the jungles of South and Southeast Asia.

Researchers have found chickens' bones in unusual amounts and out of natural jungle range, thus denoting a breeding place. Bones of domestic chickens from about 6000-4000 BC have been found in Yangshao and Peiligan, China, from a time when the Holocene climate was not naturally suitable for the *Gallus* species. Archaeological data is lacking for Thailand and southeast Asia.

Later traces are found about 3000-2000 BC in Harappa and Mohenjo-Daro, Pakistan, and, according to linguistic researchers, in Austronesian populations travelling across southeast Asia and Oceania. A northern road spread chicken to the Tarim basin of central Asia, modern day Iran. The chicken reached Europe (Romania, Turkey, Greece, Ukraine) about 3000 BC, and the Indus Valley about 2500 BC. Introduction into Western Europe came far later, about the 1st millennium BC. Phoenicians spread chickens along the Mediterranean coasts, to Iberia. Breeding increased under the Roman Empire, and was reduced in the Middle Ages. Middle East traces of chicken go back to a little earlier than 2000 BC, in Syria; chicken went southward only in the 1st millennium BC. The chicken reached Egypt for purposes of cock fighting about 1400 BC, and became widely bred only in Ptolemaic Egypt (about 300 BC). Little is known about the chicken's introduction into Africa. Three possible ways of introduction in about the early first millennium AD could have been through the Egyptian Nile Valley, the East Africa Roman-Greek or Indian trade, or from Carthage and the Berbers, across the Sahara. The earliest known remains are from Mali, Nubia, East Coast, and South Africa and date back to the middle of the first millennium AD. Domestic chicken in the Americas before Western conquest is still an ongoing discussion, but blue-egged chicken, found only in the Americas and Asia, suggest an Asian origin for early American chickens.

A lack of data from Thailand, Russia, the Indian subcontinent, Southeast Asia and Sub-Saharan Africa makes it difficult to lay out a clear map of the spread of chickens in these areas; better description and genetic analysis of local breeds threatened by extinction may also help with research into this area.

Under natural conditions, most birds lay only until a clutch is complete, and they will then incubate all the eggs. Many domestic hens will also do this–and are then said to 'go broody'. The broody hen will stop laying and instead will focus on the incubation of the eggs (a full clutch is usually about 12 eggs). She will 'sit' or 'set' on the nest, protesting or pecking in defense if disturbed or removed, and she will rarely leave the nest to eat, drink, or dust-bathe. While brooding, the hen maintains the nest at a constant temperature and humidity, as well as turning the eggs regularly during the first part of the incubation. To stimulate broodiness, an owner may place many artificial eggs in the nest, or to stop it they may place the hen in an elevated cage with an open wire floor.

At the end of the incubation period (about 21 days), he eggs, if fertile, will hatch. Development of the egg starts only when incubation begins, so they all hatch within a day or two of each other, despite perhaps being laid over a period of two weeks or so. Before hatching, the hen can hear the chicks peeping inside the eggs, and will gently cluck to stimulate them to break out of their shells. The chick begins by 'pipping'; pecking a breathing hole with its egg tooth towards the blunt end of the egg, usually on the upper side. It will then rest for some hours, absorbing the remaining egg yolk and withdrawing the blood supply from the membrane beneath the shell (used earlier for breathing through the shell). It then enlarges the hole, gradually turning round as it goes, and eventually severing the blunt end of the shell completely to make a lid. It crawls out of the remaining shell, and its wet down dries out in the warmth of the nest.

The hen will usually stay on the nest for about two days after the first egg hatches, and during this time the newly hatched chicks live off the egg yolk they absorb just before hatching. Any eggs not fertilized by a rooster will not hatch, and the hen eventually loses interest in these and leaves the nest. After hatching, the hen fiercely guards the chicks, and will brood them when necessary to keep them warm, at first often returning to the nest at night. She leads them to food and water; she will call them to edible items, but seldom feeds them directly. She continues to care for them until they are several weeks old, when she will gradually lose interest and eventually start to lay again.

Modern egg-laying breeds rarely go broody, and those that do often stop part-way through the incubation. However, some "utility" (general purpose) breeds, such as the Cochin, Cornish and Silkie, do regularly go broody, and they make excellent mothers, not only for chicken eggs but also for those of other species—even those with much smaller or larger eggs and different incubation periods, such as quail, pheasants, turkeys or geese. Chicken eggs can also be hatched under a broody duck, with varied success.

More than 50 billion chickens are reared annually as a source of food, for both their meat and their eggs. Chickens farmed for meat are called broiler chickens, whilst those farmed for eggs are called egg-laying hens. In total, the UK alone consumes over 29 million eggs per day. Some hens can produce over 300 eggs per year. Chickens will naturally live for 6 or more years, but broiler chickens typically take less than six weeks to reach slaughter size. For laying hens, they are slaughtered after about 12 months, when the hens' productivity starts to decline.

The vast majority of poultry are raised using intensive farming techniques. According to the Worldwatch Institute, 74 per cent of the world's poultry meat, and 68 per cent of eggs are produced this way. One alternative to intensive poultry farming is free range farming.

Friction between these two main methods has led to long term issues of ethical consumerism. Opponents of intensive farming argue that it harms the environment, creates human health risks and is inhumane. Advocates of intensive farming say that their highly efficient systems save land and food resources due to increased productivity, stating that the animals are looked after in state-of-the-art environmentally controlled facilities.

Incubation can successfully occur artificially in machines that provide the correct, controlled environment for the developing chick. The average incubation period for chickens is 21 days but may depend on the temperature and humidity in the incubator. Temperature regulation is the most critical factor for a successful hatch. Variations of more than 1°F (-17°C) from the optimum temperature of 99.5°F (37.5°C) will reduce hatch rates. Humidity is also important because the rate at which eggs lose water by evaporation depends on the ambient relative humidity. Evaporation can be assessed by candling, to view the size of the air sac, or by measuring weight loss. Relative humidity should be increased to around 70 per cent in the last three days of incubation to keep the membrane around the hatching chick from drying out after the chick cracks the shell. Lower humidity is usual in the first 18 days to ensure adequate evaporation. The position of the eggs in the incubator can also influence hatch rates. For best results, eggs should be placed with the pointed ends down and turned regularly (at least three times per day) until one to three days before hatching. If the eggs aren't turned, the embryo inside may stick to the shell and may hatch with physical defects. Adequate ventilation is necessary to provide the embryo with oxygen. Older eggs require increased ventilation.

Many commercial incubators are industrial-sized with shelves holding tens of thousands of eggs at a time, with rotation of the eggs a fully automated process. Home incubators are boxes holding from half a dozen to 75 eggs;

they are usually electrically powered, but in the past some were heated with an oil or paraffin lamp.

Chicken eggs are widely used in many types of dishes, both sweet and savory, including many baked goods. Eggs can be scrambled, fried, hard-boiled, soft-boiled, pickled, and poached. The albumen, or egg white, contains protein but little or no fat, and can be used in cooking separately from the yolk. Egg whites may be aerated or whipped to a light, fluffy consistency and are often used in desserts such as meringues and mousse. Ground egg shells are sometimes used as a food additive to deliver calcium. Some people prefer to just have a female, and raise it for the eggs.

The meat of the chicken, also called 'chicken', is a type of poultry meat. Because of its relatively low cost, chicken is one of the most used meats in the world. Nearly all parts of the bird can be used for food, and the meat can be cooked in many different ways. Popular chicken dishes include roasted chicken, fried chicken, chicken soup, Buffalo wings, tandoori chicken, butter chicken, and chicken rice. Chicken is also a staple of many fast food restaurants.

In Indonesia the chicken has great significance during the Hindu cremation ceremony. A chicken is considered a channel for evil spirits which may be present during the ceremony. A chicken is tethered by the leg and kept present at the ceremony for its duration to ensure that any evil spirits present during the ceremony go into the chicken and not the family members present. The chicken is then taken home and returns to its normal life.

In ancient Greece, the chicken was not normally used for sacrifices, perhaps because it was still considered an exotic animal. Because of its valor, the cock is found as an attribute of Ares, Heracles, and Athena. The alleged last words of Socrates as he died from hemlock poisoning, as recounted by Plato, were "Crito, I owe a cock to Asclepius; will you remember to pay the debt?", signifying that death was a cure for the illness of life.

The Greeks believed that even lions were afraid of cocks. Several of Aesop's Fables reference this belief.

In the New Testament, Jesus prophesied the betrayal by Peter: "Jesus answered, 'I tell you, Peter, before the rooster crows today, you will deny three times that you know me.'" (Luke 22:34) Thus it happened (Luke 22:61), and Peter cried bitterly. This made the cock a symbol for both vigilance and betrayal.

Earlier, Jesus compares himself to a mother hen when talking about Jerusalem: "O Jerusalem, Jerusalem, you who kill the prophets and stone those sent to you, how often I have longed to gather your children together, as a hen gathers her chicks under her wings, but you were not willing." (Matthew 23:37; also Luke 13:34).

In many Central European folk tales, the devil is believed to flee at the first crowing of a cock.

In traditional Jewish practice, a kosher animal is swung around the head and then slaughtered on the afternoon before Yom Kippur, the Day of Atonement, in a ritual called kapparos. A chicken or fish is typically used because it is commonly available (and small enough to hold). The sacrifice of the animal is to receive atonement, for the animal symbolically takes on all the person's sins in kapparos. The meat is then donated to the poor. A woman brings a hen for the ceremony, while a man brings a rooster. Although not actually a sacrifice in the biblical sense, the death of the animal reminds the penitent sinner that his or her life is in God's hands.

The Talmud speaks of learning "courtesy toward one's mate" from the rooster. This might refer to the fact that when a rooster finds something good to eat, he calls his hens to eat first.

The chicken is one of the Zodiac symbols of the Chinese calendar. Also in Chinese religion, a cooked chicken as a religious offering is usually limited to ancestor veneration and worship of village deities. Vegetarian deities such as the Buddha are not one of the recipients of such offerings. Under some observations, an offering of chicken is presented with "serious" prayer (while roasted pork is offered during a joyous celebration). In Confucian Chinese Weddings, a chicken can be used as a substitute for one who is seriously ill or not available (*e.g.* sudden death) to attend the ceremony. A red silk scarf is placed on the chicken's head and a close relative of the absent bride/groom holds the chicken so the ceremony may proceed. However, this practice is rare today.

A cockatrice was supposed to have been born from an egg laid by a rooster, as well as killed by a Rooster's call.

An early domestication of chickens in Southeast Asia is probable, since the word for domestic chicken (*manuk*) is part of the reconstructed Proto-Austronesian language . Chickens, together with dogs and pigs, were the domestic animals of the Lapita culture, the first Neolithic culture of Oceania.

The first pictures of chickens in Europe are found on Corinthian pottery of the 7th century BC. The poet Cratinus (mid-5th century BC, according to the later Greek author Athenaeus) calls the chicken 'the Persian alarm'. In Aristophanes's comedy *The Birds* (414 BC) a chicken is called 'the Median bird', which points to an introduction from the East. Pictures of chickens are found on Greek red figure and black-figure pottery.

In ancient Greece, chickens were still rare and were a rather prestigious food for symposia. Delos seems to have been a centre of chicken breeding.

The Romans used chickens for oracles, both when flying ('ex avibus', Augury) and when feeding ('auspicium ex tripudiis', Alectryomancy). The hen ('gallina') gave a favourable omen ('auspicium ratum'), when appearing from the left (Cic.,de Div. ii.26), like the crow and the owl.

For the oracle 'ex tripudiis' according to Cicero (Cic. de Div. ii.34), any bird could be used, but normally only chickens ('pulli') were consulted. The chickens were cared for by the pullarius, who opened their cage and fed them pulses or a special kind of soft cake when an augury was needed. If the chickens stayed in their cage, made noises ('occinerent'), beat their wings or flew away, the omen was bad; if they ate greedily, the omen was good.

Chickens were spread by Polynesian seafarers and reached Easter Island in the 12th century AD, where they were the only domestic animal, with the possible exception of the Polynesian Rat (*Rattus exulans*). They were housed in extremely solid chicken coops built from stone.

In 249 BC, the Roman general Publius Claudius Pulcher had his chickens thrown overboard when they refused to feed before the battle of Drepana, saying "If they won't eat, perhaps they will drink." He promptly lost the battle against the Carthaginians and 93 Roman ships were sunk. Back in Rome, he was tried for impiety and heavily fined.

In 161 BC, a law was passed in Rome that forbade the consumption of fattened chickens. It was renewed a number of times, but does not seem to have been successful. Fattening chickens with bread soaked in milk was thought to give especially delicious results. The Roman gourmet Apicius offers 17 recipes for chicken, mainly boiled chicken with a sauce. All parts of the animal are used: the recipes include the stomach, liver, testicles and even the pygostyle (the fatty 'tail' of the chicken where the tail feathers attach).

The Roman author Columella gives advice on chicken breeding in his eighth book of his treatise on agriculture. He identifies Tanagrian, Rhodic, Chalkidic and Median (commonly misidentified as Melian) breeds, which have an impressive appearance, a quarrelsome nature and were used for cockfighting by the Greeks. For farming, native (Roman) chickens are to be preferred, or a cross between native hens and Greek cocks. Dwarf chickens are nice to watch because of their size but have no other advantages.

Per Columella, the ideal flock consists of 200 birds, which can be supervised by one person if someone is watching for stray animals. White chickens should be avoided as they are not very fertile and are easily caught by eagles or goshawks.

One cock should be kept for five hens. In the case of Rhodian and Median cocks that are very heavy and therefore not much inclined to sex, only three hens are kept per cock. The hens of heavy fowls are not much inclined to brood; therefore their eggs are best hatched by normal hens. A hen can hatch no more than 15-23 eggs, depending on the time of year, and supervise no more than 30 hatchlings. Eggs that are long and pointed give more male, rounded eggs mainly female hatchlings.

Per Columella, chicken coops should face southeast and lie adjacent to the kitchen, as smoke is beneficial for the animals. Coops should consist of three rooms and possess a hearth. Dry dust or ash should be provided for dust-baths.

According to Columella, chicken should be fed on barley groats, small chick-peas, millet and wheat bran, if they are cheap. Wheat itself should be avoided as it is harmful to the birds. Boiled ryegrass (*Lollium* sp.) and the leaves and seeds of alfalfa (*Medicago sativa* L.) can be used as well. Grape marc can be used, but only when the hens stop laying eggs, that is, about the middle of November; otherwise eggs are small and few. When feeding grape marc, it should be supplemented with some bran. Hens start to lay eggs after the winter solstice, in warm places around the first of January, in colder areas in the middle of February. Parboiled barley increases their fertility; this should be mixed with alfalfa leaves and seeds, or vetches or millet if alfalfa is not at hand. Free-ranging chickens should receive two cups of barley daily.

Columella advises farmers to slaughter hens that are older than three years, because they no longer produce sufficient eggs.

Capons were produced by burning out their spurs with a hot iron. The wound was treated with potter's chalk.

For the use of poultry and eggs in the kitchens of ancient Rome see Roman eating and drinking.

An unusual variety of chicken that has its origins in South America is the araucana, bred in southern Chile by

Mapuche people. Araucanas, some of which are tailless and some of which have tufts of feathers around their ears, lay blue-green eggs. It has long been suggested that they predate the arrival of European chickens brought by the Spanish and are evidence of pre-Columbian trans-Pacific contacts between Asian or Pacific Oceanic peoples, particularly the Polynesians and South America. In 2007, an international team of researchers reported the results of analysis of chicken bones found on the Arauco Peninsula in south central Chile. Radiocarbon dating suggested that the chickens were Pre-Columbian, and DNA analysis showed that they were related to prehistoric populations of chickens in Polynesia. These results appeared to confirm that the chickens came from Polynesia and that there were transpacific contacts between Polynesia and South America before Columbus's arrival in the Americas.

CHAPTER 8

EGG (FOOD)

Eggs laid by females of many different species, including birds, reptiles, amphibians, and fish, have probably been eaten by mankind for millennia. Bird and reptile eggs consist of a protective eggshell, albumen (egg white), and vitellus (egg yolk), contained within various thin membranes.

Egg yolks and whole eggs store a lot of protein and choline. For this reason, the USDA (United States Department of Agriculture) categorizes eggs as *Meats* within the Food Guide Pyramid.

Popular choices for egg consumption are chicken, duck, roe, and caviar. The egg most often humanly consumed by far is the produce of the chicken.

Most commercially produced chicken eggs intended for human consumption are unfertilized, since the laying hens are kept without roosters. Fertile eggs can be purchased and eaten as well, with little nutritional difference. Fertile eggs will not contain a developed embryo, as refrigeration prohibits cellular growth for an extended amount of time (although sometimes the embryo is allowed to develop on purpose, as in balut).

Bird eggs are a common food and one of the most versatile ingredients used in cooking. They are important in many branches of the modern food industry. The most commonly used bird eggs are those from the chicken. Duck and goose eggs, and smaller eggs such as quail eggs are occasionally used as a gourmet ingredient, as are the largest bird eggs, from ostriches. Gull eggs are considered a delicacy in England, as well as in some Scandinavian countries, particularly in Norway. In some African countries, guineafowl eggs are commonly seen in marketplaces, especially in the spring of each year. Pheasant eggs and emu eggs are perfectly edible but less widely available. Sometimes they are obtainable from farmers, poulterers, or luxury grocery stores. Most wild birds' eggs are protected by laws in many countries, which prohibit collecting or selling them, or permit these only during specific periods of the year.

Chicken eggs are widely used in many types of dishes, both sweet and savory, including many baked goods. Eggs can be scrambled, fried, hard-boiled, soft-boiled, pickled, and refrigerated. They can also be eaten raw, though this is not recommended for people who may be especially susceptible to salmonella, such as the elderly, the infirm, or pregnant women. In addition, the protein in raw eggs is only 51 per cent bio-available, whereas that of a cooked egg is nearer 91 per cent bio-available, meaning the protein of cooked eggs is nearly twice as absorbable as the protein from raw eggs. As an ingredient, egg yolks are an important emulsifier in the kitchen.

The albumen, or egg white, contains protein but little or no fat, and can be used in cooking separately from the yolk. Egg whites may be aerated or whipped to a light, fluffy consistency and are often used in desserts such as meringues and mousse. Ground egg shells are sometimes used as a food additive to deliver calcium. Every part of an egg is edible, although the eggshell is generally discarded.

Although the age of the egg and the conditions of its storage have a greater influence, the bird's diet does affect the flavour of the egg. For example, when a brown-egg chicken breed eats rapeseed or soy meals, its intestinal microbes metabolize them into fishy-smelling triethylamine, which ends up in the egg. The unpredictable diet of free-range hens will produce unpredictable eggs.

Egg white coagulates, or solidifies, when it reaches temperatures between 144°F and 149°F (62.2°C – 65°C). Egg yolk coagulates at slightly higher temperatures, between 149°F and 158°F (65°C-70°C).

If a boiled egg is overcooked, a greenish ring sometimes appears around egg yolk. This is a manifestation of the iron and sulfur compounds in the egg. It can also occur when there is an abundance of iron in the cooking water . The green ring does not affect the egg's taste; overcooking, however, harms the quality of the protein Chilling the egg for a few minutes in cold water until the egg is completely cooled prevents the greenish "ring" from forming on the surface of the yolk.

Cooking also increases the risk of atherosclerosis due to increased oxidization of the cholesterol contained in the egg yolk.

Careful preservation of edible eggs is extremely important, as an improperly handled egg can contain elevated levels of *Salmonella,* bacteria that can cause severe food poisoning. The simplest method to preserve an egg is to treat it with salt. Salt draws water out of bacteria and molds, which prevents their growth. The Chinese salted duck egg is made by immersing duck eggs in brine, or coating them individually with a paste of salt and mud or clay. The eggs stop absorbing salt after about a month, having reached chemical equilibrium. Their yolks take on an orange-red colour and solidify, but the white remains liquid. They are boiled before consumption and often served with rice congee.

Another method is to make pickled eggs, by boiling them first and immersing them in a mixture of vinegar, salt, and spices like ginger or allspice. Frequently, beetroot juice is added to impart a red colour to the eggs. If the eggs are immersed in it for a few hours, the distinct red, white, and yellow colours can be seen when the eggs are sliced. If marinated for several days or more, the red colour will reach the yolk. If the eggs are marinated in the mixture for several weeks or more, the vinegar will dissolve much of the shell's calcium carbonate and penetrate the egg, making it acidic enough to inhibit the growth of bacteria and molds. Pickled eggs made this way will generally keep for a year or more without refrigeration.

A century egg or hundred-year-old egg is preserved by coating an egg in a mixture of clay, wood ash, salt, lime, and rice straw for several weeks to several months, depending on the method of processing. After the process is completed, the yolk becomes a dark green, cream-like substance with a strong odor of sulfur and ammonia, while the white becomes a dark brown, transparent jelly with a comparatively mild, distinct flavour. The transforming agent in a century egg is its alkaline material, which gradually raises the pH of the egg from around 9 to 12 or more. This chemical process breaks down some of the complex, flavourless proteins and fats of the yolk into simpler, flavourful ones, which in some way may be thought of as an 'inorganic version' of fermentation.

For those who do not consume eggs, alternatives used in baking include other rising agents or binding materials, such as ground flax seeds or potato starch flour. Tofu can also act as a partial binding agent, since it is high in lecithin due to its soy content. Applesauce can be used, as well as arrowroot and banana. Extracted soybean lecithin, in turn, is often used in packaged foods as an inexpensive substitute for egg-derived lecithin.

Other egg substitutes are made from just the white of the egg for those who worry about the high cholesterol and fat content in eggs. These products usually have added vitamins and minerals as well as vegetable-based emulsifiers and thickeners such as xanthan gum or guar gum. These allow the product to maintain the nutrition and several culinary properties of real eggs, making possible foods like Hollandaise sauce, custard, mayonnaise, and most baked goods with these substitutes.

Bird eggs have been valuable foodstuff since prehistory, in both hunting societies and more recent cultures where birds were domesticated. The chicken was probably domesticated for its eggs from jungle fowl native to tropical and subtropical Southeast Asia and India before 7500 BCE. Chickens were brought to Sumer and Egypt by 1500 BCE, and arrived in Greece around 800 BCE, where the quail had been the primary source of eggs. In Thebes, Egypt, the tomb of Haremhab, built about 1420 BCE, shows a depiction of a man carrying bowls of ostrich eggs and other large eggs, presumably those of the pelican, as offerings. In ancient Rome, eggs were preserved using a number of methods, and meals often started with an egg course. The Romans crushed the shell in their plate to prevent evil spirits from hiding there. In the Middle Ages, eggs were forbidden during Lent because of their richness. It is possible that the word *mayonnaise* was derived from *moyeu*, the mediaeval French word for the yolk meaning *centre* or *hub*.

Egg scrambled with acidic fruit juices were popular in France in the 17th century; this may have been the origin of lemon curd.

The dried egg industry developed in the 19th century, before the rise of the frozen egg industry. In 1878, a company in St. Louis, Missouri started to transform egg yolk and white into a light-brown, meal-like substance by using a drying process. The production of dried eggs significantly expanded during World War II, for use by the United States Armed Forces and its allies.

The egg carton was invented by Joseph Coyle in Smithers, British Columbia, to solve a dispute about broken eggs between a farmer in Bulkley Valley and the owner of the Aldermere Hotel. Early egg cartons were made of paper.

The shape of an egg is an ovate spheroid with one end larger than the other end. The egg has cylindrical symmetry along the long axis.

An egg is surrounded by a thin, hard shell. Inside, the egg yolk is suspended in the egg white by one or two spiral bands of tissue called the chalazae (from the Greek word *khalazi*, meaning hailstone or hard lump.)

The larger end of the egg contains the air cell that forms when the contents of the egg cool down and contract after it is laid. Chicken eggs are graded according to the size of this air cell, measured during candling. A very fresh egg has a small air cell and receives a grade of AA. As the size of the air cell increases, and the quality of the egg decreases, the grade moves from AA to A to B. This provides a way of testing the age of an egg: as the air cell increases in size, the egg becomes less dense and the larger end of the egg will rise to increasingly shallower depths when the egg is placed in a bowl of water. A very old egg will actually float in the water and should not be eaten.

Egg shell colour is caused by pigment deposition during egg formation in the oviduct and can vary according to species and breed, from the more common white or brown to pink or speckled blue-green. In general, chicken breeds with white ear lobes lay white eggs, whereas chickens with red ear lobes lay brown eggs. Although there is no significant link between shell colour and nutritional value, there is often a cultural preference for one colour over another. For example, in most regions of the United States, chicken eggs are generally white; while in the northeast of that country, and in countries as diverse as Costa Rica, Ireland, and the United Kingdom, they are generally light-brown. In Brazil and Poland, white chicken eggs are generally regarded as industrial, and brown or reddish ones are preferred.

The yolk in a newly laid egg is round and firm. As the yolk ages it absorbs water from the albumen, which increases its size and causes it to stretch and weaken the vitelline membrane (the clear casing enclosing the yolk). The resulting effect is a flattened and enlarged yolk shape.

Yolk colour is dependent on the diet of the hen; if the diet contains yellow/orange plant pigments known as xanthophylls, then they are deposited in the yolk, colouring it. Lutein is the most abundant pigment in egg yolk. A colourless diet can produce an almost colourless yolk. Yolk colour is for example enhanced if the diet includes products such as yellow corn and marigold petals. In the US, the use of artificial colour additives is forbidden.

Eggs add protein to a person's diet, as well as various other nutrients.

Chicken eggs are the most commonly eaten eggs. They supply all essential amino acids for humans, and provide several vitamins and minerals, including vitamin A, riboflavin (vitamin B_2), folic acid (vitamin B_9), vitamin B_6, vitamin B_{12}, choline, iron, calcium, phosphorus and potassium. They are also a single-food source of protein.

All of the egg's vitamin A, D, and E are in the egg yolk. The egg is one of the few foods that naturally contain vitamin D. A large egg yolk contains approximately 60 Calories (250 kilojoules); the egg white contains about 15 Calories (60 kilojoules). A large yolk contains more than two-thirds of the recommended daily intake of 300 mg of cholesterol (although one study indicates that the human body may not absorb much cholesterol from eggs). The yolk makes up about 33 per cent of the liquid weight of the egg. It contains all of the fat, slightly less than half of the protein, and most of the other nutrients. It also contains all of the choline, and one yolk contains approximately half of the recommended daily intake. Choline is an important nutrient for development of the brain, and is said to be important for pregnant and nursing women to ensure healthy fetal brain development.

The diet of the laying hens can greatly affect the nutritional quality of the eggs. For instance, chicken eggs that are especially high in omega 3 fatty acids are produced by feeding laying hens a diet containing polyunsaturated fats and kelp meal. Pastured raised free-range hens which forage largely for their own food also tend to produce eggs with higher nutritional quality in having less cholesterol and fats while being several times higher in vitamins and omega 3 fatty acids than standard factory eggs Focusing on the protein and crude fat content, a 2010 USDA study determined that there were no significant differences of these two macronutrients in consumer chicken eggs.

Cooked eggs are easier to digest, as well as having a lower risk of salmonellosis.

More than half the calories found in eggs come from the fat in the yolk; a large (50 gram) chicken egg contains approximately 5 grams of fat. People on a low-cholesterol diet may need to reduce egg consumption; however, only 27 per cent of the fat in egg is saturated fat (palmitic, stearic and myristic acids) that contains LDL cholesterol. The egg white consists primarily of water (87%) and protein (13%) and contains no cholesterol and little, if any, fat.

There is debate over whether egg yolk presents a health risk. Some research suggests dietary cholesterol increases the ratio of total to HDL cholesterol and, therefore, adversely affects the body's cholesterol profile; whereas other studies show that moderate consumption of eggs, up to one a day, does not appear to increase heart disease risk in healthy individuals. Harold McGee argues that the cholesterol in the yolk is not what causes a problem, because fat (in particular, saturated) is much more likely to raise cholesterol levels than the actual consumption of cholesterol. A 2007 study of nearly 10,000 adults demonstrated no correlation between moderate (6 per week) egg consumption and cardiovascular disease or strokes except in the sub-population of diabetic patients that presented an increased risk of coronary heart disease. Other research supports the idea that a high egg intake increases cardiovascular risk in diabetic patients.

Consumption of eggs has been linked to an increased risk of type 2 diabetes in both men and women. A 2008 study using data on over 50,000 individuals collected by the Physicians' Health Study I (1982–2007) and the Women's Health Study (1992-2007) determined that the "data suggest that high levels of egg consumption (daily) are associated with an increased risk of type 2 diabetes." However, a study published in 2010 found no link between egg consumption and type 2 diabetes.

A health issue associated with eggs is contamination by pathogenic bacteria like *Salmonella enteritidis*. Contamination of eggs exiting a female bird via the cloaca may also occur with other members of the *Salmonella* genus, so care must be taken to prevent the egg shell from becoming contaminated with fecal matter. In commercial practice, eggs are quickly washed with a sanitizing solution within minutes of being laid. The risk of infection from raw or undercooked eggs is dependent in part upon the sanitary conditions under which the hens are kept.

Health experts advise people to refrigerate eggs, use them within two weeks, cook them thoroughly, and never consume raw eggs. As with meat, containers and surfaces that have been used to process raw eggs should not come in contact with ready-to-eat food.

A study by the U.S. Department of Agriculture in 2002 (Risk Analysis April 2002 22(2):203-18) suggests the problem is not as prevalent as once thought. It showed that of the 69 billion eggs produced annually, only 2.3 million are contaminated with *Salmonella* — equivalent to just one in every 30,000 eggs — thus showing that *Salmonella* infection is quite rarely induced by eggs. However, this has not been the case in other countries where *Salmonella enteritidis* and *Salmonella typhimurium* infections due to egg consumptions are major concerns. Egg shells act as hermetic seals that guard against bacteria entering, but this seal can be broken through improper handling or if laid by unhealthy chickens. Most forms of contamination enter through such weaknesses in the shell. In the UK, the British Egg Industry Council award the lions stamp to eggs that, among other things, come from hens that have been vaccinated against *Salmonella*.

One of the most common food allergies in infants is eggs. Infants usually have the opportunity to grow out of this allergy during childhood, if exposure is minimized. Allergic reactions against egg white are more common than reactions against egg yolks.

In addition to true allergic reactions, some people experience a food intolerance to egg whites.

Food labelling practices in most developed countries now include eggs, egg products and the processing of foods on equipment that also process foods containing eggs in a special allergen alert section of the ingredients on the labels.

Antibiotic Resistance

Information obtained by the Canadian Integrated Programme for Antimicrobial Resistance (CIPARS) "strongly indicates that cephalosporin resistance in humans is moving in lockstep with use of the drug in poultry production." According to the Canadian Medical Association Journal, the unapproved antibiotic ceftiofur is routinely injected into eggs in Quebec and Ontario to discourage infection of hatchlings. Although the data are contested by the industry, antibiotic resistance in humans appears to be directly related to the antibiotic's use in eggs.

Chicken Egg Grading

The US Department of Agriculture grade eggs by the interior quality of the egg (see Haugh unit) and the appearance and condition of the egg shell. Eggs of any quality grade may differ in weight (size).

U.S. Grade AA eggs have whites that are thick and firm; yolks that are high, round, and practically free from defects; and clean, unbroken shells. Grade AA and Grade A eggs are best for frying and poaching, where appearance is important.

U.S. Grade A eggs have characteristics of Grade AA eggs except the whites are 'reasonably' firm. This is the quality most often sold in stores.

U.S. Grade B eggs have whites that may be thinner and yolks that may be wider and flatter than eggs of higher grades. The shells must be unbroken, but may show slight stains. This quality is seldom found in retail stores because they are usually used to make liquid, frozen, and dried egg products, as well as other egg-containing products.

In other countries, such as Australia and European Union countries, eggs are graded by the hen farming method instead, *e.g.*, from free range hens, battery cages, etc.

Chicken eggs are also graded by size, for the purpose of sales.

Commercial factory farming operations often involve raising the hens in small crowded cages, preventing the chickens from engaging in natural behaviours such as wing-flapping, dust-bathing, scratching, pecking, perching and nest-building. Such restrictions can lead to pacing and escape behaviour.

Many hens confined to battery cages, and some raised in cage-free conditions, are de-beaked to prevent harming each other and cannibalism. According to critics of the practice, this can cause hens severe pain to the point where some may refuse to eat and starve to death. Some hens may be force molted to increase egg quality and production level after the molting. Molting can be induced by extended feed withdrawal, water withdrawal or controlled lighting programmes.

Laying hens are often slaughtered between 100–130 weeks of age, when their egg productivity starts to decline. Due to modern selective breeding, laying hen strains differ from meat production strains. As male birds of the laying strain do not lay eggs and are not suitable for meat production, they are generally culled at the hatchery.

Free-range eggs are considered by some advocates to be an acceptable substitute to factory-farmed eggs. Free-range laying hens are given outdoor access instead of being contained in crowded cages. Questions on the actual living conditions of free-range hens have been raised, as there is no legal definition or regulations for eggs labelled as free-range in the US.

In the US, increased public concern for animal welfare has pushed various egg producers to release eggs under a variety of different standards. The most widespread standard in use is used by United Egg Producers and is a volunteer programme known as *United Egg Producers Certified* (UEP Certified). The programme includes guidelines with regard to housing, feed, water, air, space allowance, beak trimming, molting, handling, and transportation; however, critics such as The Humane Society have alleged UEP Certification misleadingly allows for a significant amount of animal cruelty. Other standards include 'Cage Free', 'Natural', 'Certified Humane', and 'Certified Organic'. Of these standards, 'Certified Humane', which carries requirements for stocking density and cage-free keeping, among others, and 'Certified Organic', which requires hens have outdoor access and are fed only organic, vegetarian feed, among other requirements, are the most stringent.

The European Union will introduce an EU-wide ban on the use of conventional battery cages for egg-laying hens. This ban is expected to come into effect from 1 January 2012, as per EU Directive 1999/74/EC. The EU will instead permit the use of 'enriched' cages that must meet certain space and amenity requirements. Egg producers in many member states have objected to the ban.

A popular Easter tradition in some parts of the world is the decoration of hard-boiled eggs (usually by dyeing but often by spray-painting). Adults often hide the eggs for children to find, an activity known as an Easter egg hunt. A similar tradition of egg painting exists in areas of the world influenced by the culture of Persia. Before the spring equinox in the Persian New Year tradition (called Norouz), each family member decorates a hard-boiled egg and sets them together in a bowl.

Although a food item, eggs are sometimes thrown at houses, cars, or people. This act, known commonly as *egging* in the various English-speaking countries, is a minor form of vandalism and, therefore, usually a criminal offense and is capable of damaging property (egg whites can degrade certain types of vehicle paint) as well as causing serious eye injury. On Halloween, for example, trick or treaters have been known to throw eggs (and sometimes flour) at property or people from whom they received nothing. Eggs are also often thrown in protests, as they are inexpensive and non-lethal, yet very messy when broken.

CHAPTER

9

DUCK (FOOD)

Duck refers to the meat of several species of bird in the Anatidae family, found in both fresh and salt water. Duck is eaten in many cuisines around the world.

The most common duck meat consumed in the United States is the Pekin duck. Because most commercially raised Pekins come from Long Island, New York, Pekins are also sometimes called 'Long Island' ducks, despite being of Chinese origin. Some specialty breeds have become more popular in recent years, notably the Muscovy duck, and the Moulard duck (a sterile hybrid of Pekins and Muscovies). Unlike most other domesticated ducks, Muscovy ducks are not descended from mallards.

According to the USDA, nearly 26 million ducks were eaten in the U.S. in 2004.

Duck meat is derived primarily from the breasts and legs of ducks. The meat of the legs is darker and somewhat fattier than the meat of the breasts, although the breast meat is darker than the breast meat of a chicken or a turkey. Being waterfowl, ducks have a layer of heat-insulating subcutaneous fat between the skin and the meat. De-boned duck breast can be grilled like steak, usually leaving the skin and fat on. Magret refers specifically to the breast of a mallard or Barbary duck that has been force fed to produce foie gras.

Internal organs such as heart and kidneys may also be eaten; the liver in particular is often used as a substitute for goose liver in foie gras.

Duck is used in a variety of dishes around the world, most of which involve roasting for at least part of the cooking process to aid in crisping the skin. Notable duck dishes include:

- *Bebek Betutu:* a famous traditional dish from Bali, Indonesia. The duck is first seasoned with pungent roots and various herbs, wrapped with banana leaves, and roasted. Chicken is also used to prepare Betutu.
- *Confit:* duck legs that have been cured (partly or fully) in salt, then marinated and poached in duck fat, typically with garlic and other herbs. The French word *confit* means 'preserved', and the French name for duck confit is 'confit de canard'.
- *Czernina:* a sweet and sour Polish soup made of duck blood and clear poultry broth. It was once considered a symbol of Polish culture until the 19th century, customarily served to young men and is even featured as a plot device in a famous epic poem called Pan Tadeusz.
- *Duck à l'orange:* a classic French dish in which the duck is roasted and served with an orange sauce.
- *Duck sauce:* a fruit-based dipping sauce for deep fried dishes in Chinese American cuisine.
- *Foie Gras:* a specially fattened and rich liver, or a pâté made from the liver, sometimes taken from a duck but usually from a goose.
- *Oritang:* a variety of *guk,* Korean soup made with duck and various vegetables.
- *Peking Duck:* a famous Chinese dish originating from Beijing, prepared since the Ming Dynasty era. It is prized

for the thin, crispy skin, with authentic versions of the dish serving mostly the skin and little meat, and eaten with pancakes, spring onions, and hoisin sauce or sweet bean sauce.

- *Pressed duck:* a complex dish originally from Rouen, France.
- *Turducken:* an American dish that comprises a turkey, stuffed with a duck, which is in turn stuffed with a chicken.
- *Zhangcha duck:* a quintessential dish of Sichuan cuisine. It is first prepared by smoking a marinated duck over tea leaves and twigs of the camphor plant, then steamed, and finally deep fried for a crisp finish. Also called tea-smoked duck.
- *Long Island roast duckling:* This is a whole roasted bird, sometimes brined previously. When done properly, most of the fat melts off during the cooking process, leaving a crispy skin and well-done meat. Some restaurants on Long Island serve this dish with a cherry sauce.

Pekin Duck

Pekin duck, or Long Island duck (*Anas platyrhynchos domestica,* or *Anas peking*, is a breed of domesticated duck used primarily for egg and meat production. It was bred from the Mallard in China. The ancestors of those ducks originated from the canals which linked waterways in Nanjing and originally had small bodies and black feathers. With the relocation of the Chinese capital to Beijing, supply barge traffic increased in the area which would often spill grain on which the ducks fed. Over time, the ducks slowly increased in size and grew white feathers. By the Five Dynasties, the new species of duck had been domesticated by Chinese farmers.

In 1873 nine ducks were exported from China to Long Island, New York in the United States and the animals and their meat are sometimes referred to as 'Long Island duckling'. It is the most popular commercial duck breed in the United States, although some farming has since relocated to Indiana from Suffolk County, New York. Around 95 per cent of duck meat consumed in the United States is Pekin duck.

Pekin duck embryos take around 28 days to develop in the egg at 99.5°F (37.5°C) and 55-75 per cent humidity. A heartbeat can usually be seen by the third day of incubation when candling the egg.

The eggs must be regularly turned during incubation. This occurs in nature when the female duck shifts her position while sitting on the eggs. For artificial incubation, machines are available which will constantly turn the eggs.

When being artificially incubated, the eggs are moved to a 'hatcher' three days before they are due to hatch. This has a slightly lower temperature and higher humidity which increases the survivability of the hatchlings while their protective down develops.

Compared with other birds, duck eggs are relatively easy to hatch as they are very forgiving of variations in temperature and humidity.

Pekin hatchlings have bright yellow plumage with an orange bill, shanks, and feet.

Hatchlings should not be given free access to swimming water unless they have been hatched naturally by other ducks. The feathers of a young duckling are not sufficiently developed to properly protect them for extended periods in the water and they do not produce enough preen oil to waterproof this plumage. In the wild, a mother duck will monitor the time her ducklings spend in the water as well as supplying additional preen oil to supplement what is produced by the hatchlings.

It can be difficult to determine the sex of the young ducklings due to the lack of external genitalia or other differences. Venting is one common method. This entails gently squeezing the duckling to cause faeces to be expelled, which forces the cloaca to open slightly, permitting the sexer to view the sexual organs. However, these are almost undifferentiated in hatchlings.

As a male duck matures it acquires a curled tail feather called a drake feather, and their vocalisations become much weaker. Conversely, the female develops a loud quack. Venting is also easier when the ducks' genitals are fully mature but is not necessary because of the readily apparent external differences between males and females.

A female may be missing feathers on the back of her neck. This is due to the male grabbing and holding the back of the female's neck during mating.

Fully mature adult Pekin ducks weigh between 8 and 11 pounds (3.6 and 5 kilograms) in captivity. Their average lifespan (if not eaten at an early age) is about 9 to 12 years. Their external feathers are white sometimes with a yellowish tinge. This is more obvious with ducks that have been reared indoors and not exposed to sunlight. The ducks have a more upright stance than dabbling ducks, and possess an upturned rump. The eyes of this duck appear to be black when seen far away, but up-close is grayish-blue coloured iris.

An adult Pekin will lay an average of 200 eggs per year if it does not try to, or is prevented from, hatching them. They will normally only lay one egg on any given day. They will lay their eggs in what they consider to be a safe place and will often lay where another duck has already laid (egg dumping). Ducks can be tricked into laying eggs where desired by placing a golf ball or similar object in a place where they might normally lay.

Pekin ducks are less 'broody' than other ducks which means they will incubate eggs less frequently and they are more likely to abandon their nest before their eggs hatch. Hens can be used to sit on the duck eggs, or they can be incubated artificially.

Pekin ducks, for the most part, are too heavy to get airborne. While some individual ducks may be lighter and capable of short bursts of vertical flight, clipping their flight feathers (pinioning) is generally unnecessary. They are gregarious and will usually group together with other ducks.

As with most waterfowl, the Pekin duck has feet perfectly adapted for paddling through water but is also capable of walking while foraging and exploring as well. If keeping ducks, be sure to remove items from their environment which may cause tripping or stumbling, and house them on natural surfaces, such as grass, hardpack, straw, or sand which is gentler on the bones and ligaments, will not abraid the sensitive surface of the webbed feet, and is easy to keep clean. Ducks are happiest when they have free access to clean, safe water in which to swim and mate.

Pets

As precocial birds, Pekin ducks make ideal companion animals for a variety of reasons. As a duck imprints on a human, the bond of trust that develops rivals that of humans and dogs, for example, and can provide enduring companionship if they are not surrounded by other ducks. Pekin ducks are very intelligent, and are capable of life-long strong and loyal bonds with humans, and often then prefer human company over the company of other ducks.

Ducks can be both outdoor and indoor companion animals, with numerous pet accessories available to help keep them comfortable and your home clean. They are successful 'indoor' pets because they are adaptable to house life (be sure to provide them with toys and stimulation). When taken on supervised outings in nature, if properly imprinted, the duck will stay with the human 'flock' member(s) and not wander away. If a predator or danger approaches, the duck will seek safety and remain with their human flock member rather than flee and become lost and separated away from the human flock member. They are excellent sentinels, like geese, and will warn the household or other animals in the yard of approaching strangers or danger.

Domestic Duck

Domesticated ducks are ducks that are raised for meat, eggs and down. Many ducks are also kept for show, as pets or for their ornamental value. Almost all of the varieties of domesticated ducks are descended from the Mallard (*Anas platyrhynchos*), apart from the Muscovy Duck (*Cairina moschata*).

Ducks have been farmed for thousands of years, possibly starting in Southeast Asia. They are not as popular as the chicken, because chickens have much more white lean meat and are easier to keep confined, making the total price much lower for chicken meat, whereas duck is comparatively expensive and, while popular in the haute cuisine, appears less frequently in mass market food industry and restaurants in the lower price range.

Ducks are farmed for their meat, eggs, and down. A minority of ducks are also kept for foie gras production. In Vietnam, their blood is used in a food called ti?t canh. Their eggs are blue-green to white depending on the breed.

Ducks can be kept free range, in cages, in barns, or in batteries. To be healthy, ducks should be allowed access to water, though battery ducks are often denied this. They should be fed a grain and insect diet. It is a popular misconception that ducks should be fed bread; bread has limited nutritional value and can be deadly when fed to developing ducklings. Ducks should be monitored for avian influenza, as they are especially prone to infection with the dangerous H5N1 strain.

The females of many breeds of domestic ducks are unreliable at sitting their eggs and raising their young. Notable exceptions include the Rouen Duck and especially the Muscovy Duck. It has been a custom on farms for centuries to put duck eggs under a broody hen for hatching; nowadays incubators are often used. However, young ducklings rely on their mother for a supply of preen oil to make them waterproof, and a chicken hen does not make as much preen oil as a duck hen; and an incubator makes none. Once the duckling sprouts its own feathers it will produce preen oil from the sebaceous gland near the base of its tail.

Domesticated ducks can be kept as pets. They can be kept in a garden or backyard, and with special accessories, have also been known to be kept in the house. They will often eat insects and slugs. A pond or deep water dish is recommended. Without access to plentiful water, ducks will not thrive.

If ducks are given access to a pond they will dabble in the mud, dredging out and eating wildlife and frogspawn, and swallow adult frogs and toads up to the size of the British common frog *Rana temporaria*, as they have been bred to be much bigger than wild ducks with a 'hull length' (base of neck to base of tail) of up to a foot or more; the wild mallard's 'hull length' is about 6 inches (150 mm). A coop should be provided for shelter from predators such as foxes, hawks, coyotes, and racoons, as many breeds of domestic ducks are unable to fly.

Ducks are also kept for their ornamental value. Breeds have been developed with crests and tufts or striking plumage. Exhibition shows are held in which ducks, along with other breeds of poultry, are exhibited in competition.

These shows can be 'open' (meaning any exhibitor who pays the required entry fee can enter), or 'closed' (accessible only to members of a given group). The most common of these is a 4-H poultry show.

Vertically Rotating Roasted Lamb, to be Served in Pieces

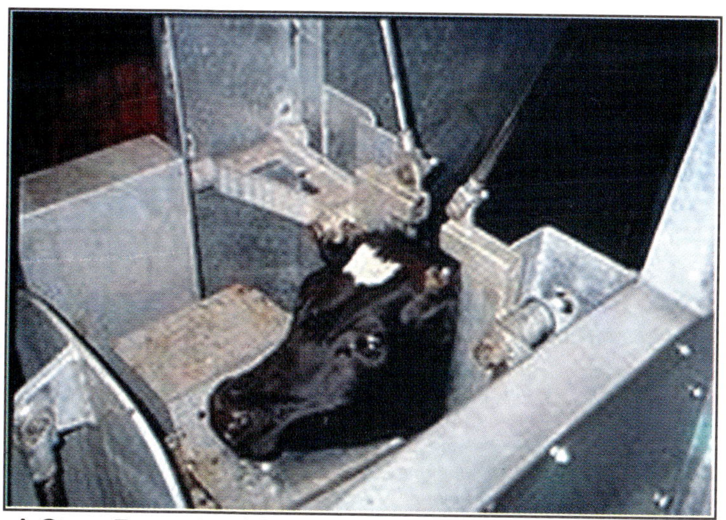

A Steer Restrained for Stunning Just Prior to Slaughter

Oven Roasted Rosemary and Lemon Chicken

Chicken in a Public Market

Marination of Chicken for Grilling

Roasted Chicken

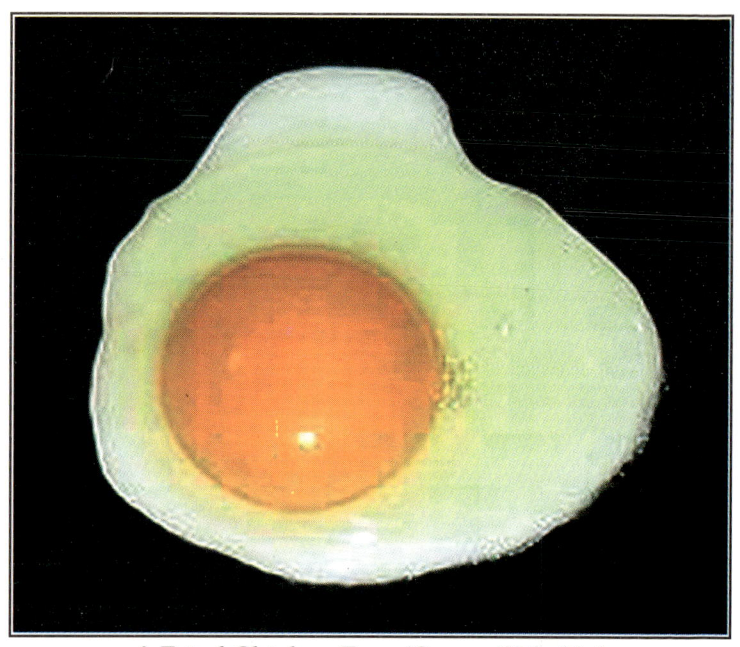

A Fried Chicken Egg, 'Sunny Side Up'

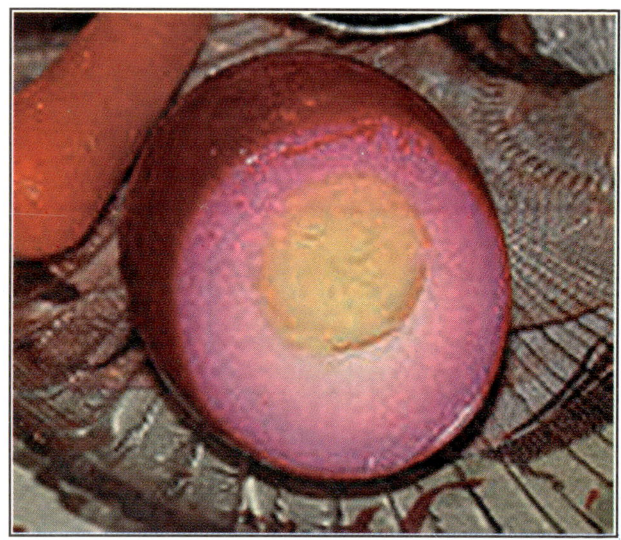

Pickled Egg, Coloured with Beetroot Juice

Various Offal Delicacies (Heads, Brains, Trotters and Tripe) for Sale in an Istanbul Meat Market

Grilled Beef Satay

Andouillette from Troyes on Sale at a Charcuterie in Montmartre, Paris

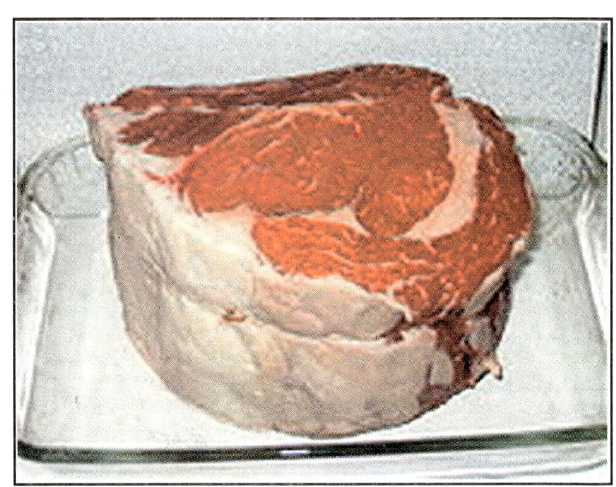

An Uncooked Rib Roast

Malaysian/Singaporean Bakkwa Jerky

Boneless Veal Cutlets

Shoulder of Lamb

Marinating Goat Chops

CHAPTER
10

AUSTRALIAN AND NEW ZEALAND MEAT PIE

An Australian or New Zealand meat pie is a hand-sized meat pie containing largely diced or minced meat and gravy, sometimes with onion, mushrooms, or cheese and often consumed as a takeaway food snack. The pie itself is similar to the United Kingdom's steak pie.

It is considered iconic in Australia and New Zealand. It was described by former New South Wales Premier Bob Carr in 2003 as Australia's 'national dish'. Across the Tasman, New Zealanders regard the meat pie as a part of New Zealand cuisine, and it forms part of the New Zealand national identity.

The popular brand Four 'N' Twenty produces 50,000 pies per hour and Australians consume an average of 12 meat pies each per year. The average consumption of meat pies in New Zealand is higher at 15 per person per year. The meat pie is heavily associated with Australian Rules Football as one of the most popular consumed food items whilst watching a game.

Manufacturers of pies in Australia tend to be state based, reflecting the long distances involved with interstate transport and lack of refrigeration capabilities in the early years of pie production. Many pies sold ready-to-eat at smaller outlets are sold unbranded and may be locally produced, produced by a brand-name vendor, or even imported, frozen pies heated prior to serving.

The Australian meat pie manufacturer Four 'N' Twenty says that its pie was invented in 1947 by L. T. McClure in a small Bendigo bakery, to become the brand Four 'N' Twenty. Due to their relationship with Australian rules football, Four 'N' Twenty has iconic status in Victoria and high popularity outside the state.

Other manufacturers predate this, and the pie manufacturer Sargent can trace their pie making back to 1906. Sargent meat pies were served at the opening of the Old Parliament House in 1927 — or rather 10,000 pies were not served and the left-over pies had to be buried nearby.

In South Australia, Balfours has been making pies since the early 1900s and remains (with Vili's) one of two major pie manufacturers in the state. Both of these pie makers supply pies to various venues hosting Australian Rules Football games.

Produced in Western Australia, Mrs Mac's Pies are now sold nationwide, found mostly in service stations and corner stores, competing with other brands in the contested takeaway hotbox market on the basis of quality and fillings other than the normal fare.

In Victoria, some of the well known and famous pie makers are Pie in the Sky from Olinda, Clarke's Pies from Mortlake, Kings Pies from Hamilton, Gillies from Bendigo, Beaumont's Pies from Geelong and Patties Pies from Bairnsdale.

In Tasmania, the main manufacturer of pies is National Pies . National Pies make typical beef mince pies, as well as 'Cottage Pies', which are topped with mashed potato. National Pies' mince pies are rectangular in shape, as opposed to most other brands, which are round.

Australian Meat Pies were introduced into the United States in 1994 by Mark Allen, of Boort, Victoria, when he and his wife, Wendy, began operation of Pacific Products, Inc. in Marietta, Georgia. Stutchbury, Michael (20 June 1995). "Pies de resistance in the Land of the Feed". *The Australian Financial Review*. Almer, Sean (3 June 1996). "Aussie strives to put meat pies into diets of Yankee sports fans". *Business Sydney*. Pacific Products was a wholesale only business, selling their pies to chain retailers throughout the United States. Although Pacific Products is no longer in business, Mark Allen and his Partner Neville Steele opened the Australian Bakery Cafe in Marietta Georgia, a retail bakery which also ships its products throughout the USA.

In 1977, during the time that American fast food restaurants moved into New Zealand, Progressive Enterprises created Georgie Pie, a fast food restaurant with a menu based on meat pies. The pies were batch made and frozen at Progressive's Mangere plant. The first Georgie Pie restaurant opened in Kelston, Auckland, and at its peak in the mid-1990s had become a chain of 32 restaurants across New Zealand. However, after a major expansion, Georgie Pie became uneconomic to run and was eventually sold to McDonald's New Zealand in 1996. The last restaurant at Mission Bay, Auckland, closed in 1998.

Former New South Wales Premier Bob Carr launched a childhood obesity summit in 2002 where he told participants that feeding children a diet of meat pies, sausage rolls and chiko rolls was akin to child cruelty.

In April 2002, the Australian Consumers Association conducted a study of 22 frozen meat pies available in supermarkets. They found three brands did not meet the minimum 25 per cent meat content requirement set by Food Standards Australia New Zealand (FSANZ), they also found that the fat content ranged from 15 to 35 grams of fat per pie. The ACA study was of a select group of frozen meat pies in supermarkets, thus the study does not account for freshly baked meat pies of which the meat content and nutritional value varies from bakery to bakery. Another study by ACA in 2006 found 5 of the 23 pie products tested had less than the minimum 25 per cent meat required.

In 2006, The ACA awarded pie manufacturer Black and Gold *"The CHOICE Shonky Award for UnAustralian Content"* for their pies found to contain just 17 per cent meat.

The meats allowed by FSANZ in a meat pie are beef, buffalo, camel, cattle, deer, goat, hare, pig, poultry, rabbit and sheep. Kangaroo meat, a leaner alternative, is also sometimes used. However, most pie manufacturers specify 'beef' in their ingredients list; typically, those using other types of meat will simply put 'meat' in the list instead. FSANZ's definition of meat includes snouts, ears, tongue roots, tendons and blood vessels. Only offal (such as brain, heart, kidney, liver, tongue, tripe) must be specified on the label. Wild animals ("slaughtered ... in the wild state") may not be used.

Controversy

In 1993, manufacturer Gartrell White lost millions of dollars after an extortionist falsely claimed to have put cyanide in Big Ben pies.

In 2007, a woman in New Zealand choked on a bone that was contained in a NZ Big Ben pie. The bone broke on its way out, ripping the woman's oesophagus. The owners of the Big Ben Pies brand, Purity Foods, had offered her an out of court settlement of up to $8000.

The Great Aussie Meat Pie Contest

Started in 1990 and held annually since, the Great Aussie Pie Contest was created to find the best everyday commercially produced meat pie produced in Australia, to promote the higher quality pie production as well as attempting to increase media attention upon the foodstuff, the iconic meat pie often dwarfed by the omnipresent advertising of fast food chains.

The contest attracts various pie makers Australia wide; the pies for the contest are judged anonymously to avoid bias towards or against specific bakeries or states. Run in parallel to the main contest is one for gourmet pies, with categories for such fillings as chicken, seafood and even vegetarian pies. As well as the main prize, certificates of excellence are awarded for entries that reach set quality standards. The main award is highly coveted due to the greatly increased sales it generates, with many people travelling interstate to sample the winning pie.

Bakels New Zealand Supreme Pie Awards

In New Zealand an annual pie competition is held since 1997, the Bakels New Zealand Supreme Pie Awards aims to recognise the best pie manufacturers in New Zealand and assisting them in producing award-winning pies and continuing to help foster and encourage developments within this category of baking.

They were entered in 11 categories — mince and gravy; chicken and vegetables; gourmet meat; bacon and egg; gourmet fruit; steak, vegetable and gravy; steak and cheese; vegetarian; mince and cheese; seafood and commercial wholesale pies. The pies were judged on presentation, the pastry on the top and bottom, the filling and the profile.

Celebrity judges included New Zealand food writers Julie Biuso and Richard Till.

Other Cultural References

In the 1970s meat pies were mentioned in an advertising jingle for General Motors Holden Australia. The jingle — *football, meat pies, kangaroos and Holden cars, they go together underneath the Southern Stars* — was an adaptation of an American jingle for the General Motors Chevrolet brand.

Fair-Go Dibbler, citizen of Fourecks (*The Last Continent*) in Terry Pratchett's *Discworld* series, is famous for selling the archetypal pie floaters to his unsuspecting customers.

In 2007, Domino's Australia and Domino's New Zealand both released a meat pie pizza, consisting of minced beef, peas, diced fresh tomato, onions, gravy, thick pastry and tomato sauce.

CHAPTER

11

MEAT SPOILAGE

The spoilage of meat occurs, if the meat is untreated, in a matter of hours or days and results in the meat becoming unappetizing, poisonous or infectious. Spoilage is caused by the practically unavoidable infection and subsequent decomposition of meat by bacteria and fungi, which are borne by the animal itself, by the people handling the meat, and by their implements. Meat can be kept edible for a much longer time — though not indefinitely — if proper hygiene is observed during production and processing, and if appropriate food safety, food preservation and food storage procedures are applied.

The organisms spoiling meat may infect the animal either while still alive ('endogenous disease') or may contaminate the meat after its slaughter ('exogenous disease'). There are numerous diseases that humans may contract from endogenously infected meat, such as anthrax, bovine tuberculosis, brucellosis, salmonellosis, listeriosis, trichinosis or taeniasis.

Infected meat, however, should be eliminated through systematic meat inspection in production, and consequently, consumers will more often encounter meat exogenously spoiled by bacteria or fungi after the death of the animal. One source of infectious organisms is bacteraemia, the presence of bacteria in the blood of slaughtered animals. The large intestine of animals contains some 3.3×10^{13} viable bacteria, which may infect the flesh after death if the carcass is improperly dressed. Contamination can also occur at the slaughterhouse through the use of improperly cleaned slaughter or dressing implements, such as powered knives, on which bacteria persist. A captive bolt pistol's bolt alone may carry about 400,000 bacteria per square centimeter. After slaughter, care must be taken not to infect the meat through contact with any of the various sources of infection in the abattoir, notably the hides and soil adhering to them, water used for washing and cleaning, the dressing implements and the slaughterhouse personnel.

Bacterial genera commonly infecting meat while it is being processed, cut, packaged, transported, sold and handled include Salmonella spp., Shigella spp., *E. coli*, B. proteus, S. epidermidis and Staph. aureus, Cl. welchii, B. cereus and faecal streptococci. These bacteria are all commonly carried by humans; infectious bacteria from the soil include Cl. botulinum. Among the molds commonly infecting meat are Penicillium, Mucor, Cladosporium, Alternaria, Sporotrichium and Thamnidium.

As these microorganisms colonize a piece of meat, they begin to break it down, leaving behind toxins that can cause enteritis or food poisoning, potentially lethal in the rare case of botulism. The microorganisms do not survive a thorough cooking of the meat, but several of their toxins and microbial spores do. The microbes may also infect the person eating the meat, although against this the microflora of the human gut is normally an effective barrier.

The presence of infectious agents can be detected with a number of tests during the production and processing of meat, but testing by itself is not sufficient to ensure adequate food safety. The industry-standard *Hazard Analysis Critical Control Points* (HACCP) system provides for a comprehensive quality management framework as a part of which such tests can be conducted. Testing methods applied include phage and serological typing, direct epifluorescence filter techniques (DEFT) and plasmid profiling.

Food Safety

Food safety is a scientific discipline describing handling, preparation, and storage of food in ways that prevent foodborne illness. This includes a number of routines that should be followed to avoid potentially severe health hazards. Food can transmit disease from person to person as well as serve as a growth medium for bacteria that can cause food poisoning. Debates on genetic food safety include such issues as impact of genetically modified food on health of further generations and genetic pollution of environment, which can destroy natural biological diversity. In developed countries there are intricate standards for food preparation, whereas in lesser developed countries the main issue is simply the availability of adequate safe water, which is usually a critical item. In theory food poisoning is 100 per cent preventable.

REGULATORY AGENCIES

Australia

Australian Food Authority is working toward ensuring that all food businesses implement food safety systems to ensure food is safe to consume in a bid to halt the increasing incidence of food poisoning, this includes basic food safety training for at least one person in each business. Smart business operators know that basic food safety training improves the bottom line, staff take more pride in their work; there is less waste; and customers can have more confidence in the food they consume. Food Safety training in units of competence from a relevant training package, must be delivered by a Registered Training Organization (RTO) to enable staff to be issued with a nationally-recognised unit of competency code on their certificate. Generally this training can be completed in less than one day. Training options are available to suit the needs of everyone. Training may be carried out in-house for a group, in a public class, via correspondence or online. Basic food safety training includes:

- Understanding the hazards associated with the main types of food and the conditions to prevent the growth of bacteria which can cause food poisoning.
- The problems associated with product packaging such as leaks in vacuum packs, damage to packaging or pest infestation, as well as problems and diseases spread by pests.
- Safe food handling. This includes safe procedures for each process such as receiving, re-packing, food storage, preparation and cooking, cooling and re-heating, displaying products, handling products when serving customers, packaging, cleaning and sanitizing, pest control, transport and delivery. Also the causes of cross contamination.
- Catering for customers who are particularly at risk of food-borne illness, including allergies and intolerance.
- Correct cleaning and sanitizing procedures, cleaning products and their correct use, and the storage of cleaning items such as brushes, mops and cloths.
- Personal hygiene, hand washing, illness, and protective clothing.

People responsible for serving unsafe food can be liable for heavy fines under this new leglislation, consumers are pleased that industry will be forced to take food safety seriously.

China

Food safety is a growing concern in Chinese agriculture. The Chinese government oversees agricultural production as well as the manufacture of food packaging, containers, chemical additives, drug production, and business regulation.

In recent years, the Chinese government attempted to consolidate food regulation with the creation of the State Food and Drug Administration in 2003, and officials have also been under increasing public and international pressure to solve food safety problems. However, it appears that regulations are not well known by the trade. Labels used for 'green' food, 'organic' food and 'pollution-free' food are not well recognized by traders and many are unclear about their meaning. A survey by the World Bank found that supermarket managers had difficulty in obtaining produce that met safety requirements and found that a high percentage of produce did not comply with established standards.

Traditional marketing systems, whether in China or the rest of Asia, presently provide little motivation or incentive for individual farmers to make improvements to either quality or safety as their produce tends to get grouped together with standard products as it progresses through the marketing channel. Direct linkages between farmer groups and traders or ultimate buyers, such as supermarkets, can help avoid this problem. Governments need to improve the condition of many markets through upgrading management and reinvesting market fees in physical infrastructure. Wholesale markets need to investigate the feasibility of developing separate sections to handle fruits and vegetables that meet defined safety and quality standards.

European Union

The parliament of the European Union (EU) makes legislation in the form of directives and regulations, many of which are mandatory for member states and which therefore must be incorporated into individual countries' national legislation. As a very large organisation that exists to remove barriers to trade between member states, and into which individual member states have only a proportional influence, the outcome is often seen as an excessively bureaucratic 'one size fits all' approach. However, in relation to food safety the tendency to err on the side of maximum protection for the consumer may be seen as a positive benefit. The EU parliament is informed on food safety matters by the European Food Safety Authority.

Individual member states may also have other legislation and controls in respect of food safety, provided that they do not prevent trade with other states, and can differ considerably in their internal structures and approaches to the regulatory control of food safety.

Germany

The Federal Ministry of Food, Agriculture and Consumer Protection (BMELV) is a Federal Ministry of the Federal Republic of Germany. History founded as Federal Ministry of Food, Agriculture and Foresting in 1949, this name did not change until 2001. Then the name changed to Federal Ministry of Consumer Protection, Food and Agriculture. At the 22nd of November 2005, the name got changed again to its current state: Federal Ministry of Food, Agriculture and Consumer Protection. The reason for this last change was that all the resorts should get equal ranking which was achieved by sorting the resorts alphabetically. Vision: A balanced and healthy diet with safe food, distinct consumer rights and consumer information for various areas of life, and a strong and sustainable agriculture as well as perspectives for our rural areas are important goals of the Federal Ministry of Food, Agriculture and Consumer Protection (BMELV). The Federal Office of Consumer Protection and Food Safety is under the control of the Federal Ministry of Food, Agriculture and Consumer Protection. It exercises several duties, with which it contributes to safer food and thereby intensifies health-based consumer protection in Germany. Food can be manufactured and sold within Germany without a special permission, as long as it does not cause any damage on consumers' health and meets the general standards set by the legislation. However, manufacturers, carriers, importers and retailers are responsible for the food they pass into circulation. They are obliged to ensure and document the safety and quality of their food with the use of in-house control mechanisms.

Hong Kong

In Hong Kong SAR, the Centre for Food Safety is in charge of ensuring food sold is safe and fit for consumption.

Pakistan

Pakistan does not have an integrated legal framework but has a set of laws, which deals with various aspects of food safety. These laws, despite the fact that they were enacted long time ago, have tremendous capacity to achieve at least minimum level of food safety. However, like many other laws, these laws remain very poorly enforced. There are four laws that specifically deal with food safety. Three of these laws directly focus issues related to food safety, while the fourth one namely Pakistan Standards and Quality Control Authority Act, is indirectly relevant to food safety. The Pure Food Ordinance, 1960 consolidates and amends the law in relation to the preparation and the sale of foods. All provinces and some northern areas have adopted this law with certain amendments. Its aim is to ensure purity of food being supplied to people in the market and, therefore, provides for preventing adulteration. The Pure Food Ordinance 1960 does not apply to cantonment areas. There is separate law for cantonments called "The Cantonment Pure Food Act, 1966". There is no substantial difference between the Pure Food Ordinance 1960 and The Cantonment Pure Food Act. Even the rules of operation are very much similar. Pakistan Hotels and Restaurant Act, 1976 applies to all hotels and restaurants in Pakistan and seeks to control and regulate the rates and standard of service(s) by hotels and restaurants. In addition to other provisions, under section 22(2), the sale of food or beverages that are contaminated, not prepared hygienically or served in utensils that are not hygienic or clean is an offence. There are no express provisions for consumer complaints in the Pakistan Restaurants Act, 1976, Pakistan Penal Code, 1860 and Pakistan Standards and Quality Control Authority Act, 1996. However, the laws do not prevent citizens from lodging complaints with the concerned government officials. However, the consideration and handling of complaints is a matter of discretion of the officials.

South Korea

Korea Food and Drug Administration

Korea Food and Drug Administration (KFDA) is working for food safety since 1945. It is part of the Government of South Korea.

IOAS Organic Certification Bodies Registered in KFDA: 'Organic' or related claims can be labelled on food products when organic certificates are considered as valid by KFDA. KFDA admits organic certificates which can be issued by:

1. IFOAM (International Federation of Organic Agriculture Movement) accredited certification bodies
2. Government accredited certification bodies — 328 bodies in 29 countries have been registered in KFDA.

National Institute of Food and Drug Safety Evaluation

National Institute of Food and Drug Safety Evaluation (NIFDS) is functioning as well. The National Institute of Food and Drug Safety Evaluation is a national organization for toxicological tests and research. Under the Korea Food and Drug Administration, the Institute performs research on toxicology, pharmacology, and risk analysis of foods, drugs, and their additives. The Institute strives primarily to understand important biological triggering mechanisms and improve assessment methods of human exposure, sensitivities, and risk by:

- conducting basic, applied, and policy research that closely examines biologically triggering harmful effects on the regulated products such as foods, food additives, and drugs; and
- operating the national toxicology program for the toxicological test development and inspection of hazardous chemical ubstances assessments.

The Institute ensures safety by:

- investigation and research on safety by its own researchers;
- contract research by external academicians and research centres.

United States

The US food system is regulated by numerous federal, state and local officials. Although the US food safety system is one of the best in the world, it is lacking in "organization, regulatory tools, and resources to address food borne illness."

Federal Level Regulation

The Food and Drug Administration publishes the Food Code, a model set of guidelines and procedures that assists food control jurisdictions by providing a scientifically sound technical and legal basis for regulating the retail and food service industries, including restaurants, grocery stores and institutional foodservice providers such as nursing homes. Regulatory agencies at all levels of government in the United States use the FDA Food Code to develop or update food safety rules in their jurisdictions that are consistent with national food regulatory policy. According to the FDA, 48 of 56 states and territories, representing 79 per cent of the U.S. population, have adopted food codes patterned after one of the five versions of the Food Code, beginning with the 1993 edition.

In the United States, federal regulations governing food safety are fragmented and complicated, according to a February 2007 report from the Government Accountability Office. There are 15 agencies sharing oversight responsibilities in the food safety system, although the two primary agencies are the U.S. Department of Agriculture (USDA) Food Safety and Inspection Service (FSIS), which is responsible for the safety of meat, poultry, and processed egg products, and the Food and Drug Administration (FDA), which is responsible for virtually all other foods.

The Food Safety and Inspection Service has approximately 7,800 inspection programme personnel working in nearly 6,200 federally inspected meat, poultry and processed egg establishments. FSIS is charged with administering and enforcing the Federal Meat Inspection Act, the Poultry Products Inspection Act, the Egg Products Inspection Act, portions of the Agricultural Marketing Act, the Humane

Slaughter Act, and the regulations that implement these laws. FSIS inspection programme personnel inspect every animal before slaughter, and each carcass after slaughter to ensure public health requirements are met. In fiscal year (FY) 2008, this included about 50 billion pounds of livestock carcasses, about 59 billion pounds of poultry carcasses, and about 4.3 billion pounds of processed egg products. At U.S. borders, they also inspected 3.3 billion pounds of imported meat and poultry products.

Industry Pressure

There have been concerns over the efficacy of safety practices and food industry pressure on U.S. regulators. A study reported by Reuters found that "the food industry is jeopardizing U.S. public health by withholding information from food safety investigators or pressuring regulators to withdraw or alter policy designed to protect consumers". A survey found that 25 per cent of U.S. government inspectors and scientists surveyed have experienced during the past year corporate interests forcing their food safety agency to withdraw or to modify agency policy or action that protects consumers. Scientists have observed that management undercuts field inspectors who stand up for food safety against industry pressure. According to Dr. Dean Wyatt, a USDA veterinarian who oversees federal slaughter house inspectors, "Upper level management does not adequately support field inspectors and the actions they take to protect the food supply. Not only is there lack of support, but there's outright obstruction, retaliation and abuse of power."

State and Local Regulation

A number of U.S. states have their own meat inspection programmes that substitute for USDA inspection for meats that are sold only in-state. Certain state programmes have been criticized for undue leniency to bad practices.

However, other state food safety programmes supplement, rather than replace, Federal inspections, generally with the goal of increasing consumer confidence in the state's produce.

For example, state health departments have a role in investigating outbreaks of food-borne disease bacteria, as in the case of the 2006 outbreak of *Escherichia coli* O157:H7 (bad *E. coli* bacteria) from processed spinach. Health departments also promote better food processing practices to eliminate these threats.

In addition to the US Food and Drug Administration, several states that are major producers of fresh fruits and vegetables (including California, Arizona and Florida) have their own state programmes to test produce for pesticide residues.

Restaurants and other retail food establishments fall under state law and are regulated by state or local health departments. Typically these regulations require official inspections of specific design features, best food-handling practices, and certification of food handlers. In some places a letter grade or numerical score must be prominently posted following each inspection. In some localities, inspection deficiencies and remedial action are posted on the Internet.

CONSUMER LABELLING

United Kingdom

Food stuffs in the UK have one of two labels to indicate the nature of the deterioration of the product and any subsequent health issues. EHO Food Hygiene certification is required to prepare and distribute food. While there is no specified expiry date of such a qualification the changes in legislation it is suggested to update every five years.

Best before indicates a future date beyond which the food product *may* lose quality in terms of taste or texture amongst others, but does not imply any serious health problems if food is consumed beyond this date (within reasonable limits).

Use by indicates a legal date beyond which it is not permissible to sell a food product (usually one that deteriorates fairly rapidly after production) due to the potential serious nature of consumption of pathogens. Leeway is sometimes provided by producers in stating display until dates so that products are not at their limit of safe consumption on the actual date stated (this latter is voluntary and not subject to regulatory control). This allows for the variability in production, storage and display methods.

United States

With the exception of infant formula and baby foods which must be withdrawn by their expiration date, Federal law does not require expiration dates. For all other foods, except dairy products in some states, freshness dating is strictly voluntary on the part of manufacturers. In response to consumer demand, perishable foods are typically labeled with a Sell by date. It is up to the consumer to decide how long after the Sell by date a package is usable. Other common dating statements are Best if used by, Use-by date, Expiration date, Guaranteed fresh <date>, and Pack date.

Australia and New Zealand

Guide to Food Labelling and Other Information Requirements: This guide provides background information on the general labelling requirements in the Code. The information in this guide applies both to food for retail sale and to food for catering purposes. Foods for catering purposes means those foods for use in restaurants, canteens, schools, caterers or self-catering institutions, where food is offered for immediate consumption. Labelling and information requirements in the new Code apply both to food sold or prepared for sale in Australia and New Zealand and food imported into Australia and New Zealand. Warning and Advisory Declarations, Ingredient Labelling, Date Marking, Nutrition Information Requirements, Legibility Requirements for Food Labels, Percentage Labelling, Information Requirements for Foods Exempt from Bearing a Label.

Issues Associated with Sell by/Use by Dates

According to the UK's Waste and Resources Action Programme, 33 per cent percent of all food produced is wasted along the chill chain or at the consumer. At the same time, a large number of people get sick every year due to spoiled food.

UK Government to Replace Sell by/Use by Dates?

According to the UK minister Hilary Benn the use by date and sell by dates are old technologies that are outdated and should be replaced by other solutions or disposed of altogether.

How to Enhance Food Safety

There is a number of ways to enhance sell by and use by dates. These include better education of consumers on how to use, transport, and store fresh food products, but also by enhancing the use by and sell by dates by adding to the package smart indicators such as TTIs (Time Temperature Indicators). These show through a visible color change whether the product is still fresh. TTIs are already in use by retailers and food producers in France (Monoprix and Carrefour), Switzerland (Kneuss), and other countries in western Europe.

Consumer Tips: How to Keep Food Safe

1. One of the simplest measures that any person can take to prevent the spread of foodborne illness is to properly wash his or her hands before preparing or eating any meal. Many people who believe they are adequately washing their hands are sorely mistaken. According to a study conducted by the American Society of Microbiology, 97 per cent of females and 92 per cent of males said they washed their hands, but those numbers turned out to be 75 per cent of females and 58 per cent of males upon observation. A proper hand-washing technique suggested by the Missouri Department of Health and Senior Services includes using soap and warm water; washing vigorously for 10-20 seconds, making sure to reach all surfaces of the hands including the wrists, between the fingers, and under the finger nails; rinsing well; drying hands with a paper towel; and using a paper towel to turn off the water. It is certainly important to wash your hands before preparing a meal and eating, but hands should also be washed after using the restroom, coughing/sneezing, touching cuts or skin infections, handling raw meat, and

touching pets or other animals. Almost half the cases of foodborne illnesses could be prevented by better hand-washing by food handlers. In addition, hand sanitizer is a helpful follow-up to hand-washing, but it should never be used to replace this valuable technique.

2. Some foods should simply never be ingested in the first place because they have such a high risk of containing harmful bacteria that can make people ill. These foods include raw milk, unpasteurized dairy products, unpasteurized juices (such as fresh apple cider), raw meat, and raw cookie dough.
3. In cases of suspected food spoilage, food should never simply be tasted, smelled, or eye-balled in order to determine its safety. It is true that in some cases, the presence of mold or other growths may indicate that a food has reached its expiration date and should not be consumed. However, some foods may look and smell fine, but if they have been stored at room temperature for over 2 hours, microscopic bacteria may have been allowed to grow. The safe temperature for foods in refrigerators is between 35°F and 45°F, and freezers should be kept at 0° F or below.
4. It is not safe to let meats thaw on the counter all day, because this allows any germs present on the food to thrive. Safer alternatives to this practice include thawing the food under running water (70°F or below) for less than 2 hours, placing the food in the refrigerator to thaw, or thawing the food in the microwave as part of the cooking process.
5. It is also important to make sure that raw meats are cooked to the appropriate internal temperature before they are consumed. Safe internal temperatures for various meats include 165°F for poultry, 155°F for ground meat, and 145°F for fish and pork. It is not sufficient to judge the doneness of meat by its internal colour. According to a study performed by the USDA, "25 per cent of hamburgers with a brown internal colour were not cooked to the

proper temperature." Instead of simply eyeballing the meat, it is essential to use a meat thermometer to judge the safety of consuming the food.

6. The cooking process is often the time that foodborne pathogens are allowed to enter the food we eat because of the prevalence of cross contamination. Cross contamination occurs when a person handling raw meats, eggs, fish, or other foods containing harmful pathogens touches cooking utensils, cutting boards, or cooking surfaces and spreads the pathogens to ready-to-eat foods in the process. This mode of transmission can be interrupted by washing hands after handling raw foods, washing utensils and cutting boards that have come in contact with raw foods, and disinfecting counter surfaces frequently.
7. Leftovers are ideally stored in the refrigerator in shallow containers (2 inches tall or less) so that the cooling process can be accelerated and the buildup of harmful bacteria can be prevented. Storing foods in larger containers may keep foods warm and allow harmful bacteria to grow.

CHAPTER

12

ENVIRONMENTAL EFFECTS OF MEAT PRODUCTION

The environmental effects of meat production include pollution and the use of resources such as fossil fuels, water, and land. This article discusses the environmental effects of livestock and poultry farming.

According to a 2006 report by the Livestock, Environment and Development Initiative, the livestock industry is one of the largest contributors to environmental degradation worldwide, and modern practices of raising animals for food contributes on a 'massive scale' to air and water pollution, land degradation, climate change, and loss of biodiversity. The initiative concluded that "the livestock sector emerges as one of the top two or three most significant contributors to the most serious environmental problems, at every scale from local to global." In 2006 FAO estimated that meat industry contributes 18 per cent of all emissions of greenhouse gasses. This figure was challenged in 2009 by two World-Watch researchers who estimated a 51 per cent minimum, however this paper has not been peer reviewed.

Animals fed on grain need more water than grain crops. In tracking food animal production from the feed through to the dinner table, the inefficiencies of meat, milk and egg production range from a 4:1 energy input to protein output ratio up to 54:1. The result is that producing animal-based food is typically much less efficient than the harvesting of grains, vegetables, legumes, seeds and fruits for direct human consumption.

Relatedly, the production and consumption of meat and other animal products is associated with the clearing of rainforests, resource depletion, air and water pollution, land and economic inefficiency, species extinction, and other environmental harms.

Although it requires less land for the livestock, factory farming requires large quantities of feed which must be grown on large areas of land. Free-range animal production requires land for grazing, which has led to encroachment on undeveloped lands as well as clear cutting of forests. Such expansion has increased the rate of species extinction and damaged the services offered by nature, such as the natural processing of pollutants.

According to the United Nations, "Ranching-induced deforestation is one of the main causes of loss of some unique plant and animal species in the tropical rainforests of Central and South America as well as carbon release in the atmosphere." The Food and Agriculture Organization (FAO) agrees, saying that "Expanding livestock production is one of the main drivers of the destruction of tropical rain forests in Latin America, which is causing serious environmental degradation in the region." An earlier FAO study found that 90 per cent of deforestation is caused by unsustainable agricultural practices. Logging and plantation forestry, though not as major contributors to *deforestation*, play a greater role in forest *degradation*.

Producing a certain quantity of food in meat requires much more water than producing the same amount of food in grain.

According to the vegetarian author John Robbins, it roughly takes 60, 108, 168, and 229 pounds of water to produce a pound of potatoes, wheat, corn and rice respectively. He reports that a pound of beef however, requires 12,000 gallons of water.

David Pimentel explained of his calculations that:

> The data we had indicated that a beef animal consumed 100 kg of hay and 4 kg of grain per 1 kg of beef produced. Using the basic rule that it takes about 1,000 liters of water to produce 1 kg of hay and grain, thus about 100,000 liters were required to produce the 1 kg of beef.

Effects on Aquatic Ecosystems

Significant negative effects of aquatic and riparian ecosystems are also associated with meat production in the United States; In the Western United States 80 per cent of stream and riparian habitats have been negatively impacted by livestock grazing. This has resulted in increased phosphates, nitrates, decreased dissolved oxygen, increased temperature, turbidity, and eutrophication events, and reduced species diversity (Belsky et al., 1999). In the Eastern United States waste release from pork farms have also been shown to cause large-scale eutrophication of bodies of water, including the Mississippi River and Atlantic Ocean.

Fossil Fuel Consumption and Greenhouse Gas Emissions

Farmer ploughing rice paddy, in Indonesia. Animals can provide a useful source of draught power to farmers in the developing world.

At a global scale, a 29 November 2006 United Nations report called the Livestock's Long Shadow — Environmental Issues and Options assesses the meat and livestock industry to contribute to about 9 per cent of total anthropogenic carbon dioxide emissions, including 37 per cent of methane and 65 per cent of nitrous oxide emissions.

At a local level, livestock represents up to half of New Zealand's greenhouse gas emissions, and nearly 20 per cent of the total methane emissions of the United States of America.

Indirect effects account for most of agricultural greenhouse gas emissions, and are attributed to emissions of nitrous oxides and other gases from concentrated livestock operations and from microbial activities in soil and water following applications of fertilizers . Greenhouse gas emissions are not limited to animal husbandry; for instance, in many countries where rice is the main cereal crop, rice cultivation is responsible for most of the methane emissions.

The production of protein from grain-fed animals requires eight times as much fossil-fuel energy as the production of plant protein. According to an article in Environmental Health Perspectives, typical feedlot husbandry of cattle requires an input of 35 kcal of fossil fuel to produce one kcal of food energy in beef, far more than that required for comparable plants.

A 2006 study at the University of Chicago concluded that a person switching from a typical American diet to a vegan diet with the same number of calories would prevent the emission of 1485 kg of carbon dioxide. The difference exceeds that of an individual switching from a Toyota Camry to the hybrid Toyota Prius, and collectively amounts to over 6 per cent of the total U.S. greenhouse gas emissions.

This view, however, reflects the situation in the developed world and does not take into account the situation in most third world countries. In the developing world, notably Asia and Africa, fossil fuels are seldom used to transport feed for farm animals. Sheep or goats, for example, require no fuel, since they graze on farmlands, while bales of hay for bovines are still transported mainly using bullock carts or similar devices. Little to no meat processing takes place in the vast majority of the developing world. Animals are also often herded to the place of slaughter (with the exception of poultry) resulting in a very low use of fossil fuels. In fact, farm animals in the developing world are used for multiple purposes, from providing draught power to transportation, while also serving as meat once they reach the end of their economic lives.

A more efficient use of animal waste may be a contributing factor in sustainability. The by-products of slaughtered animals can be used to provide biogas. Trains running on this fuel are already in operation in Sweden. The use of biogas to run mass transit is likely only possible as a side effect of industrial agriculture.

The detrimental environmental effects of meat production has become a strong argument in favour of the reduction or abandonment of the consumption of meat, most notably for vegetarianism. Individual commitment is being increasingly supported by local initiatives, such as the meat-free days of the Belgian city of Ghent (or Veggiedag) which imposes vegetarian-only food in public canteens for civil servants and elected concillors, soon in all schools, and promotes vegetarian eating options in town through the distribution of 'veggie street maps'.

The UN has admitted a report linking livestock to global warming exaggerated the impact of eating meat on climate change. Dr. Frank Mitloehner, from the University of California at Davis (UCD), said meat and milk production generates less greenhouse gas than most environmentalists claim and that the emissions figures were calculated differently to the transport figures, resulting in an "apples-and-oranges analogy that truly confused the issue". The meat figure had been reached by adding all greenhouse-gas emissions associated with meat production, including fertilizer production, land clearance, methane emissions and vehicle use on farms, whereas the transport figure had only included the burning of fossil fuels. In the original press release in which Dr. Mitloehner's assertions appear, it transpires that his work was funded by a $26,000 grant from the Beef Checkoff Program. In addition, his comments do not state that the UN's calculations are false, but rather that they considered the entire commodity chain, which they did not do for transport.

CHAPTER 13

MEAT ANALOGUE

A meat analogue, also called a meat substitute, mock meat, faux meat, or imitation meat, approximates the aesthetic qualities (primarily texture, flavour, and appearance) and/or chemical characteristics of specific types of meat.

Generally, *meat analogue* is understood to mean a food made from non-meats, sometimes without other animal products such as dairy. The market for meat imitations includes vegetarians, vegans, non-vegetarians seeking to reduce their meat consumption for health or ethical reasons, and people following religious dietary laws, such as Kashrut or Halal. Buddhist cuisine features the oldest known use of meat analogues.

Meat analogue may also refer to a meat-based and/or less-expensive alternative to a particular meat product, such as surimi.

Some vegetarian meat analogues are based on centuries-old recipes for seitan (wheat gluten), rice, mushrooms, legumes, tempeh, or pressed-tofu, with flavouring added to make the finished product taste like chicken, beef, lamb, ham, sausage, seafood, etc. Yuba is another soy-based meat analogue, made by layering the thin skin which forms on top of boiled soy milk. Some more recent meat analogues include textured vegetable protein (TVP), which is a dry bulk commodity derived from soy, soy concentrate, mycoprotein-based Quorn which uses egg white as a binder making them unsuitable for vegans, and modified defatted peanut flour.

Dairy analogues may be composed of processed rice, soy (tofu, soymilk, soy protein isolate), almond, cashew, gluten (such as with the first non-dairy creamers), nutritional yeast, or a combination of these, as well as flavoring to make it taste like milk, cheeses, yogurt, mayonnaise, ice cream, cream cheese, sour cream, whipped cream, buttermilk, rarebit, or butter. Many dairy analogues contain casein, which is extracted dried milk proteins, making them unsuitable for vegans.

Egg substitutes may be composed of tofu, tapioca starch, or similar products that recreate the leavening and binding effects of eggs in baked goods. Many people use fruit products such as banana paste or applesauce as egg analogues in baking.

Lab-grown Animal Tissue

Biologists have long researched methods for growing muscle tissue in laboratory conditions, and the technology is ready for commercial use. PETA has offered a $1 million prize to the first company that can bring lab-grown chicken meat to consumers by 2012.

Surimi and Similar Meat-based Meat Analogues

Surimi, a processed hash of fish plus flavourings, is used to make products such as imitation crab meat. In some regions, 'surimi' refers only to products made from fish, but elsewhere may refer to other products (*e.g.*, turkey dogs produced from turkey in North America), which are then also called 'surimi'.

Examples of surimi include:

- Surimi from fish, such as imitation crab, imitation shrimp, or imitation lobster

- Surimi from turkey, such as hot dogs, brats, sausage, salami, lunch meats, loafs, burgers, bacon, ham, or ground
- Other processed poultry products, such as emu, in the same forms described above for turkey.

Surimi products are often marketed as 'imitation' meats (*e.g.*, 'imitation crab meat', 'imitation shrimp').

In vitro Meat

In vitro meat, also known as cultured meat, is an animal flesh product that has never been part of a complete, living animal. Several current research projects are growing *in vitro* meat experimentally, although no meat has yet been produced for public consumption. The first-generation products will most likely be chopped meat, and a long-term goal is to grow fully developed muscle tissue. Potentially, any animal's muscle tissue could be grown through the *in vitro* process. With the costs of conventional meat farming techniques constantly increasing and the rising world population (reaching 9.2 billion people by the year 2050 *in vitro* meat may be one of several new technologies needed to maintain food supplies by the year 2050. Conventional meat production may simply become too expensive for the average consumer to support.

However, it is suggested that the high costs of food (which are projected to last until 2018 due to the decreased number of crop plantings prior to the 2009 growing season in Canada, the United States, and Europe) in developed countries are linked to packaging and advertising as opposed to the actual cost of the food product. While the total number of cash crop plantings started to increase again at the 2009 planting season, prices have only begun to stabilize. The UN's World Food Programme does not expect the price of wheat and corn — which are required to maintain livestock — to return to pre-2008 levels due to the rising cost of commodity goods in the emerging markets. A few scientists claim that this technology is ready for commercial use and simply needs a company to back it. Cultured meat is currently prohibitively expensive, but it is anticipated that the cost could be reduced to about twice as expensive as conventionally produced chicken.

In vitro meat should not be confused with imitation meat, which is a vegetarian food product produced from vegetable protein, usually from soy or gluten. The terms 'synthetic meat' and 'artificial meat' may refer to either. *In vitro* meat has also been described, somewhat derisively, as 'laboratory-grown' meat.

Most meat is animal muscle. The process of developing *in vitro* meat involves taking muscle cells and applying a protein that helps the cells to grow into large portions of meat. Once the initial cells have been obtained, additional animals would not be needed — akin to the production of yogurt cultures.

There are, loosely, two approaches for production of *in vitro* meat: loose muscle cells and structured muscle, the latter one being vastly more challenging than the former. Muscles consist of muscle fibers, long cells with multiple nuclei. They don't proliferate by themselves, but arise when precursor cells fuse. Precursor cells can be embryonic stem cells or satellite cells, specialized stem cells in muscle tissue.

Theoretically, it is relatively simple to culture them in a bioreactor and then make them fuse. For the growth of real muscle, however, the cells should grow 'on the spot', which requires a perfusion system akin to a blood supply to deliver nutrients and oxygen close to the growing cells, as well as to remove the waste products. In addition, other cell types, such as adipocytes, need to be grown, and chemical messengers should provide clues to the growing tissue about the structure. Lastly, muscle tissue needs to be physically stretched or 'exercised' to properly develop.

In vitro meat does not necessarily involve genetic engineering, a common misconception. In fact, the cells involved are natural cells which would grow in the normal method.

History

Modern research into *in vitro* meat arose out of experiments conducted by NASA, attempting to find improved forms of long-term food for astronauts in space. The technique was approved by the U.S. Food and Drug Administration (FDA) in 1995, and NASA has been conducting experiments since 2001, producing *in vitro* meat from turkey cells. The first edible form was produced by the NSR/Touro Applied BioScience Research Consortium in 2000: goldfish cells grown to resemble fish fillets.

In 2001, dermatologist Wiete Westerhof from the University of Amsterdam, medical doctor Willem van Eelen, and businessman Willem van Kooten announced that they had filed for a worldwide patent on a process to produce *in vitro* meat. In the process, a matrix of collagen is seeded with muscle cells, which are then bathed in a nutritious solution and induced to divide.

Scientists in Amsterdam study the culture medium, while the University of Utrecht studies the proliferation of muscle cells, and the Eindhoven University of Technology is researching bioreactors. Van Eelen said that he had thought of the idea of *in vitro* meat for years, since he was held in a Japanese POW camp.

Jon F. Vein of the United States has also secured a patent (U.S. Patent 6,835,390) for the production of tissue-engineered meat for human consumption, wherein muscle and fat cells would be grown in an integrated fashion to create food products such as beef, poultry and fish.

The first peer-reviewed journal article published on the subject of laboratory-grown meat appeared in a 2005 issue of *Tissue Engineering*. Of course, the basic concept dates back further. Winston Churchill said in the 1930s, "Fifty years hence, we shall escape the absurdity of growing a whole chicken in order to eat the breast or wing, by growing these parts separately under a suitable medium."

In 2008, PETA offered a $1 million prize to the first company that brings lab-grown chicken meat to consumers by 2012. The Dutch government has put US$4 million into experiments into *in vitro* meat.

The *In Vitro* Meat Consortium, a group formed by international researchers interested in the technology, held the first international conference on the production of *in vitro* meat, hosted by the Food Research Institute of Norway in April 2008, to discuss commercial possibilities. Time Magazine declared *in vitro meat* production to be one of the 50 breakthrough ideas of 2009. In November 2009, scientists from the Netherlands announced they had managed to grow meat in the laboratory using the cells from a live pig.

DIFFERENCES FROM CONVENTIONAL MEAT

Health

Large scale production of *In vitro* meat may require artificial growth hormones to be added to the culture for meat production, which is not necessary in conventional meat production. No procedure has been presented to produce large scale *in vitro* meat without the use of antibiotics to prevent bacterial infections.

Because *in vitro* meat has yet to be placed on the market, the health risks have not yet been fully investigated. This question is one of the main focuses of scientists working on *in vitro* meat, and the aim is to produce healthier meat than conventional meat, most notably by reducing its fat content and controlling nutrients.

Researchers have suggested that omega-3 fatty acids could be added to *in-vitro* meat as a health bonus. In a similar way, the omega-3 fatty acid content of conventional meat can also be increased by altering what the animals are fed. Time Magazine has suggested that the *in-vitro* process may also decrease exposure of the meat to bacteria and disease.

Artificiality

Although *in vitro* meat consists of natural meat cells, consumers may find such a high-technology approach to food production distasteful. Technology in cuisine tends to remain stagnant for a long period of time as people are often wary of new cooking methods. *In vitro* meat has been disparagingly described as Frankenmeat, reflecting a sentiment that it is unnatural and therefore wrong.

If *in vitro* meat turns out to be different in appearance, taste, smell, texture, or other factors, it may not be commercially competitive with conventionally produced meat. The lack of fat and bone may also be a disadvantage, for these parts make appreciable culinary contributions. Many food items, such as surimi, designed to substitute for other ingredients (for reasons from morality to expense) have become independently sought out for their own properties. However, the lack of bones and/or fat may make many traditional meats like Buffalo wings more palatable to small children.

Environmental

A few people have speculated that *in-vitro* meat might require fewer resources and produce less greenhouse gas and other waste than conventional meat production. This includes the patent holder for *in-vitro* meat, the journalist Brendan I. Koerner, and Hanna Tuomisto, a PhD student from Oxford University. Margaret Mellon of the Union of Concerned Scientists, a science-based lobby group dedicated to environmental and social issues, has a different view, and thinks that the energy and fossil fuel requirements of large scale *in-vitro* meat production in a factory make it more environmentally destructive than producing food off the land.

Economic Differences

The production of *in-vitro* meat is currently very expensive (about US$1 million for a 250 g piece of beef and it would take considerable investment to switch to large scale production. However, the *in vitro* Meat Consortium has estimated that with improvements to current technology there could be considerable reductions in the cost of *in vitro* meat. They estimate that it could be produced for 3500•/tonne, which is about twice the cost of unsubsidized conventional European chicken production.

Ethical Considerations

Animal welfare groups are in favour of the production of *in vitro* meat because it does not have a nervous system and therefore cannot feel pain.

Potential Usage

The original NASA research on *in vitro* meat was intended for use on long space voyages or stays; it would be a sustainable food source alongside hydroponic or aeroponically grown vegetables.

RESEARCH

Challenges

The science for *in vitro* meat is an outgrowth of the field of biotechnology known as tissue engineering. The technology is simultaneously being developed along with other uses for tissue engineering such as helping those with muscular dystrophy and, similarly, growing transplant organs. There are several obstacles to overcome if it has any chance of succeeding; at the moment, the most notable ones are scale and cost.

Proliferation of muscle cells: Although it is not very difficult to make stem cells divide, for meat production it is necessary that they divide at a quick pace, producing the solid meat. This requirement has some overlap with the medical branch of tissue engineering.

Culture medium: Proliferating cells need a food source to grow and develop. The growth medium should be a well-balanced mixture of ingredients and growth factors. Scientists have already identified possible growth media for turkey, fish, sheep and pig muscle cells. Depending on the motives of the researchers, the growth medium has additional requirements.

Commercial: The growth medium should be inexpensive to produce. A plant-based medium may be less expensive than fetal bovine serum.

Environmental: The production of the growth medium shouldn't have a negative effect on the environment. This means that the production should be energetically favorable. Additionally, the ingredients should come from completely renewable sources. Minerals from mined sources are in this case not possible, nor are synthetically produced nutrients which use non-renewable sources.

Animal welfare: The growth medium should be devoid of animal sources (except for the initial "mining" of the original stem cells).

Non-Allergenic: While plant based growth media are "more realistic," will be cheaper, and reduce possibility of infectious agents, there is also the possibility that plant-based growth media may cause allergic reactions to some consumers.

Bioreactors: Nutrients and oxygen need to be delivered close to each growing cell, on the scale of millimeters. In animals this job is handled by blood vessels. A bioreactor should emulate this function in an efficient manner. The usual approach is the creation of a sponge-like matrix in which the cells can grow, and perfusing it with the growth medium.

Initiatives

Perhaps the first research into *in vitro* meat was performed by M. A. Benjaminson from Touro College. His research group managed to grow muscle tissue from goldfish in a laboratory setting with several kinds of growth media.

In 2004, a group of researchers started the non-profit organization New Harvest, with the goal of promoting research into *in vitro* meat. Among the founders are Jason Matheny and Vladimir Mironov. According to their website, cultured meat in a processed form, like sausages, hamburgers, or chicken nuggets, may become commercially available within several years. One of the first places of businesses to accept this *in vitro* meat would be fast food restaurants. Since they do not disclose which farmer or rancher provided them with food, *in vitro* meat in fast food restaurants is often seen as an inevitable advancement.

In April 2005, a research project into cultured meat started in The Netherlands, and in 2008, it was reported that most research into *in vitro* meat is being conducted by Dutch scientific teams. The research is carried out under the lead of Henk Haagsman, a meat science researcher at the University of Amsterdam, the Eindhoven University of Technology and Utrecht University, in cooperation with sausage manufacturer Stegeman. The Dutch government granted a two million euro subsidy for the project.

On April 21, 2008, PETA announced a $1 million X-Prize style reward for the first group to successfully produce synthetic meat that is comparable to and commercially viable against naturally sourced meat products.

In Fiction

In *Two Planets* (original German title: *Auf Zwei Planeten*) (1897) by Kurd Lasswitz, 'synthetic meat' is one of the varieties of synthetic food introduced on Earth by the Martians.

In *Illegal Alien* (1997) by Robert J. Sawyer, the monofilament used to cut artificial meat is a suspected murder weapon.

In the book *Neuromancer* (1984) by William Gibson, artificial meat, called vatgrown flesh, is mentioned as food sold in stores, cheaper than meat from living animals.

In *The Space Merchants* (1952) by Frederik Pohl and C.M. Kornbluth, artificial meat is grown in huge lumps tens of metres in diameter, workmen walking on top of it harvesting slices with big knives. The lump of meat is called 'Chicken Little'.

In the *Terro-Human Future History* stories (1952–84) by H. Beam Piper, 'carniculture vats' were a common source of meat for food, even though livestock was raised for meat on worlds with appropriate biospheres. Several of Piper's protagonists (such as Lucas Trask in *Space Viking*) found 'vat-grown' meat acceptable, but considered the 'real thing' more palatable.

In *Stars in My Pocket Like Grains of Sand* (1984) by Samuel R. Delany, the main character's society uses vat-grown meat cultured from humans as the primary protein source. Interaction between this society and societies using 'natural' meat are (briefly) explored.

Claude Zidi's 1976 comedy film *L'aile ou la cuisse* starring Louis de Funès as top-notch gourmet and Julien Guiomar as the infamous Tricatel who secretly produces artificial food.

In *Assimilating our Culture, That's What they're Doing!*, one of Larry Niven's short stories set in the Draco Tavern, a man who visits the tavern is depressed by the fact that he has licenced his own genome to an alien race, who are mass-producing headless clones of him for the meat market on their home planet.

Two *Bob the Angry Flower* comic strips, The Vegetarian's Dilemma and Meat Sheets, touch on points relating to artificially produced meat.

In the short story collection 'The State of the Art' by Iain M. Banks, one of the stories includes a party where the main course is vat grown meat from cells of notable human villains and megalomaniacs, with 'stewed Idi Amin' and 'Richard Nixon Burgers' among others.

In Margaret Atwood's *Oryx and Crake*, 'Chicky Knobs' were chickens with only a mouth and a digestive tract that were genetically engineered for meat products.

Although not called '*in vitro* meat', the creation of zombification in the Xbox 360 game Dead Rising was the result of US scientists trying to mass produce meat for consumption. The engineered wasps that were to facilitate this escaped from the Santa Cabeza complex and 'zombified' the populace, resulting in military intervention.

Two of the survivors of that incident, Carlito and Isabella Keyes, started a new outbreak in the Southwest town of Willamette in revenge, where the game takes place.

A popular urban legend describes a genetically engineered vat-grown creature, dubbed 'Animal 57', as the source of meat for various fast-food chains.

In Rudy Rucker's *Ware Tetralogy* almost all of the meat was tank grown, including human meat.

Meat on *Star Trek* is created by devices called replicators.

In *Mass Effect 2* the Normandy's pilot remarks how he prefers natural cow meat over 'vat-grown' beef.

In *Crest of the Stars* a space station's on-board meat culture facility is briefly displayed, and it is referred to provide a reliable source of sustenance for years (serving a crew of several dozen).

In an episode of the American Broadcasting Company (ABC) show Better Off Ted, they show scientists growing a 'meat blob'.

CHAPTER 14

BUSHMEAT

Bushmeat initially referred to the hunting of wild animals in West and Central Africa and is a calque from the French *viande de brousse*. Nowadays the term is commonly used for meat of terrestrial wild animals, killed for subsistence or commercial purposes throughout the humid tropics of the Americas, Asia, and Africa. To reflect the global nature of hunting of wild animals Resolution 2.64 of the IUCN General Assembly in Amman in October 2000 referred to *wild meat* rather than *bushmeat*. A more worldwide term is game. The term *bushmeat crisis* tends to be used to describe unsustainable hunting of often endangered wildlife in West and Central Africa and the humid tropics, depending on interpretation. African hunting predates recorded history; by the 21st century it had become an international issue.

Many conservation organizations have come together to address the bushmeat crisis through the formation of the Bushmeat Crisis Task Force, whose mission is to build a public, professional and government constituency aimed at identifying and supporting solutions that effectively respond to the bushmeat crisis in Africa and around the world.

Bushmeat hunting is common in many parts of the world where hunting of animals from the wild is performed. The *bushmeat trade* refers to the sale of any wild species, though Western sources tend to focus on the trade specifically involving great apes. Though some bushmeat hunters have been targeting gorillas, chimpanzees, bonobos, and other primate species, great apes constitute less than 1 per cent of bushmeat from all species sold on the market. This rate of harvest, combined with habitat loss and alteration, has led to very severe population declines; if this trend is unchecked, extinction is likely. The number of animals and great apes killed has distressed many conservationists and advocates of animal rights and great ape personhood.

The issue of bushmeat hunting is highly politicized, with little support for the practice outside the forests and cities where it is conducted. International efforts to stop it have been launched, especially in the United States, United Kingdom, and Canada. In the countries where the hunting occurs, orphaned apes are deemed unable to survive on their own, but also deemed too small to be worth shooting and cutting up. They are raised and returned to the wild as part of these efforts.

In Cameroon, where gorilla populations are especially endangered, the Wildlife Protectors Fund launched an education campaign to teach children about Koko the gorilla, who is part of a long-term psychology experiment in an American research sanctuary.

Logging concessions operated by European and Malaysian companies in African forests have been closely linked to the bushmeat trade. Because they provide roads, trucks and other access to remote forests, they are the primary means for the transportation of hunters and meat between forests and urban centres. Some, including the Congolaise Industrielle du Bois (CIB) in Republic of Congo, have partnered with governments and international conservation organizations to regulate the bushmeat trade within the concessions where they operate. Numerous solutions are needed; because each country has different circumstances, traditions and laws, no one solution will work in every location.

Some species are legal to hunt and not endangered, and others not so. Only about 1 per cent of the bushmeat trade is in ape meat. However, the apes' small numbers and the attractiveness of hunting them (being a large animal, a gorilla can offer a good 'payoff' for each cartridge) means the impact on hunting them is considerable. Orphans of the bushmeat trade are often sold as pets, as young apes do not have enough meat on them to eat. The Pan African Sanctuary Alliance (PASA) is a member organization of sanctuaries that provide care for bushmeat orphans and education for local communities.

Armed conflict has a direct impact on the killing of great apes for bushmeat. This is largely because of the breakdown of law and order. A well documented case was the killing and eating of mountain gorillas during the military insurrection around Virunga National Park in the eastern Democratic Republic of Congo in January 2007.

Apes reproduce relatively slowly, at about one-fourth the rate of most other mammals. A study in Gabon, the wealthiest country in the region with 80 per cent of its forest cover still in place, showed that it had suffered at least a 56 per cent decline in its ape population over seventeen years.

Apes may harbour pathogens that can in theory affect humans. Ebola for instance may also be found in chimps and gorillas and bonobos, and might spread to humans by handling the meat and consumption of such great apes.

African squirrels (*Heliosciurus, Funisciurus*) have been implicated as reservoirs of the monkeypox virus in the Democratic Republic of the Congo and their use as bushmeat may be an important means of transmission to humans.

Research has shown that Human Immunodeficiency Virus (HIV), the virus which causes AIDS originated from a similar virus in chimpanzees called Simian Immunodeficiency Virus

(SIV); researchers believe that HIV probably initially jumped into humans after people in Africa came into contact with infected bush meat.

The bushmeat trade is considered by some anti-globalization activists to be one of many ways in which globalization affects life on the planet, due to the lumber trade (as described in the Factors section above). There is no way (other than by researching the corporations involved, or their countries of origin) to tell which lumber has been produced in a way that assists the hunting of apes, and which has not. It has been suggested that the only way to eliminate the bushmeat trade might be industry-specific protocols, along the lines of the Cocoa Protocol. Although some argue against Western interference with African culture, claiming that the West should take a value-neutral perspective on eating apes, many African cultures greatly respect or fear apes, and frown on their consumption. Some have suggested that the economic incentive to hunt bushmeat has led to an erosion of these traditional values, and that Western interference is therefore appropriate.

It has also been proposed by Dr. Peter Arcese, an associate professor of forest sciences at the University of British Columbia, that farming infrastructure needs to be created and the international exploitation of African fisheries needs to stop. The fisheries are being overfished by mainly EU-subsidized fleets and could collapse within a few decades. Reduced fishery landings in Africa increase demand for bushmeat, which is leading many species to face extinction, and a humanitarian crisis could easily follow. In some locations the biomass of mammals in parks has been reduced by 70 per cent since 1967 because of bushmeat harvesting. Since wildlife monitoring is limited to a few countries, the full extent and future outlook of bushmeat is not currently known.

Small villages and indigenous communities in Amazonia, sub-Saharan Africa, and other tropical areas still rely heavily on plants and animals for life's necessities (housing, food, fuel) as they always have. The free availability of forest products has long been a sustainable buffer against poverty in tropical forest communities. But as human populations expand, populations of animals diminish, biodiversity decreases, and this relationship grows less sustainable worldwide. "The sad reality is that those who most depend upon wild sources of food are usually the ones who pay the heaviest price for biodiversity loss," says Dr Susan Lieberman, Director WWF's International Species Programme.TRAFFIC: The Wildlife Trade Monitoring Network.

A major factor in the decline of tropical wildlife species is the harvesting of wildlife for sale, especially by outsiders. This practice flourishes as transportation to markets becomes easier. Modern firearms mean easy hunting. New logging roads and motorized boats provide quick transport from deep forests to city markets. Markets in cities along the Amazon and other tropical rivers offer a bounty of forest and river animals, alive and dead, for meat, medicine, pets, or for blackmarket traders who will smuggle live animals into wealthy countries such as the United States for the pet trade or medical research.

Meat on the Bone

Meat on the bone, also called bone-in meat is meat that is sold with some or all of the bones included in the cut or portion, i.e. meat that has not been filleted. The phrase 'on the bone' can also be applied to specific types of meat, most commonly ham on the bone , and to fish . Meat or fish on the bone may be cooked and served with the bones still included or the bones may be removed at some stage in the preparation.

Examples of meat on the bone include T-bone steaks, chops, spare ribs, chicken leg portions and whole chicken. Examples of fish on the bone include unfilleted plaice and some cuts of salmon.

Meat on the bone is used in many traditional recipes.

The principal advantage of cooking meat on the bone is that it adds flavour and texture. Albumen and collagen in the bones release gelatine when boiled which adds substance to stews, stocks, soups and sauces . The bone also conducts heat within the meat so that it cooks more evenly and prevents meat drying out and shrinking during cooking.

Cooking Meat on the Bone

Meat on the bone typically cooks faster than boneless meat when roasted in a joint. However, individual portions such as chops can take longer to cook than their filleted equivalents.

Value for Money

Meat on the bone is quicker and easier to butcher as there is no filleting involved. Filleting is a skilled process that adds to labour and wastage costs as meat remaining on the bones after filleting is of low value (although it can be recovered). As a result meat on the bone can be better value for money however relative value can be hard to judge as the bone part of the product is inedible. Different portions may contain a greater or lesser proportion of bone.

Ease of Handling

The presence of bones may make meat products more bulky, less regular in shape and less easy to pack. Bones may make preparation and carving more difficult however bones can sometimes be used as handles to make the meat easier to eat.

Import Restrictions

Foot-and-mouth disease (FMD) is a contagious disease affecting cloven-hoofed animals. Because FMD rarely infects humans but spreads rapidly among animals, it is a much greater threat to the agriculture industry than to human health.

FMD can be contracted by contact with infected meat, with meat on the bone representing a higher risk than filleted meat . As a result, import of meat on the bone remains more restricted that of filleted meat in many countries.

Injury

Meat and fish served on the bone can present a risk of accident or injury. Small, sharp fish bones are the most likely to cause injury although sharp fragments of meat bone can also cause problems. Typical injuries include bones being swallowed and becoming trapped in the throat and bones being trapped under the tongue.

Discarded bones can also present a risk of injury to pets or wild animals as some types of cooked meat bone break into sharp fragments when chewed .

Bovine Spongiform Encephalopathy (BSE)

Bovine spongiform encephalopathy (BSE), also known as 'mad cow disease', is a fatal brain disease affecting cattle. It is believed by most scientists that the disease may be transmitted to human beings who eat the brain or spinal cord of infected carcasses. In humans, it is known as *new variant Creutzfeldt-Jakob disease* (vCJD or nvCJD), and is also fatal.

The largest outbreak of BSE was in the United Kingdom, with several other countries affected to a lesser extent. The outbreak started in 1984, and continued into the 1990s, leading to increasing concern among governments and beef consumers as the risk to humans became known, but could not be quantified. Many countries banned or restricted the import of beef products from countries affected by BSE.

Animal brain and spinal cord had already been removed from the human and animal food chain when, in 1997, prion infection was also detected in the dorsal root ganglia within the spinal column of infected animals. As a result, beef on the bone was banned from sale in the UK as a precaution. This led to criticism that the government was overreacting. The European Union also considered banning beef and lamb on the bone. The UK ban lasted from December 1997 to December 1999, when it was lifted and the risk from beef on the bone declared negligible.

CHAPTER 15

SALMON AS FOOD

Salmon is the common name for Salmonidae. Several other fish in the family are called trout; the difference is often said to be that salmon migrate and trout are resident, a distinction that holds true for the *Salmo* genus. Salmon live along the coasts of both the North Atlantic (one migratory species *Salmo salar*) and Pacific Oceans (approximately a dozen species of the genus *Oncorhynchus*), as well as having been introduced into the Great Lakes of North America.

Typically, salmon are anadromous, they are born in fresh water, migrate to the ocean, then return to fresh water to reproduce. However, there are populations of several species that are restricted to fresh water through their life. Folklore has it that the fish return to the exact spot where they were born to spawn; tracking studies have shown this to be true, and this homing behaviour has been shown to depend on olfactory memory. Salmon are intensively produced in aquaculture in many parts of the world.

Salmon eggs are laid in freshwater streams typically at high latitudes. The eggs hatch into *alevin* or *sac fry*. The fry quickly develop into *parr* with camouflaging vertical stripes. The parr stay for 6 months to three years in their natal stream before becoming *smolts,* which are distinguished by their bright silvery colour with scales that are easily rubbed off. It is estimated that only 10 per cent of all salmon eggs survive to this stage. The smolt body chemistry changes, allowing them to live in salt water. Smolts spend a portion of their out-migration time in brackish water, where their body chemistry becomes accustomed to osmoregulation in the ocean.

The salmon spend about one to five years (depending on the species) in the open ocean where they gradually become sexually mature. The adult salmon then return primarily to their natal stream to spawn. In Alaska, the crossing-over to other streams allows salmon to populate new streams, such as those that emerge as a glacier retreats. The precise method salmon use to navigate has not been established, though their keen sense of smell is involved. Atlantic salmon spend between one and four years at sea. (When a fish returns after just one year's sea feeding it is called a *grilse* in Canada, the UK and Ireland.) Prior to spawning, depending on the species, salmon undergo changes. They may grow a hump, develop canine teeth, develop a *kype* (a pronounced curvature of the jaws in male salmon). All will change from the silvery blue of a fresh run fish from the sea to a darker colour. Salmon can make amazing journeys, sometimes moving hundreds of miles upstream against strong currents and rapids to reproduce. Chinook and sockeye salmon from central Idaho, for example, travel over 900 miles (1,400 km) and climb nearly 7,000 feet (2,100 m) from the Pacific ocean as they return to spawn. Condition tends to deteriorate the longer the fish remain in fresh water, and they then deteriorate further after they spawn, when they are known as *kelts.* In all species of Pacific salmon, the mature individuals die within a few days or weeks of spawning, a trait known as semelparity. Between 2 per cent and 4 per cent of Atlantic salmon kelts survive to spawn again, all females. However, even in those species of salmon that may survive to spawn more than once (iteroparity), post-spawning mortality is quite high (perhaps as high as 40 to 50%.)

To lay her roe, the female salmon uses her tail (caudal fin), to create a low-pressure zone, lifting gravel to be swept downstream, excavating a shallow depression, called a *redd*. The redd may sometimes contain 5,000 eggs covering 30 square feet (2.8 m^2). The eggs usually range from orange to red. One or more males will approach the female in her redd, depositing his sperm, or milt, over the roe. The female then covers the eggs by disturbing the gravel at the upstream edge of the depression before moving on to make another redd. The female will make as many as 7 redds before her supply of eggs is exhausted.

Each year, the fish experiences a period of rapid growth, often in summer, and one of slower growth, normally in winter. This results in rings (annuli) analogous to the growth rings visible in a tree trunk. Freshwater growth shows as densely crowded rings, sea growth as widely spaced rings; spawning is marked by significant erosion as body mass is converted into eggs and milt.

Freshwater streams and estuaries provide important habitat for many salmon species. They feed on terrestrial and aquatic insects, amphipods, and other crustaceans while young, and primarily on other fish when older. Eggs are laid in deeper water with larger gravel, and need cool water and good water flow (to supply oxygen) to the developing embryos. Mortality of salmon in the early life stages is usually high due to natural predation and human-induced changes in habitat, such as siltation, high water temperatures, low oxygen concentration, loss of stream cover, and reductions in river flow. Estuaries and their associations wetlands provide vital nursery areas for the salmon prior to their departure to the open ocean. Wetlands not only help buffer the estuary from silt and pollutants, but also provide important feeding and hiding areas.

Pacific species belong to the genus *Oncorhynchus*, some examples include:

- Cherry salmon or seema (*Oncorhynchus masou*) is found only in the western Pacific Ocean in Japan, Korea and Russia. There is also a landlocked subspecies known as the *Taiwanese salmon* or *Formosan salmon* (*Oncorhynchus masou formosanum*) in central Taiwan's Chi Chia Wan Stream.
- Chinook salmon (*Oncorhynchus tshawytscha*) is also known in the USA as King or Blackmouth Salmon, and as Spring Salmon in British Columbia. Chinook are the largest of all Pacific salmon, frequently exceeding 30 lb (14 kg). The name Tyee is used in British Columbia to refer to Chinook over 30 pounds. Chinook salmon are known to range as far north as the Mackenzie River and Kugluktuk in the central Canadian arctic.
- Chum salmon (*Oncorhynchus keta*) is known as Dog, Keta, or Calico salmon in some parts of the USA. This species has the widest geographic range of the Pacific species: south to the Sacramento River in California in the eastern Pacific and the island of Kyushu in the Sea of Japan in the western Pacific; north to the Mackenzie River in Canada in the east and to the Lena River in Siberia in the west.
- Coho salmon (*Oncorhynchus kisutch*) is also known in the USA as Silver salmon. This species is found throughout the coastal waters of Alaska and British Columbia and up most clear-running streams and rivers. It is also now known to occur, albeit infrequently, in the Mackenzie River.
- Pink salmon (*Oncorhynchus gorbuscha*), known as humpies in south east and south west Alaska, are found from northern California and Korea, throughout the northern Pacific, and from the Mackenzie River in Canada to the Lena River in Siberia, usually in shorter coastal streams. It is the smallest of the Pacific species, with an average weight of 3.5 lb (1.6 kg) to 4 lb (1.8 kg).

- Sockeye salmon (*Oncorhynchus nerka*) is also known in the USA as Red salmon. This lake-rearing species is found south as far as the Klamath River in California in the eastern Pacific and northern Hokkaido island in Japan in the western Pacific and as far north as Bathurst Inlet in the Canadian Arctic in the east and the Anadyr River in Siberia in the west. Although most adult Pacific salmon feed on small fish, shrimp and squid; sockeye feed on plankton that they filter through gill rakers. Kokanee salmon is a land-locked form of sockeye salmon.

Other Species

The huchen or Danube salmon (*Hucho hucho*), the largest permanent fresh water salmonid species.

Salmon Fisheries

The salmon has long been at the heart of the culture and livelihood of coastal dwellers. Many people of the Northern Pacific shore had a ceremony to honor the first return of the year. For many centuries, people caught salmon as they swam upriver to spawn. A famous spearfishing site on the Columbia River at Celilo Falls was inundated after great dams were built on the river. The Ainu, of northern Japan, trained dogs to catch salmon as they returned to their breeding grounds *en masse*. Now, salmon are caught in bays and near shore.

Salmon population levels are of concern in the Atlantic and in some parts of the Pacific but in Alaska stocks are still abundant. Fish farming of Pacific salmon is outlawed in the United States Exclusive Economic Zone, however, there is a substantial network of publicly funded hatcheries, and the State of Alaska's fisheries management system is viewed as a leader in the management of wild fish stocks. Some of the most important Alaskan salmon sustainable wild fisheries are located near the Kenai River, Copper River, and in Bristol Bay. In Canada, returning Skeena River wild salmon support commercial, subsistence and recreational fisheries, as well as the area's diverse wildlife on the coast and around communities hundreds of miles inland in the watershed. The status of wild salmon in Washington is mixed. Out of 435 wild stocks of salmon and steelhead, only 187 of them were classified as healthy; 113 had an unknown status, 1 was extinct, 12 were in critical condition and 122 were experiencing depressed populations. The Columbia River salmon population is now less than 3 per cent of what it was when Lewis and Clark arrived at the river. The commercial salmon fisheries in California have been either severely curtailed or closed completely in recent years, due to critically low returns on the Klamath and or Sacramento Rivers, causing millions of dollars in losses to commercial fishermen. Both Atlantic and Pacific salmon are popular sportfish. Salmon populations now exist in all the Great Lakes. Coho stocks were planted in the late 1960s in response to the growing population of non-native alwifes by the state of Michigan. Now Chinook (King), Atlantic, and Coho (silver) salmon are annually stocked in all Great Lakes by mosts bordering states and provinces. These populations are not self sustaining and do not provide much in the way of a commercial fishery, but have led to the development of a thriving sportfishery.

Salmon aquaculture is the major economic contributor to the world production of farmed fin-fish, representing over U$1 billion annually. Other commonly cultured fish species include: tilapia, catfish, sea bass, carp, bream, and trout. Salmon farming is very big in Chile, Norway, Scotland, Canada and the Faroe Islands, and is the source for most salmon consumed in America and Europe. Atlantic salmon are also, in very small volumes, farmed in Russia and the island of Tasmania, Australia.

Salmon are carnivorous and are currently fed a meal produced from catching other wild fish and other marine organisms. Salmon farming leads to a high demand for wild forage fish. Salmon require large nutritional intakes of protein, and consequently, farmed salmon consume more fish than they generate as a final product. To produce one pound of farmed salmon, products from several pounds of wild fish are fed to them. As the salmon farming industry expands, it requires more wild forage fish for feed, at a time when seventy five percent of the worlds monitored fisheries are already near to or have exceeded their maximum sustainable yield. The industrial scale extraction of wild forage fish for salmon farming then impacts the survivability of the wild predator fish who rely on them for food.

Work continues on substituting vegetable proteins for animal proteins in the salmon diet. Unfortunately though, this substitution results in lower levels of the highly valued Omega-3 content in the farmed product.

Intensive salmon farming now uses open-net cages which have low production costs but have the drawback of allowing disease and sea lice to spread to local wild salmon stocks.

On a dry-dry basis, it takes 2-4 kg of wild caught fish to produce one kg of salmon.

Another form of salmon production, which is safer but less controllable, is to raise salmon in hatcheries until they are old enough to become independent. They are then released into rivers, often in an attempt to increase the salmon population. This system is referred to as ranching and was very common in countries like Sweden before the Norwegians developed salmon farming, but is seldom done by private companies, as anyone may catch the salmon when they return to spawn, limiting a company's chances of benefiting financially from their investment. Because of this, the method has mainly been used by various public authorities and non profit groups like the Cook Inlet Aquaculture Association as a way of artificially increasing salmon populations in situations where they have declined due to overharvest, construction of dams, and habitat destruction or fragmentation. Unfortunately, there can be negative consequences to this sort of population manipulation, including genetic 'dilution' of the wild stocks, and many jurisdictions are now beginning to discourage supplemental fish planting in favour of harvest controls and habitat improvement and protection. A variant method of fish stocking, called ocean ranching, is under development in

Alaska. There, the young salmon are released into the ocean far from any wild salmon streams. When it is time for them to spawn, they return to where they were released where fishermen can then catch them.

An alternative method to hatcheries is to use spawning channels. These are artificial streams, usually parallel to an existing stream with concrete or rip-rap sides and gravel bottoms. Water from the adjacent stream is piped into the top of the channel, sometimes via a header pond to settle out sediment. Spawning success is often much better in channels than in adjacent streams due to the control of floods which in some years can wash out the natural redds. Because of the lack of floods, spawning channels must sometimes be cleaned out to remove accumulated sediment. The same floods which destroy natural redds also clean them out. Spawning channels preserve the natural selection of natural streams as there is no temptation, as in hatcheries, to use prophylactic chemicals to control diseases.

Farm raised salmon are fed the carotenoids astaxanthin and canthaxanthin, so that their flesh colour matches wild salmon.

According to Canadian biologist Dorothy Kieser, myxozoan parasite *Henneguya salminicola* is commonly found in the flesh of salmonids. It has been recorded in the field samples of salmon returning to the Queen Charlotte Islands. The fish responds by walling off the parasitic infection into a number of cysts that contain milky fluid. This fluid is an accumulation of a large number of parasites.

Henneguya and other parasites in the myxosporean group have a complex lifecycle where the salmon is one of two hosts. The fish releases the spores after spawning. In the *Henneguya* case, the spores enter a second host, most likely an invertebrate, in the spawning stream. When juvenile salmon out-migrate to the Pacific Ocean, the second host releases a stage infective to salmon. The parasite is then carried in the salmon until the next spawning cycle. The myxosporean parasite that causes whirling disease in trout, has a similar lifecycle. However, as opposed to whirling disease, the *Henneguya* infestation does not appear to cause disease in the host salmon — even heavily infected fish tend to return to spawn successfully.

According to Dr. Kieser, a lot of work on *Henneguya salminicola* was done by scientists at the Pacific Biological Station in Nanaimo in the mid-1980s, in particular, an overview report which states that "the fish that have the longest fresh water residence time as juveniles have the most noticeable infections. Hence in order of prevalence coho are most infected followed by sockeye, chinook, chum and pink." As well, the report says that, at the time the studies were conducted, stocks from the middle and upper reaches of large river systems in British Columbia such as Fraser, Skeena, Nass and from mainland coastal streams in the southern half of B.C. "are more likely to have a low prevalence of infection." The report also states "It should be stressed that *Henneguya*, economically deleterious though it is, is harmless from the view of public health. It is strictly a fish parasite that cannot live in or affect warm blooded animals, including man".

According to Klaus Schallie, Molluscan Shellfish Programme Specialist with the Canadian Food Inspection Agency, "*Henneguya salminicola* is found in southern B.C. also and in all species of salmon. I have previously examined smoked chum salmon sides that were riddled with cysts and some sockeye runs in Barkley Sound (southern B.C., west coast of Vancouver Island) are noted for their high incidence of infestation."

Sea lice, particularly *Lepeophtheirus salmonis* and various *Caligus* species, including *Caligus clemensi* and *Caligus rogercresseyi*, can cause deadly infestations of both farm-grown and wild salmon. Sea lice are ectoparasites which feed on mucus, blood, and skin, and migrate and latch onto the skin of wild salmon during free-swimming, planktonic *nauplii* and *copepodid* larval stages, which can persist for several days. Large numbers of highly populated, open-net salmon farms can create exceptionally large concentrations of sea lice; when exposed in river estuaries containing large numbers of open-net farms, many young wild salmon are infected, and do not survive as a result. Adult salmon may survive otherwise critical numbers of sea lice, but small, thin-skinned juvenile salmon migrating to sea are highly vulnerable. On the Pacific coast of Canada, the louse-induced mortality of pink salmon in some regions is commonly over 80 per cent.

Environmental Pressures

The population of wild salmon declined markedly in recent decades, especially north Atlantic populations which spawn in the waters of western Europe and eastern Canada, and wild salmon in the Snake and Columbia River system in northwestern United States. The decline is attributed to the following factors:

Disease transfer from open net cage salmon farming, especially sea lice. The European Commission (2002) concluded "The reduction of wild salmonid abundance is also linked to other factors but there is more and more scientific evidence establishing a direct link between the number of lice-infested wild fish and the presence of cages in the same estuary." It is reported that wild salmon on the west coast of Canada are being driven to extinction by sea lice from nearby salmon farms.

For Atlantic salmon smolts, it takes as few as eight sea lice to kill the fish. On the Pacific Coast where the smolt are much smaller, only one or two can be critical, often resulting in death. In the Atlantic, sea lice have been a proven factor in both Norwegian and Scottish salmon declines. In the Western Atlantic there has been little research at sea, but sea lice numbers in the period post-2000 do not appear to be a significant factor in the critical decline of endangered inner Bay of Fundy salmon. The situation may have been different in the 1980s and 1990s, but we are unlikely ever to know the factual history in that regard.

Overfishing in general but especially commercial netting in the Faroes and Greenland. Several seafood sustainability guides have recommendations on which salmon fisheries are sustainable and which have negative impacts on Salmon populations.

Ocean and river warming which can delay spawning and accelerate transition to smolting.

Ulcerative dermal necrosis (UDN) infections of the 1970s and 1980s which severely affected adult salmon in freshwater rivers.

Loss of suitable freshwater habitat, especially degradation of stream pools and reduction of suitable material for the excavation of redds. Historically stream pools were, to a large extent, created by beavers . With the extirpation of the beaver, the nurturing function of these ponds was lost.

Reduction of the retention of the nutrients brought by the returning adult salmon in stream pools. Without stream pools, dead adult salmon tend to be washed straight back down the streams and rivers.

The construction of dams, weirs, barriers and other 'flood prevention' measures, which bring severe adverse impacts to river habitat and on the accessibility of those habitats to salmon. This is particularly true in the northwest USA, where large numbers of dams have been built in many river systems, including over 400 in the Columbia River Basin.

Other environmental factors such as light intensity, water flow, or change in temperature dramatically affects salmon during their migration season.

Loss of invertebrate diversity and population density in rivers because of modern farming methods and various sources of pollution, thus reducing food availability.

Reduction in freshwater base flow in rivers and disruption of seasonal flows, because of diversions and extractions, hydroelectric power generation, irrigation schemes, barge transportation, and slackwater reservoirs, which inhibit normal migratory processes and increase predation for salmon.

Loss of suitable low gradient stream habitats due to agricultural practices such as the removal of riparian plants, destabilization of stream banks by livestock and irrigation processes.

There are efforts to relieve this situation. As such, several governments and NGOs are sharing in research and habitat restoration efforts.

In the western Atlantic, the Atlantic Salmon Federation has developed a major sonic tracking technology programme to understand the high at-sea mortality since the early 1990s. Ocean arrays are deployed across the Baie des Chaleurs and between Newfoundland and Labrador at the Strait of Belle Isle. Salmon have now been tracked half way from rivers such as the Restigouche to Greenland feeding grounds. Now the first line of the Ocean Tracking Network initiative is installed by DFO and Dalhousie University of Halifax from Halifax to the edge of the continental shelf. First results include Atlantic salmon travelling from the Penobscot River in Maine, the 'anchor river' for US Atlantic salmon populations.

In the northern Atlantic, the North Atlantic Salmon Fund, led by Icelandic Entrepreneur Orri Vigfússon, has since 1989 worked closely with governments and fishermen for conservation. The conservation efforts are not limited to oceans, and a sustainable angling scheme has been developed in rivers, notably in Vopnafjörður, Iceland.

Results overall are showing that estuary problems exist for some rivers, but issues involving feeding grounds at sea are impacting populations as well. In 2008 returns were markedly improved for Atlantic salmon on both sides of the Atlantic Ocean, but no one knows if this is a temporary improvement or sign of a trend.

A great threat to Pacific salmon conservation is commercial fishing. There are many methods of harvest for the commercial salmon fishing industry, such as trolling, seining, and gillnetting. Gillnets are an extremely size-selective method of harvest, where a long net is placed in the path of the salmon's migration to their natal stream in hopes of entangling the salmon for commercial harvest. Gillnets are extremely size-selective; fish too small to be caught pass through the net, fish too large cannot be entangled, only catching fish that fall somewhere in between. By selectively harvesting certain sized fish, governed by the mesh-size of the gillnet, some age-class and length-class fish are selectively removed from the population, progressively leaving phenotypically smaller spawners. Fecundity generally decreases with length. So, smaller fish produce fewer eggs than larger fish. There is also concern regarding the genetic information passed down from the fish. If the majority of spawning fish in a particular salmon run has gotten smaller due to the size-selective fishing methods, the run could eventually evolve to become smaller.

Gillnet Size-Selectivity

Gillnets are designed to harvest a specific sized fish. For example, Washington Department of Fish and Wildlife's 2010 Commercial Regulations had a 7-inch minimum mesh size restriction for Chinook, and a 5-inch minimum – 5.5-inch maximum for sockeye. Gillnetting only targets the fish which are small enough to enter the net, but large enough to be tangled in it. Possible problems arising from this selective harvest are smaller reproducing adult fish, as well as the unexpected mortality of the fish which sustain injuries from the gillnet but are not retained in the fishery. Most salmon populations include several age classes, allowing for fish of different ages, and sizes, to reproduce with each other. A recent 2009 study looked at 59 years of catch and escapement data of Bristol Bay sockeye to determine age and size at maturity trends attributable to the selectivity of commercial gillnet harvests. The study found that the larger females (>550 mm) of all age classes were most susceptible to harvest. The study suggests that smaller, younger fish were more likely to successfully traverse the gillnet fishery and reproduce than the larger fish. The study also found that the average length of sockeye harvested from 1946–2005 was 8 mm larger than the sockeye who escaped the gillnet fishery to spawn, reducing the fecundity of the average female by 5 per cent, or 104 eggs.

Gillnet-related Mortality

If a salmon enters a gillnet, but manages to escape, it often sustains injuries. These injuries can lead to a lower degree of reproductive success. A study aimed at quantifying mortality of Bristol Bay sockeye salmon due to gillnet-related injuries found that 11-29 per cent of sockeye sustained fishery-related injuries attributable to gillnets, 51 per cent of those fish were expected to not reproduce.

Salmon and Beavers

Beavers are archetypal ecosystem engineers; in the process of clear cutting and damming, beavers alter their ecosystem extensively. Beaver ponds can provide critical habitat for juvenile salmon. An example of this was seen in the years following 1818 in the Columbia River Basin. In 1818, the British government made an agreement with the U.S. government to allow U.S. citizens access to the Columbia catchment . At the time, the Hudson's Bay Company sent word to trappers to extirpate all furbearers from the area in an effort to make the area less attractive to U.S. fur traders. In response to the elimination of beavers from large parts of the river system, salmon runs plummeted, even in the absence of many of the factors usually associated with the demise of salmon runs. Salmon recruitment can be affected by beavers' dams because dams can:

- Slow the rate at which nutrients are flushed from the system; nutrients provided by adult salmon dying throughout the fall and winter remain available in the spring to newly-hatched juveniles.
- Provide deeper water pools where young salmon can avoid avian predators.
- Increase productivity through photosynthesis and by enhancing the conversion efficiency of the cellulose-powered detritus cycle.
- Create low-energy environments where juvenile salmon put the food they ingest into growth rather than into fighting currents.

- Increase structural complexity with many physical niches where salmon can avoid predators.

Beavers' dams are able to nurture salmon juveniles in Estuarine tidal marshes where the salinity is less than 10ppm. Beavers build small dams of generally less than 2 feet (0.61 m) high in channels in the Myrtle zone. These dams can be overtopped at high tide and hold water at low tide. This provides refuges for juvenile salmon so they don't have to swim into large channels where they are subject to predation.

Salmon as Food

Salmon is a popular food. Classified as an 'oily fish', salmon is considered to be healthy due to the fish's high protein, high omega-3 fatty acids, and high vitamin D content. Salmon is also a source of cholesterol, with a range of 23–214 mg/100 g depending on the species. According to reports in the journal *Science,* however, farmed salmon may contain high levels of dioxins. PCB (polychlorinated biphenyl) levels may be up to eight times higher in farmed salmon than in wild salmon. Omega-3 content may also be lower than in wild-caught specimens, and in a different proportion to what is found naturally. Omega-3 comes in three types, ALA, DHA and EPA; wild salmon has traditionally been an important source of DHA and EPA, which are important for brain function and structure, among other things. This means if the farmed salmon is fed on a meal which is partially grain, then the amount of omega-3 it contains will be present as ALA (alpha-linolenic acid). The body can itself convert ALA omega-3 into DHA and EPA, but at a very inefficient rate (2–15%). Nonetheless, according to a 2006 study published in the Journal of the American Medical Association, the benefits of eating even farmed salmon still outweigh any risks imposed by contaminants. The type of omega-3 present may not be a factor for other important health functions.

A simple rule of thumb is that the vast majority of Atlantic salmon available on the world market are farmed (greater than

99%), whereas the majority of Pacific salmon are wild caught (greater than 80%). Farmed Atlantic salmon outnumber wild Atlantic salmon 85-to-1.

Salmon flesh is generally orange to red, although there are some examples of white-fleshed wild salmon. The natural colour of salmon results from carotenoid pigments, largely astaxanthin but also canthaxanthin, in the flesh. Wild salmon get these carotenoids from eating krill and other tiny shellfish. Because consumers have shown a reluctance to purchase white-fleshed salmon, astaxanthin (E161j), and very minutely canthaxanthin (E161g), are added as artificial colourants to the feed of farmed salmon, because prepared diets do not naturally contain these pigments. In most cases, the astaxanthin is made chemically; alternatively it is extracted from shrimp flour.

Another possibility is the use of dried red yeast, which provides the same pigment. However, synthetic mixtures are the least expensive option. Astaxanthin is a potent antioxidant that stimulates the development of healthy fish nervous systems and enhances the fish's fertility and growth rate. Research has revealed canthaxanthin may have negative effects on the human eye, accumulating in the retina at high levels of consumption. Today, the concentration of carotenoids (mainly canthaxanthin and astaxanthin) exceeds 8 mg/kg of flesh, and all fish producers try to reach a level that represents a value of 16 on the 'Roche Colour Card', a colour card used to show how pink the fish will appear at specific doses. This scale is specific for measuring the pink colour due to astaxanthin and is not for the orange hue obtained with canthaxanthin. The development of processing and storage operations, which can be detrimental on canthaxanthin flesh concentration, has led to an increased quantity of pigments added to the diet to compensate for the degrading effects of the processing. In wild fish, carotenoid levels of up to 25 mg are present, but levels of canthaxanthin are, in contrast, minor.

Canned salmon in the U.S. is usually wild Pacific catch, though some farmed salmon is available in canned form. Smoked salmon is another popular preparation method, and can either be hot or cold smoked. Lox can refer either to cold smoked salmon or to salmon cured in a brine solution (also called gravlax). Traditional canned salmon includes some skin (which is harmless) and bone (which adds calcium). Skinless and boneless canned salmon is also available.

CHAPTER

16

MEAT PROCESSING IN INDIA

India has a livestock population of 470 million, which includes 205 million cattle and 90 million buffaloes. India's livestock population is largest in the world with 50 per cent of world's buffaloes, 20 per cent of cattle and one-sixth of total production, but only 1 per cent of total meat production is converted to value added products. The country produces about 450 million broilers and 30 billion eggs annually. Animals, which are generally used for production of meat, are cattle, buffaloes, sheep and goat, pigs and poultry.

Methuen is also slaughtered for meat in North East and Sikkim. Rabbit meat is also used as a specialty in Kerala and some other states.

The world's largest cattle population grazes in Indian pastures. Today India's free ranging, steroid and fat-free meat is winning worldwide acceptance. 40,000 Veterinary centres and numerous research stations ensure that India's meat and poultry products meet the most stringent quality checks worldwide. Which is why they are a favourite in Malaysia, UAE, Philippines, Iran and Oman.

Major products: Frozen and packed meat and poultry mainly in fresh form and egg powder.

The production of meat and meat products has shown an impressive growth.

Meat Processing

The total meat production in the country is 4 million tonnnes, which includes beef, buffalo meat, mutton, goat meat, pork and poultry meat. However, only about 1 per cent of the total meat is converted into value added products like sausages, ham becon, luncheon meat, kababs, meatballs etc. The total meat export during 1999-2000 was worth Rs. 845.00 crores consisting mostly of mutton and buffalo meat out of which 70 per cent was contributed by export of buffalo meat.

Buffalo meat is surplus in India. There is a vast scope to set up modern slaughter facilities and cold store chains in meat and poultry processing sector. India's current level of meat and meat-based exports is around Rs. 8,000 million. In the last six years foreign investment in this segment stood at Rs. 5,000 million which is more than 50 per cent of the total investment made in this sector.

The current level of exports of meat and meat products from India is US$ 190 million, the major destinations being the countries in the Middle East and South East Asia. Meat processing sector has attracted a total investment of US$ 471.1 million in the last six years i.e., since the initiation of the liberalisation process including Foreign Investment of US$ 116.1 million.

Major Markets

Buffalo meat — Malaysia, Philippines, UAE, Iran, Jordan, sheep/goat Meat Saudi Arabia, UAE, Oman, Bahrain, Kuwait Animal Products Portugual, France, UK, Spain, Netherlands Processed Meat Seychelles, Germany, Oman, Congo, Sri Lanka. The current level of exports of meat and meat products from India is US$ 190 million, the major destinations being the countries in the Middle East and South East Asia.

The total meat production in the country is 4 million tonnnes.

Production

(a) *Livestock Population:* India is rich in its livestock wealth. It accounts for nearly 16 per cent of the world cattle population, more than half of world buffalo population and about 17 per cent of world's goat population.

(b) *Production of Meat:* As per FAO data, the world production of various kinds of meat is 216.25 million metric tons of which India's share is 4.42 million metric tons accounting for about 2 per cent of world meat production.

Meat Production Centres

The major meat production centres for exports are as under: India is rich in its livestock wealth. It accounts for nearly 16 per cent of the world cattle population, more than half of world buffalo population and about 17 per cent of world's goat population.

- Aurangabad, Nanded, Bombay and Satara in Maharashtra
- Goa
- Medak Dist. In Andhara Pradesh.
- Derabassi in Punjab
- Aligarh, Unnao and Ghaziabad in UP
- Cochin in Kerala

In addition, the exporters source their meat requirement from various Municipal Slaughter Houses throughout the country. Some of the slaughter houses from where the exporters source their requirement are Deonar abattoir, Mumbai, Meerut, Jaipur, Saharanpur, Bareily, Hapur, Muradabad, Khurja, Gangoh, Hyderabad, Aligarh, Muzzaffarnagar, Buland Sahar and Meerut slaughter houses.

Slaughter Houses in India

There are nearly 3600 Municipal Slaughter houses in the country. These slaughter houses are primarily catering to the domestic market. However, exporters have been also procuring the meat from some of these Municipal Slaughter houses. Most of these slaughter houses are very old and have out-lived their utility. They lack essential amenities such as water, light, drainage, lairage, holding pens, etc. The Government felt the need to improve and modernize the conditions of slaughter houses catering to exports. In view of above, schemes were formulated by APEDA, Deptt. of Animal Husbandry and Dairying, Ministry of Agriculture and Ministry of Food Processing Industries. Under the Schemes were formulated by APEDA, Deptt. of Animal Husbandry and Dairying, Ministry of Agriculture and Ministry of Food Processing Industries to improve exports.

Meat Processing schemes, financial assistance is provided for upgrading the abattoir and meat processing plants.

Consumption

Indian Council of Medical Research (ICMR) has recommended daily allowance of meat as 34 grams per day, whereas in India the per capita meat consumption is as low as 14 grams per day. According to Anthropological Survey of India study, more than 80 per cent of Indian population are non-vegetarian. A large proportion of non-vegetarians has no religious or social taboo for consumption of Sheep, Goat and Poultry meat.

Consumption of beef, buffaloe meat and pork has religious taboos.

Surplus for Export

As mentioned above, the slaughter rate in case of bovine animals is very low, whereas the slaughter rate is high in case of Sheep and Goat (as high as 38% in goats). The demand for meat of bovine animals in domestic market is negligible as the domestic consumers have a preference for Sheep, Goat and Poultry meat. We have therefore, enough potential for production of buffalo meat for export.

Infrastructure Facilities

(i) India has several integrated mechanized slaughterhouse-cum meat processing plants and has facilities for slaughtering, processing, freezing packing and cold storage of meat. Refer containers are easily available. India has several integrated mechanized slaughter-house-cum meat processing plants and has facilities for slaughtering, processing, freezing packing and cold storage of meat. For factory stuffing of frozen meat. Some of the exporters have started backward integration for rearing of animals wherein they provide veterinary health coverage and concentrated feed in the catchment area. Skilled and technical manpower for slaughtering, processing, packaging etc. of meat is adequately available in the country.

(ii) The Government of India has notified three agencies namely State Directorates of Animal Husbandry, EIA and DMI for inspection of meat prior to export. However, the inspection of meat is mainly done by the State Animal Husbandry Departments. The State Government laboratories are not equipped adequately and do not have skilled staff to conduct various examinations of meat. These laboratories need to be further strengthened in terms of modern testing facilities and skilled manpower.

(iii) We also need to have semi-modern and modern abattoirs to produce quality meat of international standards. Transportation of refer containers through railway needs further strengthening. Export:

(a) *Products for exports:* Frozen buffalow meat, sheep and goat meat, animal casings (wet salted and dried). In processed meat products corned buffaloe meat is also exported from India in small quantities.

(b) *Major Destinations:* The major markets for export of meat and meat products are as under:

- Buffalo Meat Malaysia (32%), UAE (22%),

- Philippines (20%),
- Iran (5%)
- Sheep and Goat Meat UAE (46%), Saudi Arabia (40%),
- Oman (8%)
- Animal Casings: Portugal (48%, France (1 5%),
- Spain (14%), Switzerland (5%)
- Comed Meat Zaire (32%), Seychelles (20%),
- UAE (19%)

(c) *Future Market:* India can predominantly play a major role in South East Asia, Africa and East Europe. International Scenario The major exporters of bovine meat are USA, Europe, Oceania (Australia and New Zealand), Brazil, Argentina and Canada. In case of Sheep and Goat Meat, Oceania accounts for 70 per cent of the world sheep meat exports followed by Europe which accounts for about 23 per cent the world sheep meat exports.

The world Markets and Trade in meat as reported by USDA is as under:

United States: Beef exports rose by about 9 per cent during 1999. The rise reflects strong markets in Mexico, Korea and Taiwan, reduced competition from Australia and New Zealand and food aid to Russia. U.S. beef imports increased by 6 per cent in 1999. As US beef supplies tighten and prices increase, Canada and Australia are expected to increase exports to the United States.

Mexico: Beef imports are expected to rise 13 per cent in 1999 to 228,000 tonnes due to lower domestic production and higher Future Market, India can predominantly play a major role in South East Asia, Africa and East Europe. consumption. About 93 per cent of Mexican imports are supplied by the United States.

Argentina: Argentina beef exports increased by 17 per cent during 1999 to 340,000 tonnes. The major markets are Germany and USA.

Brazil: Brazilian beef exports have grown sharply in 1999 to 485,000 tonnes. Brazil is under taking an FMD eradication programme aimed at having Brazil FMD free by 2004. Two FMD outbreaks reported to have occurred during early 1999.

European Union: Beef consumption in the EU continues to remain low following the 1996 BSE scare. Intervention stock of EU beef stood at about 510,000 tonnes at the beginning of 1999, of which Germany had the largest share, followed by UK, France and Ireland. Many importing countries refuse to purchase intervention beef due to it's lack of traceability and length of time in storage, despite it's low price. EU beef exports suffered a decline in 1998 as a result of crisis in Russia which is EU's top export market.

Russian Federation: Russian beef production continues to fall sharply reflecting the reduced inventories as well as low slaughter weights due to feed grain shortage. Import of beef was 500,000 tonnes during 1999, of which 195,000 tonnes is to be supplied by EU and USA under food aid programme.

China: China's beef imports were negligible at 6,000 tonnes in 1998. Australia is the major supplier to Chinese Market.

New Zealand: Beef exports declined in 1999 as New Zealand is concentrating on rebuilding it's cattle herd which declined meat Processing sharply after 1997-98 drought. Beef exports are mainly to USA, Japan, Hong Kong and Singapore.

Australia: Although overall beef exports are expected to decline but higher prices in the United States are encouraging, increased Australian exports to the United States. Potential for Value Added Products Till date India has targeted the bulk customers in the export of buffalo meat. A small quantity as branded product in Consumer packs have shown their presence in the super markets. Except corned beef, we are not exporting any other product of processed meat category. Whereas there is a demand for ethnic Indian meat product like Kabab, Gushtaba, Akhani, Korma etc., still there is a great potential for European processed meat products like Sausages, Ham, Salami, Burger, Smoked meat etc. If we are able to produce processed meat products, it would add value and help in earning more foreign exchange.

Investment Opportunities There is a large potential for setting up of modern slaughter facilities and development of cold chains in meat and poultry processing sector. The market has not been tapped fully for ready-to-eat and semi-processed meat products in the domestic market as well as for exports to neighboring countries especially to the Middle East. Buffalo meat is surplus in the country and has good export potential. Poultry production and egg processing industries have come up in the country in a big way and we are exporting egg powder, There is a demand for ethnic Indian meat product like Kabab, Gushtaba, Akhani, Korma etc. There is a large potential for setting up of modern slaughter facilities and development of cold chains in meat and poultry processing sector. frozen egg yolk, albumin powder to Europe, Japan and some other countries. Meat products have a growth rate of 10 per cent whereas the growth rate of eggs and broilers is 16 per cent and 20 per cent respectively.

Most of the production of meat and meat products continues to be in the unorganised sector. However, some branded products have also come up in the domestic market. At present, poultry export from India is mostly to Maldives and Oman. Some other markets can be explored for export of poultry meat products like Japan, Malaysia, Indonesia and Singapore.

Steps initiated by APEDA Standards have been laid down for export of raw chilled and frozen meat as well as for processed meat products.

These include standards for abattoirs, processing plants and for various meat products. Registration of abattoirs and meat processing plants and animal casings processing plants for export is regularly undertaken by APEDA. The plants are periodically inspected by a committee consisting of officials of various Government departments and Trade. The plants confirming to the laid down standards are registered with

APEDA. Steps have been initiated to grade the plants on the basis of adoption of international quality systems such as HACCP. The plants implementing these quality systems will be graded as Grade A, while others will be graded as grade B. A list of Grade A plants will be sent to all importing countries. A committee has been constituted by APEDA for this purpose.

Training programmes are being organised to create awareness among meat workers, supervisors and Managers for sanitation and hygiene. Efforts are being made to upgrade the Municipal Slaughter Houses which largely cater to the requirement of meat exporters.

Efforts are also necessary for the modernisation of quality control laboratories of the State Animal Husbandry Department under plan schemes.

Recommendations

- Identification of FMD free areas particularly where export oriented abattoirs are located and notification of these Disease Free Zones by OIE.
- Identification and upgradation of municipal slaughter houses for export purpose.
- Need for modernising the Quality Control laboratories of the State Government.
- Need for strict laboratory inspection of meat and meat products.
- Training programmes for meat workers regarding hygiene and sanitation need to be organized regularly.
- Rearing of Male Buffalo Calves on scientific lines so as to fatten them quickly.

CHAPTER

17

VACUUM PACKED MEAT

The chilled storage life of beef and lamb is greatly extended by vacuum packaging; however, vacuum-packed meat eventually spoils. Some indicators of spoilage include surface discolouration or 'greening' of the meat and/or the drip, evidence of gas production in the pack, and off odours that may be noticeable when packs are opened. This information sheet outlines the factors that influence the storage life of vacuum-packed meat, and the types of bacteria that are able to grow and cause spoilage.

If the package becomes punctured or the seals come apart, the pack is termed a 'leaker'. Air comes in contact with the meat and spoilage will be rapid. Pack integrity is mentioned later. The factors that affect the storage life of meat in intact packs are discussed below:

- Temperature is very important for microbial growth. Growth rates at 0-1°C are only about half those at 5°C and are further reduced below 0°C. As vacuum-packed meat does not freeze until minus 2°C, storage should ideally be at 0±0.5°C.

- The growth of many microorganisms is inhibited by the exclusion of oxygen and presence of carbon dioxide. After evacuation and sealing of vacuum packs, most of the residual oxygen is consumed by natural muscle respiration or microbial activity on the meat, and carbon dioxide is produced. This carbon dioxide is absorbed into the meat.
- Meat pH and availability of nutrients can significantly affect the type of and growth of bacteria. The normal pH of meat is in the range 5.4-5.8. A high pH (>6.0) can permit the growth of spoilage bacteria, but is only significant in some circumstances (as discussed later). A high pH is the result of stress in the live animal, though some muscles routinely have a higher ultimate pH than 5.7.
- If the meat has a high level of initial contamination, it is possible that unfavourable bacteria could become dominant before the favourable lactic acid bacteria become established.

Vacuum packaging does not prevent the growth of all bacteria, but those that do grow are different species from those that grow on meat exposed to air. When chilled meat is stored in air, spoilage is mainly due to the growth and metabolism of *Pseudomonas* bacteria. As the numbers of pseudomonads reach around 100 million per g at the meat surface, they produce a putrid odour and slime forms.

Vacuum-packed meat is stored in the absence of oxygen and the microorganisms mentioned above (e.g. *Pseudomonas*) have restricted growth. Instead, the bacterial population will consist mainly of lactic acid bacteria. These should be the predominant organisms present in significant numbers if the:

- Low oxygen atmosphere is maintained;
- pH of the meat remains below 5.8; and
- Temperature is controlled below 4°C.

Lactic acid bacteria grow slowly at chill temperatures. Even when the count is high (100 million per g) they do not produce unpleasant odours and the product is still in good condition. Lactic acid bacteria could grow to 10-100 million per g after about 6 weeks of storage. They will stay at this level for the rest of the life of the product but do not produce signs of spoilage until several weeks after the maximum population of bacteria is reached.

In this situation, a total plate count (TPC) is NOT a useful indication of the microbiological quality of the product. If the total count is made up of mostly lactic acid bacteria, counts of more than 10 million per g do not indicate incipient spoilage or any processing or storage problem. For vacuum packs that have been aged for several weeks, only total counts in excess of 100 million per g should be regarded with suspicion; however, an *E. coli* count is a useful indicator of the quality of vacuum-packed meat. High *E. coli* counts (greater than 100 per g) on stored meat could indicate temperature abuse because *E. coli* does not grow below 7°C. A high *E. coli* count may also indicate a food safety issue.

Practicable Storage Life

Generally, the storage life of vacuum-packed beef is at least 10-12 weeks and that of lamb is 8-10 weeks or greater depending on the primal cut, processing conditions, packaging materials and maintenance of a low storage temperature. With storage temperatures below 0°C and use of packaging film with very low oxygen transmission rate, commercial storage life of beef is now.

If the total aerobic count on fresh meat is within the 'Good' category before vacuum packaging, and if cold chain parameters are maintained, then the storage lives mentioned above should be achievable. Storage at 0°C or below is recommended whenever possible because storage at higher temperatures will reduce the storage life of the product — by up to 50 per cent if held at 5°C.

Nature of Spoilage

A range of odours and flavours has been reported for vacuum-packaged beef and lamb. Aged vacuum-packed, commercially sterile meat will eventually develop cooked aromas that are described as sour, milky or cheesy and flavours that are sour, lactic-like or caramel-like. As stated earlier, lactic acid bacteria will dominate the bacterial flora of these packs. After 14-16 weeks, bitter or liver-like flavours develop. Even though spoilage may have occurred after extended storage, it is most unlikely that any pathogenic bacteria will have grown on vacuum-packed meat if the meat has been stored at less than 4°C.

Very occasionally, meat from a pack that is dominated by lactic acid bacteria is characterised by an aroma of hydrogen sulphide that rapidly dissipates when the meat is removed from the pack. Certain isolates of *Lactobacillus* have been shown to produce hydrogen sulphide.

If vacuum-packed meat has a pH greater than 6.0, if the storage temperature is 5-10°C, or if there is residual oxygen in the pack due to using a packing film with a high oxygen transmission rate, there may be an increased growth of spoilage bacteria such as *Brochothrix thermosphacta, Shewanella putrefaciens,* and psychrotrophic enterobacteria. In high pH meat, off odours may be detected when the bacterial count is just over 1 million per g at the surface. These bacteria will cause a range of off odours and off flavours, and in the case of *Shewanella putrefaciens,* spoilage is indicated by a greening of the meat surface and a strong hydrogen sulphide odour (like rotten eggs). When *Brochothrix* is a major component of the bacterial population, the aroma is variously described as 'cheesy', 'dairy like' or 'bready'. Odours and flavours in high pH meat from spoiled vacuum packs have been described as 'faecal' or 'sulphury'. Hydrogen sulphide and various other sulphur containing compounds have been detected in such meat. *Enterobacter* and other enterobacteria have been shown to produce these.

If off odours are evident when vacuum packs are opened, selective counts of these organisms can be useful in identifying why storage problems have arisen.

With the combination of low temperature, low oxygen availability and low pH, lactic acid bacteria will dominate the bacterial flora on the meat, as stated earlier. Other bacteria cannot grow or grow very poorly in these conditions and do not spoil the meat.

Random Spoilage of Vacuum-packed Cuts

Random premature spoilage of individual vacuum-packs in cartons indicates that spoilage is probably not a direct result of temperature abuse; temperature abuse is more likely to result in whole cartons being spoiled. If pack leakage can be ruled out, it is more likely that random spoilage has occurred because of a higher pH in the spoiled cut. As discussed previously, a higher pH will cause spoilage sooner because microbial flora (other than the more favourable lactic acid bacteria) will develop.

Probably the most common cause of premature spoilage of vacuum-packaged meat is loss of integrity. 'Leakers' are usually noticeable because leakage is normally accompanied by loss of vacuum in the pack. Packs of boneless primals may be leaking because of poor seals or because of puncture or scuffing of the film during processing or transport.

With bone-in primals, leakage is often due to sharp ends of bones piercing the pack and poor seals. Cut bone ends and smearing of bone dust on ends of cuts are also a source of spoilage because bone marrow provides a high pH environment.

CHAPTER

18

POTTED MEAT FOOD PRODUCT

A potted meat food product or potted meat is a food made using a method of food preservation-canning, consisting of cooked meat product, seasoned, often creamed, minced, or ground, which is filled into cans, sealed and heat processed in a retort to commercial sterility.

Various meats such as beef, pork, chicken, turkey and variety (non-skeletal) meats are used. It is produced internationally as a source of affordable meat. Its long shelf life and precooking makes it suitable for emergency food supplies, and for military and camping uses, although the high content of fat, protein, and/or preservatives may make it unsuitable for frequent consumption. The final product typically has a spreadable consistency, and typically contains high amounts of salt, as a preservative.

Canned meats have a mixed reputation on account of the taste, texture, ingredients, preparation and nutrition. The canning process produces a product with a generally homogeneous texture and flavor. The low-cost ingredients used also affect the quality. For example, mechanically separated chicken or turkey is a paste-like product made by forcing crushed bone and tissue through a sieve to separate bone from tissue. In the United States, mechanically separated poultry has been used in poultry products since 1969, after the National Academy of Sciences found it safe for use. On November 3, 1995, the Food Safety and Inspection Service (FSIS) of the U.S. Department of Agriculture (USDA) published a final rule in the Federal Register on mechanically separated poultry, stating that it was safe to use without restrictions. However, it must be labelled as "mechanically separated chicken or turkey" in the ingredient statement. The final rule became effective on November 4, 1996.

Ingredients

Armour Star: Mechanically separated chicken, beef tripe, partially defatted cooked beef fatty tissue, beef hearts, water, partially defatted cooked pork fatty tissue, salt, and less than two per cent: mustard, natural flavorings, dried garlic, dextrose, sodium erythorbate, and sodium nitrite.

Hormel: Beef tripe, mechanically separated chicken, beef hearts, partially defatted cooked beef fatty tissue, meat broth, vinegar, salt, flavouring, sugar, and sodium nitrite.

Libby's: Mechanically separated chicken, pork skin, partially defatted cooked pork fatty tissue, partially defatted cooked beef fatty tissue, vinegar, less than two per cent of: salt, spices, sugar, flavourings, sodium erythorbate and sodium nitrite.

Spam (Food)

Spam is a canned precooked meat product made by the Hormel Foods Corporation. The labeled ingredients in the classic variety of Spam are chopped pork shoulder meat with ham meat added, salt, water, modified potato starch as a binder, and sodium nitrite as a preservative. Spam's gelatinous glaze, or aspic, forms from the cooling of meat stock. The product has become part of many jokes and urban legends about mystery meat, which has made it part of pop culture and folklore.

Varieties of Spam vary by region and include Spam Classic, Spam Hot and Spicy, Spam Less Sodium, Spam Lite, Spam Oven Roasted Turkey, Hickory Smoked, and Spam Spread.

Spam which is sold in North America, South America, and Australia is produced in Austin, Minnesota, (also known as *Spam Town USA*) and in Fremont, Nebraska. Spam for the UK market is produced in Denmark by Tulip under licence from Hormel. Spam is also made in the Philippines and in South Korea. In 2007, the seven billionth can of Spam was sold. On average, 3.8 cans are consumed every second in the United States.

Introduced on July 5, 1937, the name 'Spam' was chosen when the product, whose original name was far less memorable (Hormel Spiced Ham), began to lose market share. The name was chosen from multiple entries in a naming contest. A Hormel official once stated that the original meaning of the name 'Spam' was 'Shoulder of Pork and Ham'. According to writer Marguerite Patten in *Spam – The Cookbook*, the name was suggested by Kenneth Daigneau, an actor and the brother of a Hormel vice president, who was given a $100 prize for creating the name. At one time and persisting to this day in certain books, the theory behind the nomenclature of Spam was that the name was a portmanteau of 'Spiced Meat and Ham'. According to the British documentary-reality show '1940's House', when Spam was offered by the United States to those affected by World War II in the UK, Spam stood for Specially Processed American Meats. *Yesterday's Britain*, a popular history published by *Reader's Digest* in 1998 [p. 140], unpacks Spam as 'Supply Pressed American Meat' and describes it as an imported 'wartime food' of the 1940s.

Many jocular backronyms have been devised, such as 'Something Posing As Meat', 'Specially Processed Artificial Meat', 'Stuff, Pork and Ham', 'Spare Parts Animal Meat' and 'Special Product of Austin Minnesota'.

According to Hormel's trademark guidelines, Spam should be spelled with all capital letters and treated as an adjective, as in the phrase 'SPAM luncheon meat'.

Nutritional Data

Spam is typically sold in cans with a net weight of 340 grams (12 ounces). A 100 gram (3.5 ounce) serving of original Spam provides 310 Calories, 13 grams of protein (26% DV), 3 grams of carbohydrates (1% DV), 27 grams of total fat (41% DV), including 10 grams of saturated fat (49% DV). The cholesterol content of Spam is 70 milligrams (23% DV). A serving also contains 57 per cent of the recommended daily intake of sodium (1369 milligrams). Spam provides the following vitamins and minerals: 0 per cent vitamin A, 1 per cent vitamin C, 1 per cent calcium, 5 per cent iron, 3 per cent magnesium, 9 per cent potassium, 12 per cent zinc, and 5 per cent copper.

Varieties

There are several different flavours of Spam products, including:

- Spam Classic — original flavour
- Spam Hot & Spicy — with Tabasco flavour
- Spam Less Sodium — '25 per cent less sodium'
- Spam Lite — '33 per cent less calories and 50 per cent less fat' — made from pork shoulder meat, ham, and mechanically separated chicken
- Spam Oven Roasted Turkey
- Spam Hickory Smoke flavour
- Spam Spread — 'if you're a spreader, not a slicer ... just like Spam Classic, but in a spreadable form"
- Spam with Bacon
- Spam with Cheese
- Spam Garlic
- Spam Golden Honey Grail — a limited-release special flavour made in honour of Monty Python's *Spamalot* Broadway musical

- Spam Mild
- Spam Hot Dogs

In addition to the variety of flavours, Spam is sold in tins smaller than the twelve-ounce standard size. Spam Singles are also available, as a single sandwich-sized slice of Spam Classic or Lite, wrapped in plastic instead of a metal container.

United States and Territories

In the United States in the aftermath of World War II, a troupe of ex-G.I. women was created by Hormel Foods to promote Spam from coast to coast. The group was known as the Hormel Girls and associated the food with being patriotic. In 1948, two years after the group's conception, the troupe had grown to 60 women with 16 forming an orchestra. The show went on to become a radio programme where the main selling point was Spam. The Hormel Girls were disbanded in 1953. Spam is still quite popular in the United States, but is sometimes associated with economic hardship because of its relatively low cost.

The residents of the state of Hawaii and the territories of Guam and the Commonwealth of the Northern Mariana Islands (CNMI) consume the most Spam per capita in the United States. On average, each person on Guam consumes 16 tins of Spam each year and the numbers at least equal this in the CNMI. Guam, Hawaii, and Saipan, the CNMI's principal island, have the only McDonald's restaurants that feature Spam on the menu. In Hawaii, Burger King began serving Spam in 2007 on its menu to compete with the local McDonald's chains. In Hawaii, Spam is so popular it is sometimes dubbed 'The Hawaiian Steak'. One popular Spam dish in Hawaii is Spam musubi, where cooked Spam is combined with rice and nori seaweed and classified as onigiri.

Spam was introduced into the aforementioned areas, in addition to other islands in the Pacific such as Okinawa and the Philippine Islands, during the U.S. military occupation in World War II. Since fresh meat was difficult to get to the soldiers on the front, World War II saw the largest use of

Spam. GIs started eating Spam for breakfast, lunch, and dinner. (Some soldiers referred to Spam as 'ham that didn't pass its physical' and 'meatloaf without basic training'.) Surpluses of Spam from the soldiers' supplies made their way into native diets. Consequently, Spam is a unique part of the history and effects of U.S. influence in the Pacific.

The perception of Spam in Hawaii is very different from that on the mainland. Despite the large number of mainlanders who eat Spam, and the various recipes that have been made from it, Spam, along with most canned food, is often stigmatized on the mainland as 'poor people food'. In Hawaii, similar canned meat products such as Treet are considered cheaper versions of canned meat than Spam. This is a result of Spam having the initial market share and its name sounding more convincing towards consumers.

Four different types of Spam. Clockwise from top left: Garlic, Oven Roasted Turkey, Hot and Spicy, and the Japanese released version (Spam Less Sodium) of Spam.

In these locales, varieties of Spam unavailable in other markets are sold. These include Honey Spam, Spam with Bacon, and Hot and Spicy Spam.

In the CNMI, lawyers from Hormel have threatened legal action against the local press for running articles decrying the ill-effects of high Spam consumption on the health of the local population.

Austin, Minnesota has a restaurant with a menu devoted exclusively to Spam, called 'Johnny's SPAMarama Menu'.

Europe

In the United Kingdom spam is often sliced, battered and deep-fried becoming known as 'spam fritters', and is still a popular way of eating Spam today. It gained popularity in the 1940s during World War II, as a consequence of the Lend-Lease Act when Hormel began to increase production towards British and Russian markets.

After World War II, Newforge Foods, part of the Fitch Lovell group, were awarded the license to produce the product in the UK (doing so at its Gateacre factory, Liverpool) where it stayed until production switched to the Danish Crown Group (owners of the Tulip Food Company in 1998, forcing the closure of the Liverpool factory and the loss of 140 jobs. By the early 1970s the name Spam was often misused to describe any tinned meat product containing pork, such as pork luncheon meat.

The image of Spam as a low cost meat product gave rise to the Scottish colloquial term 'Spam valley' to describe certain affluent housing areas where residents appear to be wealthy but in reality may be living at poverty levels.

Asia

In Okinawa, Japan, Spam has become very popular. The product is added into onigiri alongside eggs, used as a staple ingredient in the traditional Okinawan dish *chanpuru*, and a Spam burger is sold by local fast food chain Jef.

In China, Spam is an increasingly popular food item, and often used in sandwiches. Hormel has had a joint-venture in Shanghai for 16 years that has been highly successful in promoting Spam. In 2005, the Chinese division of Spam was one of the most profitable parts of the Hormel company. This development is caused, in part, by the increasing per capita income in Shanghai, coupled with the expansion of their food diet towards more meat.

In Hong Kong, Spam is commonly served with instant noodles and fried eggs, and is a popular item in *cha chaan teng*. Spam is less popular than Ma Ling Meats, its main competitor in the Hong Kong processed meat market. Although recent controversies surrounding high salt content in Ma Ling products may allow Spam to gain market share.

In the Philippines, Spam is a popular meal, most commonly eaten with fried rice and eggs or as a sandwich with pandesal. It is often eaten for breakfast. During the rescue efforts after the catastrophic typhoon of 2009, Hormel Foods donated over 30,000 pounds of Spam to the Philippines branch of the Red Cross.

In South Korea, Spam is popular in households as an accompaniment to rice. A local television advertisement claims that it is the most tasty when consumed with white rice and *gim* (laver seaweed used for some types of handrolls). Spam is also an original ingredient in *budae jjigae* ('army base stew'), a spicy stew with different types of preserved meat.

Spam and similar meat preserves can be bought in gift sets that may contain nothing but the meat preserve or include other products such as food oil or tuna. When invited to another person's home, guests may present their hosts with such a set, or with other food gifts such as fresh fruit, beverages or *tteok*.

The surfeit of Spam in both North and South Korea during the Korean War led to the establishment of the Spam *kimbap* (sushi roll). because of a scarcity of fish and other traditional kimbap products such as kimchi or fermented cabbage, Spam was added to a rice roll with kimchi and cucumber and wrapped in seaweed. Spam was also used by US soldiers in Korea as a means of trading for items, services or information around their bases. Spam is also remarkably popular to a majority of the population, and outranks Coca-Cola and KFC in status as a foodstuff.

In Israel, a kosher variant of Spam, known as *Loof*, was produced by Richard Levi, and mostly used as part of field rations by the Israeli Defence Forces. A Glatt kosher version was also produced. It was phased out of field rations during the early 2000s and was finally removed from rations when production ceased in 2009.

In Popular Culture

In the 1960s, the original Mercury astronauts were referred to as 'Spam in a can' by aircraft test pilots, as a derogatory reference to their restricted role as being unable to control the flight of the Mercury spacecraft in which they were launched.

In 1970, the Monty Python comedy group televised a sketch 'Spam' in which almost every breakfast meal served in a restaurant included Spam. The dialog hyped the menu as being 'Spam, Spam, Spam and more Spam'.

In the 1990s, excessive, unwanted e-mail was termed 'spam' after the phenomenon of marketers drowning out e-mail discussions, by flooding Usenet newsgroups and individuals' email with junk mail advertising messages. This was due to some early internet users who flooded forums with the word 'spam' recounting the repetitive and unwanted presence of Spam in the Monty Python sketch. This phenomenon has been reported in court decisions handed down in lawsuits against spammers - see, for example, *CompuServe Inc. v. Cyber Promotions, Inc.*, 962 F.Supp. 1015, n. 1 (S.D.Ohio 1997).

The Python programming language, named after Monty Python, prefers to use the words 'spam', 'ham', and 'eggs' as metasyntactic variables, instead of the traditional words 'foo' or 'bar' or 'baz'.

In 2004, the Broadway musical comedy *Spamalot* was created as a parody of the 1975 Monty Python film *Monty Python and the Holy Grail*.

Spam is celebrated in a small local festival in Austin, Minnesota, where Hormel corporate headquarters are located. The event, known as Spam Jam, is a carnival-type celebration that coincides with local Fourth of July festivities, featuring parades and fireworks that often relate to the popular luncheon meat. Austin is also home to the Spam Museum, and the plant that produces Spam for most of North America and Europe. In addition to the periodic celebration, there is a national recipe competition where submissions are accepted at the top forty state fairs in the nation.

Hawaii also holds an annual version of Spam Jam in Waikiki during the last week of April.

The small town of Shady Cove, Oregon is home to the annual Spam Parade and Festival, with the city allocating $1500 for it.

The Spam Jam is not to be confused with Spamarama, which is a yearly festival held around April Fool's Day in Austin, Texas. The theme of Spamarama is gentle parody of Spam, rather than straightforward celebration: the event at the heart of the festival is a Spam cook-off that originated as a challenge to produce an appetizing recipe for the meat. The festival includes light sporting activities and musical acts, in addition to the cook-off.

Food Preservation

Food preservation is the process of treating and handling food to stop or slow down spoilage (loss of quality, edibility or nutritional value).

Preservation usually involves preventing the growth of bacteria, yeasts, fungi, and other micro-organisms (although some methods work by introducing benign bacteria, or fungi to the food), as well as retarding the oxidation of fats which cause rancidity. black preservation also includes processes which inhibit natural discoloration that can occur during food preparation, such as the enzymatic browning reaction in apples after they are cut.

Many processes designed to preserve food will involve a number of food preservation methods. Preserving fruit, by turning it into jam, for example, involves boiling (to reduce the fruit's moisture content and to kill bacteria, yeasts, etc), sugaring (to prevent their re-growth) and sealing within an airtight jar (to prevent recontamination). There are many traditional methods of preserving food that limit the energy inputs and reduce carbon footprint.

Maintaining or creating nutritional value, texture and flavour is an important aspect of food preservation, although, historically, some methods drastically altered the character of the food being preserved. In many cases these changes have now come to be seen as desirable qualities — cheese, yoghurt and pickled onions being common examples.

Preservation Processes

Preservation processes include:

- Heating to kill or denature micro-organisms (*e.g.* boiling)
- Oxidation (*e.g.* use of sulfur dioxide)
- Toxic inhibition (*e.g.* smoking, use of carbon dioxide, vinegar, alcohol etc.)
- Dehydration (drying)
- Osmotic inhibition (*e.g.* use of syrups)
- Low temperature inactivation (*e.g.* freezing)
- Ultra high water pressure (*e.g.* fresherized, a kind of 'cold' pasteurization, the pressure kills naturally occurring pathogens, which cause food deterioration and affect food safety.)
- Combinations of these methods

Drying

One of the oldest methods of food preservation is by drying, which reduces water activity sufficiently to prevent or delay bacterial growth.

Refrigeration

Refrigeration preserves food by slowing down the growth and reproduction of micro-organisms and the action of enzymes which cause food to rot. The introduction of commercial and domestic refrigerators drastically improved the diets of many in the Western world by allowing foods such as fresh fruit, salads and dairy products to be stored safely for longer periods, particularly during warm weather.

Freezing

Freezing is also one of the most commonly used processes commercially and domestically for preserving a very wide range of food including prepared food stuffs which would not have required freezing in their unprepared state. For example, potato waffles are stored in the freezer, but potatoes themselves require only a cool dark place to ensure many months' storage. Cold stores provide large volume, long-term storage for strategic food stocks held in case of national emergency in many countries.

'Heat treating' Heat treating is when you *treat* a preseving food with *heat.*

Vacuum Packing

Vacuum-packing stores food in a vacuum environment, usually in an air-tight bag or bottle. The vacuum environment strips bacteria of oxygen needed for survival, slowing spoiling. Vacuum-packing is commonly used for storing nuts to reduce loss of flavor from oxidation. Chips are vacuum packed.

Salt

Salting or curing draws moisture from the meat through a process of osmosis. Meat is cured with salt or sugar, or a combination of the two. Nitrates and nitrites are also often used to cure meat and contribute the characteristic pink colour, as well as inhibition of Clostridium botulinum.

Sugar

Sugar is used to preserve fruits, either in syrup with fruit such as apples, pears, peaches, apricots, plums or in crystallized form where the preserved material is cooked in sugar to the point of crystallisation and the resultant product is then stored dry. This method is used for the skins of citrus fruit (candied peel), angelica and ginger. A modification of this process produces glacé fruit such as glacé cherries where the fruit is preserved in sugar but is then extracted from the syrup and sold, the preservation being maintained by the sugar content of the fruit and the superficial coating of syrup. The use of sugar is often combined with alcohol for preservation of luxury products such as fruit in brandy or other spirits. These should not be confused with fruit flavoured spirits such as cherry brandy or Sloe gin.

Artificial Food Additives

Preservative food additives can be *antimicrobial;* which inhibit the growth of bacteria or fungi, including mold, or *antioxidant;* such as oxygen absorbers, which inhibit the oxidation of food constituents.

Common antimicrobial preservatives include calcium propionate, sodium nitrate, sodium nitrite, sulfites (sulfur dioxide, sodium bisulfite, potassium hydrogen sulfite, etc.) and disodium EDTA. Antioxidants include BHA and BHT. Other preservatives include formaldehyde (usually in solution), glutaraldehyde (kills insects), ethanol and methylchloroisothiazolinone.

Pickling

Pickling is a method of preserving food in an edible anti-microbial liquid. Pickling can be broadly categorized as chemical pickling for example, In chemical pickling, the food is placed in an edible liquid that inhibits or kills bacteria and other micro-organisms. Typical pickling agents include brine (high in salt), vinegar, alcohol, and vegetable oil, especially olive oil but also many other oils. Many chemical pickling processes also involve heating or boiling so that the food being preserved becomes saturated with the pickling agent. Common chemically pickled foods include cucumbers, peppers, corned beef, herring, and eggs, as well mixed vegetables such as piccalilli.

In fermentation pickling, the food itself produces the preservation agent, typically by a process that produces lactic acid. Fermented pickles include sauerkraut, nukazuke, kimchi, surströmming, and curtido. Some pickled cucumbers are also fermented.

In commercial pickles, a preservative like sodium benzoate or EDTA may also be added to enhance shelf life. You can also say adding salt and oil is also pickling.

Lye

Sodium hydroxide (lye) makes food too alkaline for bacterial growth. Lye will saponify fats in the food, which will change its flavour and texture. Lutefisk uses lye in its preparation, as do some olive recipes. Modern recipes for century eggs also call for lye. Masa harina and hominy use agricultural lime in their preparation and this is often misheard as 'lye'.

Canning and Bottling

Canning involves cooking food, sealing it in sterile cans or jars, and boiling the containers to kill or weaken any remaining bacteria as a form of sterilization. It was invented by Nicolas Appert. Foods have varying degrees of natural protection against spoilage and may require that the final step occur in a pressure cooker. High-acid fruits like strawberries require no preservatives to can and only a short boiling cycle, whereas marginal fruits such as tomatoes require longer boiling and addition of other acidic elements. Low acid foods, such as vegetables and meats require pressure canning. Food preserved by canning or bottling is at immediate risk of spoilage once the can or bottle has been opened.

Lack of quality control in the canning process may allow ingress of water or micro-organisms. Most such failures are rapidly detected as decomposition within the can causes gas production and the can will swell or burst. However, there have been examples of poor manufacture (underprocessing) and poor hygiene allowing contamination of canned food by the obligate anaerobe *Clostridium botulinum,* which produces an acute toxin within the food, leading to severe illness or death. This organism produces no gas or obvious taste and remains undetected by taste or smell. Its toxin is denatured by cooking, though. Cooked mushrooms, handled poorly and then canned, can support the growth of Staphylococcus aureus, which produces a toxin that is not destroyed by canning or subsequent reheating.

Jellying

Food may be preserved by cooking in a material that solidifies to form a gel. Such materials include gelatine, agar, maize flour and arrowroot flour. Some foods naturally form a protein gel when cooked such as eels and elvers, and sipunculid worms which are a delicacy in the town of Xiamen in Fujian province of the People's Republic of China. Jellied eels are a delicacy in the East End of London where they are eaten with mashed potatoes. Potted meats in aspic, (a gel made from gelatine and clarified meat broth) were a common way of serving meat off-cuts in the UK until the 1950s. Many jugged meats are also jellied.

Potting

A traditional British way of preserving meat (particularly shrimp) is by setting it in a pot and sealing it with a layer of fat. Also common is potted chicken liver; compare pâté.

Jugging

Meat can be preserved by jugging, the process of stewing the meat (commonly game or fish) in a covered earthenware jug or casserole. The animal to be jugged is usually cut into pieces, placed into a tightly-sealed jug with brine or gravy, and stewed. Red wine and/or the animal's own blood is sometimes added to the cooking liquid. Jugging was a popular method of preserving meat up until the middle of the 20th century.

Irradiation

Irradiation of food is the exposure of food to ionizing radiation; either high-energy electrons or X-rays from accelerators, or by gamma rays (emitted from radioactive sources as Cobalt-60 or Caesium-137). The treatment has a range of effects, including killing bacteria, molds and insect pests, reducing the ripening and spoiling of fruits, and at higher doses inducing sterility. The technology may be compared to pasteurization; it is sometimes called 'cold pasteurization', as the product is not heated. Irradiation is not effective against viruses or prions, it cannot eliminate toxins already formed by microorganisms, and is only useful for food of high initial quality.

The radiation process is unrelated to nuclear energy, but it may use the radiation emitted from radioactive nuclides produced in nuclear reactors. Ionizing radiation is hazardous to life (hence its usefulness in sterilisation); for this reason irradiation facilities have a heavily shielded irradiation room where the process takes place. Radiation safety procedures ensure that neither the workers in such facility nor the environment receive any radiation dose from the facility. Irradiated food does not become radioactive, and national and international expert bodies have declared food irradiation as wholesome. However, the wholesomeness of consuming such food is disputed by opponents and consumer organizations. National and international expert bodies have declared food irradiation as 'wholesome'; UN-organizations as WHO and FAO are endorsing to use food irradiation. International legislation on whether food may be irradiated or not varies worldwide from no regulation to full banning. Irradiation may allow lower quality or contaminated foodstuffs to be rendered marketable.

It is estimated that about 500,000 tons of food items are irradiated per year worldwide in over 40 countries. These are mainly spices and condiments with an increasing segment of fresh fruit irradiated for fruit fly quarantine.

Pulsed Electric Field Processing

Pulsed electric field (PEF) processing is a method for processing cells by means of brief pulses of a strong electric field. PEF holds potential as a type of low temperature alternative pasteurization process for sterilizing food products. In PEF processing, a substance is placed between two electrodes, then the pulsed electric field is applied. The electric field enlarges the pores of the cell membranes which kills the cells and releases their contents. PEF for food processing is a developing technology still being researched. There have been limited industrial applications of PEF processing for the pasteurization of fruit juices.

Modified Atmosphere

Modifying atmosphere is a way to preserve food by operating on the atmosphere around it. Salad crops which are notoriously difficult to preserve are now being packaged in sealed bags with an atmosphere modified to reduce the oxygen (O_2) concentration and increase the carbon dioxide (CO_2) concentration. There is concern that although salad vegetables retain their appearance and texture in such conditions, this method of preservation may not retain nutrients, especially vitamins. Grains may be preserved using carbon dioxide by one of two methods; either using a block of dry ice placed in the bottom and the can is filled with grain or the container can be purged from the bottom by gaseous carbon dioxide from a cylinder or bulk supply vessel.

Carbon dioxide prevents insects, and depending on concentration, mold, and oxidation from damaging the grain. Grain stored in this way can remain edible for five years.

Nitrogen gas (N_2) at concentrations of 98 per cent or higher is also used effectively to kill insects in grain through hypoxia . However, carbon dioxide has an advantage in this respect as it kills organisms through hypercarbia and depending on concentration hypoxia and, requiring concentrations of above 35 per cent , or so. This makes carbon dioxide preferable for fumigation in situations where a hermetic seal cannot be maintained.

Burial in the Ground

Burial of food can preserve it due to a variety of factors: lack of light, lack of oxygen, cool temperatures, pH level, or desiccants in the soil. Burial may be combined with other methods such as salting or fermentation.

Many root vegetables are very resistant to spoilage and require no other preservation than storage in cool dark conditions, for example by burial in the ground, such as in a storage clamp.

Century eggs are created by placing eggs in alkaline mud (or other alkaline substance) resulting in their 'inorganic' fermentation through raised pH instead of spoiling. The fermentation preserves them and breaks down some of the complex, less flavourful proteins and fats into simpler more flavourful ones.

Most foods can be preserved in soil that is very dry and salty (thus a desiccant), or soil that is frozen.

Cabbage was traditionally buried in the fall in northern farms in the USA for preservation. Some methods keep it crispy while other methods produce sauerkraut A similar process is used in the traditional production of kimchi.

Sometimes meat is buried under conditions which cause preservation. If buried on hot coals or ashes, the heat can kill pathogens, the dry ash can desiccate, and the earth can block oxygen and further contamination. If buried where the earth is very cold, the earth acts like a refrigerator.

Controlled Use of Micro-organism

Some foods, such as many cheeses, wines, and beers will keep for a long time because their production uses specific micro-organisms that combat spoilage from other less benign organisms. These micro-organisms keep pathogens in check by creating an environment toxic for themselves and other micro-organisms by producing acid or alcohol. Starter micro-organisms, salt, hops, controlled (usually cool) temperatures, controlled (usually low) levels of oxygen and/or other methods are used to create the specific controlled conditions that will support the desirable organisms that produce food fit for human consumption.

High Pressure Food Preservation

High pressure food preservation refers to high pressure used for food preservation. "Pressed inside a vessel exerting 70,000 pounds per square inch (480 MPa) or more, food can be processed so that it retains its fresh appearance, flavour, texture and nutrients while disabling harmful microorganisms and slowing spoilage." By 2001, adequate commercial equipment was developed so that by 2005 the process was being used for products ranging from orange juice to guacamole to deli meats and widely sold.

REFERENCES

Egan, A.F., Eustace, I.J., Shay, B.J. (1988) Meat Packaging — Maintinaing the Quality and Prolonging the Storage Life of Chilled Beef, Pork and Lamb. Proceedings of Meat 88. "Shattering The Meat Myth: Humans Are Natural Vegetarians". Huffington Post. 2009-06-11.

Rejecting Meat 'Keeps Weight Low', BBC News, March 14, 2006.

Lawrie, R.A.; Ledward, D. A. (2006). *Lawrie's Meat Science* (7th ed.). Cambridge: Woodhead Publishing Limited. ISBN 978-1-84569-159-2

"Beef, Variety Meats and By-products, Kidneys, Raw". *Nutrition Facts.com*. http://www.nutritiondata.com/facts/beef-products/3466/2. Retrieved 2009-12-23.

"Lamb, Variety Meats and By-products, Tongue, Cooked, Braised". *Nutrition Facts.com*.

Budiansky, Stephen (1999). *The Covenant of the Wild: Why Animals Chose Domestication*. Yale University Press. ISBN 03-0007-993-1.

Pugh, David G. (2001). *Sheep and Goat Medicine*. Elsevier Health Sciences. ISBN 07-2169-052-1.

Weaver, Sue (2005). *Sheep: Small-scale Sheep Keeping for Pleasure and Profit*. 3 Burroughs Irvine, CA 92618: Hobby Farm Press, An Imprint of Bowtie Press, A Division of Bowtie Inc. ISBN 19-3199-349-1.

Ensminger, Dr. M.E.; Dr. R.O. Parker (1986). *Sheep and Goat Science, Fifth Edition*. Danville, Illinois: The Interstate Printers and Publishers Inc. ISBN 08-1342-464-X.

Green-Armytage, Stephen (October 2000). *Extraordinary Chickens*. Harry N. Abrams. ISBN 08-1093-343-8.

Smith, Page; Charles Daniel (April 2000). *The Chicken Book*. University of Georgia Press. ISBN 08-2032-213-X.

Rombauer, Irma S., *et al. Joy of Cooking*, Scribner, 1997. ISBN 06-8481-870-1.

Davidson, Alan (1999). *Oxford Companion to Food*. Oxford: Oxford University Press. p. 593.

Riddervold, Astri. *Food Conservation*. ISBN 978-09-0732-540-6.

Annis, P.C. and Dowsett, H.A. 1993. Low Oxygen Disinfestation of Grain: Exposure Periods Needed for High Mortality. Proc. International Conference on Controlled Atmosphere and Fumigation. Winnipeg, June 1992, Caspit Press, Jerusalem, pp. 71-83.

Hauther,W. and Worth, M., Zapped! Irradiation and the Death of Food, Food and Water Watch Press, Washington, DC, 2008.

Campbell, Belinda; Clapton, Barbara; Tipton, Catherine (2002). *Food Technology*. Heinemann. p. 20.

"9 CFR Part 318, *et al.*; Poultry Products Produced by Mechanical Separation and Products In Which Such Poultry Products Are Used; Final Rule" (PDF). U.S. Department of Agriculture.

INDEX

C

D

E

W

Y

Z